EUTHANASIA, DEATH WITH DIGNITY
AND THE LAW

Euthanasia, Death with Dignity and the Law

HAZEL BIGGS
University of Kent, Canterbury

·HART·
PUBLISHING
OXFORD – PORTLAND OREGON
2001

Oxford and Portland, Oregon

Published in North America (US and Canada) by
Hart Publishing
c/o International Specialized Book Services
5804 NE Hassalo Street
Portland, Oregon
97213-3644
USA

Distributed in the Netherlands, Belgium and Luxembourg by
Intersentia, Churchillaan 108
B2900 Schoten
Antwerpen
Belgium

Hart Publishing Ltd is a specialist legal publisher based in Oxford, England.
To order further copies of this book or to request a list of other
publications please write to:

Hart Publishing Ltd, Salter's Boatyard, Folly Bridge, Abingdon Road,
Oxford OX1 4LB
Telephone: +44 (0)1865 245533 or Fax: +44 (0)1865 794882
e-mail: mail@hartpub.co.uk
WEBSITE: http://www.hartpub.co.uk

British Library Cataloguing in Publication Data
Data Available
ISBN 1-84113-091-5

Typeset by Hope Services (Abingdon) Ltd.

And Finally. . . . .

Acknowledgements

I am indebted to a great many people as a consequence of writing this book. Thankfully, nearly everybody has a view on euthanasia which has made the research and development of these ideas fruitful and informative. Many of those to whom I owe thanks will remain unnamed but their contributions, made either by engaging in discussions when I needed to clarify my own thinking, or by not pressurising me despite my repeated cries of "after the book is finished we will. . ." have been invaluable.

The book is a transformation of my PhD thesis so I am grateful to Steve Uglow, who supervised much of the initial research, and to both Derek Morgan and Wade Mansell, before whom I defended my thesis and who subsequently provided some interesting suggestions for improvement.

Paul Conaghan provided great assistance with proof reading, and was patient in the extreme. Liz Cable and the support staff at Kent Law School have helped to keep me going throughout long days of writing, revising, printing and photocopying, amidst teaching and administrative duties. And I could not have produced the final text in coherent format without help from Mark Dean. Numerous other colleagues have taken time to express an interest in the book's progress, and the concern and attention of my insightful and talented LLM students has been heart-warming.

Most of all my heartfelt thanks go to Peter Biggs, and our three sons, Michael Jonathan and Timothy, who have been long suffering silent partners in the writing process. I owe profound thanks to them, to my parents and other family members, and not least to Ted and Vic Biggs whose support has been unflinching. The writing of this book has been an experience from which I have gained much that will be of use in the future, but for now, the triumph is in finally seeing it in print.

Contents

Table of Cases

Table of Legislation

Introduction

Medicine Men, Outlaws and Voluntary Euthanasia

During the final weeks of writing this book the news media contained yet another flurry of stories concerning euthanasia and end-of-life decisions. It was reported from Holland that after many years of judicial toleration euthanasia was finally to be formally legalised, while in Britain, a man who admitted on a radio talk show that years previously he had assisted his terminally ill mother to die, was sought and questioned by the police prior to the exhumation of his mother's body. Shortly before, *Eastenders*, a well known BBC soap opera, ran a story where, despite her religious and moral reservations, one of the regular characters had assisted her best friend to die and was left to cope with the consequences. The closing months of 2000 also witnessed three cases where the courts were required to clarify the lawfulness of clinical end of life decisions in the light of the implementation of the Human Rights Act 1998.[1] It is a familiar pattern where interest in euthanasia never seems to wane and, fuelled by examples such as these, the debate remains as polarised as ever. Taking into account the level of interest and the polarisation of views expressed, this book seeks to analyse the issues from the perspectives of law, medicine and ethics to consider whether legal reform is necessary to enable people to die with dignity.

The ability to choose, and have those choices respected, is revered as a way of maintaining control, which can in turn help to preserve personal dignity in dying. Voluntariness is a central element here, since choice dictates volition and volunterism denotes self-determination, all of which are associated with dignity. But does that mean that voluntary euthanasia should be legally permissible? And, if it were no longer outlawed, would euthanasia in fact offer an appropriate mechanism by which people could exercise choice over the time and circumstances of their dying?

Recent decades have witnessed social changes that have encouraged and empowered us to select options according to personal preferences in every other area of social life. Nowhere is this more apparent than in the realm of health care, where British patients have been transformed into clients, who consume health care services and rightly demand information along with their perceived entitlements. Heightened public awareness of the scope, successes and failures of medicine, have led to consultation and involvement in medical decisions

---

[1] *A National Health Service Trust* v. *D* [2000] Fam Law 803, and *NHS Trust 'A'* v. *M; NHS Trust 'B'* v. *H*, Family Division (Dame Elizabeth Butler-Sloss) 25 October 2000, unreported.

becoming the norm and increasingly regarded as a right. In this environment the ability to make choices about health and welfare has become a legitimate expectation. Yet, even where death is imminent and inevitable, and after careful consideration of all the alternatives, it is not lawful to seek and receive a deliberate medical intervention that will result in death.

Concentrating on the rights and responsibilities of patients and health care professionals, this discussion focuses on medical decision-making at the end of life. Specifically, what decisions may legitimately be taken, when, and by whom? Choice is a central theme, especially where a person's ideal choice might be to die sooner than would be considered natural by her professional and emotional carers. At present a patient's request for a specific course of action as a preferred medical option is futile. Any medical practitioner carrying out that wish will be outlawed as a result, hence clinical and legal boundaries prevent deliberate assistance in the exercise of terminal choices. Dignity dictates however, that it is not only important to be able to make relevant choices for oneself. The ability to influence the choices made by others who have the power to determine the extent and nature of the medical treatments that may or may not be delivered, is also crucial.

The argument is not necessarily one about institutionalising euthanasia, or providing bureaucratic mechanisms by which it can be legitimated. What is more significant is recognition and respect for considered choices, while avoiding sanctions for compassionate health professionals who voluntarily opt to assist. The chapters of this book will therefore consider the process and context of end-of-life decision-making, from the perspectives of clinicians, patients and others who will be affected.

In the past the question of inappropriately prolonging life was not a consideration. Rather, people would have died for want of effective medical treatments. Hence many of the dilemmas presented here arise only because medical progress has generated situations that would previously have resolved themselves spontaneously and rapidly. In her analysis of the relationship between law and medicine, Sheila McLean suggests that advances in medicine have inevitably resulted in the need for serious moral choices to be made, and that when medicine fails to provide a socially acceptable answer many of these are referred to the law for solutions. Within this it becomes apparent that perhaps neither law nor medicine are the appropriate disciplines to resolve the profound dilemmas emanating from advances in biotechnology. McLean argues that:

> "the approach of the courts is characterised by sophistry, thereby avoiding asking and answering the ultimate question—namely what are the true values and principles which society should apply to the new reality".[2]

In terms of decision-making at the end of life the new reality is currently less well defined than we might imagine. So, to paraphrase Peter Singer, we now need to

---

[2] S A M McLean, *Old Law, New Medicine: Medical Ethics and Human Rights* (London, Pandora Press, 1999) at 158.

rethink life and death in order to provide satisfactory answers to the moral choices presented.[3]

Euthanasia is associated with a range of different practices and situations, not all of which apply to the present discussion. Voluntary euthanasia and the value of voluntary autonomous choices, whether taken in advance or contemporaneously, provide the central focus, so that the debate revolves around the making of autonomous medical decisions in a changing medical environment. Those who are physically able, and hold no moral objections, might of course contemplate suicide. But suicide is rarely regarded as dignified and a more certain clinical route would be preferable to many.

To achieve this, attention must be paid to enabling people to make decisions, to having those decisions acknowledged and recorded, and to ensuring that they are accepted and acted upon when they become applicable. Simultaneously, it must be recognised that people can and do change their opinions depending on the circumstances in which they find themselves. For example, people may have significantly different views about death and dying when they are healthy than when faced with the imminent reality.[4] It is demonstrable that terminally ill people do not commit suicide or refuse life prolonging treatments in great numbers, a fact that is sometimes cited in arguments opposing the use of advance directives if upholding their provisions might result in death.[5] Of course the studies cited may show that people change their minds, suggesting that over reliance on advance directives could be dangerous in some circumstances. But few would contend that the terms of a living will should be upheld if there was doubt about its validity or applicability in the circumstances that have arisen. Nevertheless, there are many situations where the value of a living will must surely outweigh these possible disbenefits. Where, for example, a terminally ill person becomes physically unable to kill herself, despite a confirmed desire so to do, the only available choice is to refuse life prolonging treatment rather than to continue a futile existence. That is to die slowly, or to die more slowly. Alternatively, it has been suggested that even where people have not needed to resort to the provisions of their living will, they are empowered by the knowledge that they could, and that they have had the opportunity to decide for themselves.[6] Effectively they feel that they are in control of their fate and then choose to play it out according to their own needs. None of these instances negates the necessity to maximise every person's ability to choose and to have those choices respected, even if they change over time.

Predicated on ideals of personal autonomy and self-determination, all choices that permit recipients of health care to feel in control of their destinies, are essential to human dignity. It is clear that the law surrounding consent to

---

[3] P Singer, *Rethinking Life and Death* (Oxford, Oxford University Press, 1995).

[4] C Ryan, "Betting Your Life" in D Dickenson et al (eds.), *Death Dying and Bereavement* 2nd edn. (London, Sage, 2000) at 291.

[5] *Ibid.*

[6] T E Quill, *Death and Dignity. Making Choices and Taking Charge* (New York, Norton, 1993).

medical treatment, and legal recognition of living wills has developed in ways designed to endorse and protect individual rights to autonomy and self-determination. In recent years autonomy and self-determination have become accepted as the foundations of ethical medical practice, but they must be approached cautiously to avoid imposing additional burdens on patients who have enough to bear. Greater recognition and use of living wills could offer security and enhance the options available to patients at the end of life, but adequate safeguards will be needed to ensure that such devices are properly validated and applied in order to protect against potential abuses. Chapters four and five will assess the value of autonomy and living wills in the wider debate about euthanasia and dignity in dying.

Many people regard euthanasia as the ultimate expression of individual autonomy and self-determination. Its proponents contend that a relaxation of the law to permit euthanasia, or clinically assisted dying in appropriate circumstances, would relieve suffering and enhance human dignity, by enabling people to maintain control of their lives until their final moments. Yet English law has steadfastly declined to adapt, and calls for permissive legal reform have been resisted in favour of the present *ad hoc* common law approach.

Alexander McCall-Smith advances a scholarly defence of this position, arguing that the current legal position is sufficiently flexible to incorporate ample scope for a benevolent approach to be adopted where appropriate.[7] Certainly it is advantageous that the criminal law judges each case according to its particular facts and merits, and that a range of defences exist, which can take into account a range of mitigating circumstances through the murder/manslaughter distinction. McCall-Smith argues however, that:

> "even intentional killing, then, may be treated with relative leniency if the accused's circumstances at the time of the act trigger sufficient sympathy on the part of the prosecution or jury and can be fitted into one of the mitigating categories".[8]

There is the rub. Any leniency permissible is only relative, a perpetrator might receive a lesser sentence, but will be sentenced nonetheless. Furthermore the accused's conduct must first be manipulated to fit the mitigating criteria accepted by the law, diminished responsibility being the most obvious. While such a defence may be available and appropriate in some cases of euthanasia, particularly in a domestic setting, it is unlikely to be either suitable or attractive where medical professionals are concerned.

Further flexibility is endorsed through the availability of the doctrine of double effect, where actions can be seen to cause both wanted and unwanted effects. If the action in question is the administration of strong palliative medication to keep a dying patient comfortable, the unwanted effect may be the incidental suppression of respiration resulting in the patient's death. Here the factual circumstances can be presented in such a way that the intentions of the person

---

[7] A McCall-Smith, "Euthanasia: the Strengths of the Middle Ground", (1999) 7 *Med LR* 194–207.
[8] *Ibid*, at 198.

giving the medication appear to be focused only on the good consequences, while denying the bad, even though these were clearly anticipated. The cause of death can then be attributed to the underlying medical condition, despite the fact that death would not have occurred at that precise time, but for the therapeutic intervention. No blame would be likely to be attributed in these circumstances, but such outcomes cannot be relied upon with any certainty. Cases where these principles have been used cause tremendous anxiety and uncertainty for those who have been impugned. And, while an acquittal may be forthcoming if the doctrine of double effect provides an efficient shield and there is sufficient sympathy in the courtroom, the alternative is always a possibility.

It is the very flexibility that many find so appealing about the criminal law, that gives rise to such confusion and uncertainty when medical professionals and patients encounter euthanasia. Doctors are entitled to ask, exactly when will double effect be an acceptable defence, and how do we know? There is no certain way to respond; theory and practice make uncomfortable collaborators in this area. Sophistry and creative legalism may be effective in the court room, but medical practice cannot always be tailored to take advantage of them. Further inconsistencies also exist. The law permits doctors to withdraw futile treatment from those who are incapable of expressing any view specifically to facilitate their demise. Competent people are permitted to decline medical treatment, even if the result will be their death. Yet action that deliberately causes death is outlawed.

Legislation permitting euthanasia, or at least some forms of assisted dying, would introduce more certainty for all concerned, but great skill would be required in the drafting and extent of any such permissive reform. Calls for legal euthanasia must be carefully framed. It is not only important to increase the potential for greater choice and opportunities to terminate life according to individual voluntary preference, it is also vital to guard against the inappropriate use of "do not resuscitate orders" and failures to treat due to inadequate provision of resources. If euthanasia were to be allowed in the name of dignity, autonomy and choice, it is essential that it is also wholly voluntary. Accordingly, this book seeks to explore a "pro-choice" option where every able person is permitted to choose the time and manner of their own dying if they want to. In the present legal climate this is impossible and those who might seek dignity through active assistance in dying are deterred. A central issue is not whether life should end, but the nature of decision-making at the end of life; who should take the decision and how?[9]

The discussion here is therefore concerned primarily with medical decision making rather than advocating that a claim of compassionate motivation should automatically absolve anyone who terminates the life of another from responsibility. This is an area where people could be vulnerable to dangerous

[9] These issues are discussed at length in H Kuse, "The Case for Active Voluntary Euthanasia" (1986) 14 *Law Ethics and Health Care* 145.

abuses, and it is appropriate therefore that any move towards permissive legal reform should incorporate professional legitimacy. Death and dying are presently regarded as the domain of medical science and easing the passing from dying into death is an accepted part of a doctor's duty, so it would seem apt for that legitimacy to be conferred upon healthcare professionals. Further, there is some evidence to suggest that assisted death is regarded as more dignified if attended by a qualified medical professional.[10] In supporting that stance the arguments presented here may be open to criticism on grounds of enhancing medical power. This is not the intention, but it must be recognised that a balance needs to be struck between permitting patients the choices they seek, and protecting the vulnerable from abuse. This may only be possible through professional guidelines and legal regulation.

Today euthanasia could be described as the ultimate doctor's dilemma. Modern medicine promotes honest and responsive relationships between doctors and patients, founded on autonomy and trust, but at the end of life doctors are constrained by law from assisting their patients to die, even if that is the considered wish of the patient concerned. Alongside that is a dilemma associated with concerns that patients might demand a right to assistance in dying, either now or in the future, and that this would alter the nature of the doctor/patient relationship.[11] Arguably that danger already exists. Medical men and women may not act to hasten death, even at the considered and voluntary request of competent patients. Any who respond to impatient pleas for help are outlawed and risk their own dignity through potential professional and legal sanction.

Whether it is possible to achieve dignity in dying, with or without euthanasia and with or without legal reform is the subject of this book. The chapters are designed to build upon one another, so that concepts and case examples are developed through repeat analysis and subtle differences in emphasis. While pursuing the core debate about euthanasia each chapter can stand alone, so that scholars interested in the law and ethics of consent, or the issues associated with living wills for example, should be able to dip into those chapters and find them informative and stimulating, even if they are not seeking a detailed knowledge of issues associated with euthanasia, death and dying. Euthanasia is contextualised through discussions of clinical decision-making at the end of life from the perspectives of law, medicine and ethics to provide an overview of the complex issues involved. Some technical discussion of the significant legal principles is essential to construction of the legal argument and as a result chapters two and three conduct a detailed examination of the law of homicide and consent respectively. Despite the complex legal analysis, both are intended to be accessible to non-law readers. Accordingly, these discussions are set against the backdrop of clinical scenarios and the factual backgrounds of the cases discussed, so

---

[10] W Macdonald, "Situational Factors and Attitudes Toward Voluntary Euthanasia" (1998) 46 *Social Science and Medicine* 73–81.

[11] L Emanuel (ed.), *Regulating How We Die: The Ethical, Medical and Legal Issues Surrounding Physician Assisted Suicide* (Harvard, Harvard University Press, 1998).

that the concepts are located within relevant practical situations. A hypothetical patient is occasionally referred to for this purpose. The female gender is used as a reference point throughout in an attempt to break down stereotypical assumptions.

This text aims to expose the inconsistencies and ambiguities associated with the present legal approach to end-of-life decision-making in order to suggest that legal reform might provide a more consistent response. It is inconsistent to permit terminal decisions to be made about people who cannot speak for themselves or make a considered choice, while those who actively and competently seek medical assistance for a permanent resolution are prohibited from so doing. Similarly, there may be little dignity in a slow death, either through incurable or terminal disease, or by the deliberate withholding of nutrition from an incapacitated person. Legal reform might aid consistency so that voluntary euthanasia could offer the opportunity for death with dignity, but in the meantime, dignity will always be compromised while the law prohibits active intervention in dying.

1

To Kill or Not to Kill; is that the Euthanasia Question?[1]

"Every day, rational people all over the world plead to be allowed to die. Sometimes they plead for others to kill them. Some of them are dying already . . . Some of them want to die because they are unwilling to live in the only way left open to them".[2]

INTRODUCTION—WHY EUTHANASIA?

Advances in medical science now allow both living and dying to be prolonged, a fact which has raised awareness of issues relating to death and dying in the community at large, popular fiction and the medical professions. Dworkin's sentiments above reflect a commonly held belief that modern medicine can compel people to endure life beyond what they perceive to be dignified bounds. Statistical evidence also supports the popular perception that some doctors do sometimes engage in excessive treatment to prolong the lives of the terminally ill.[3] As a result, recent years have seen repeated calls for legal reform to permit euthanasia and assisted death.[4]

In modern Western culture death has traditionally been a private affair occurring behind closed doors and with minimal observation or discussion. Yet in Britain today approximately seventy per cent of all deaths occur under the bright lights of hospital where the natural processes of dying are often transformed into a medical event and subordinated to technology. Advanced scientific medical knowledge has increased the average life expectancy in the United Kingdom by twenty five years during this century.[5] As a result the numbers of people aged eighty and over rose nearly threefold between 1951 and 1988, from 0.7 million to two million. Increasing longevity by this magnitude is expected to

---

[1] This chapter has formed the basis of an article entitled, "Euthanasia and Death with Dignity: Still poised on the Fulcrum of Homicide" [1996] *Crim L R* 878–88.

[2] R Dworkin, *Life's Dominion* (London, Harper-Collins, 1993) at 179.

[3] See for example, J Brody, "Doctors Admit Ignoring Patients Wishes" *The New York Times* Jan 1993, which reports on a survey conducted by the *American Journal of Public Health* in January 1993.

[4] G Williams, "Euthanasia" (1973) 41 *Medico-Legal Journal*, R Veatch, *Death, Dying and the Biological Revolution* (New Haven, Nash Publications, 1976), I Kennedy, "Euthanasia", in A Grubb (ed.), *Choices and Decisions in Health Care* (Chichester, Wiley 1993).

[5] *Social Trends*, Table 1.2, Age sex structure of the population (London, HMSO, 1990) at 24.

cause a rise in the numbers of new cancer patients of 0.5 per cent a year over the next twenty years,[6] and the numbers of those suffering from chronic and incurable disease will grow proportionately. Alongside this, growing awareness of patient's rights to self-determination, has stimulated public, academic, medical and legal debate about euthanasia, assisted dying and treatment withdrawal.[7]

Central to this discourse is the dilemma encountered by doctors attempting to provide appropriate care while respecting patient autonomy. Medical decisions in the terminal stages of life are frequently questioned by patients and their relatives, while the options available to the personnel responsible for those decisions are strictly defined by the law. As a consequence, the legal system is repeatedly being called upon to define the boundary between patient's rights and doctor's responsibilities with regard to potentially life-limiting treatment decisions.[8] The following hypothetical case illustrates many of the issues exposed when modern medicine views death as defeat, and strives to maintain life at all costs. Just imagine a scene of impending despair at a hospital near by. An anxious relative sits at the bedside of a hospital patient expecting the imminent arrival of the Grim Reaper and the ultimate departure of a loved one. But the deathly visitation is not forthcoming and the patient lingers on interminably. The prospect of recovery is negligible but the expectation of death recedes with the passage of time. Eventually, it is apparent that medical technology has exceeded its ability to preserve life and has embarked on an odyssey of prolonging the dying process.

The options available for the continuing care and treatment of this patient are readily apparent. She can be maintained indefinitely in her present condition, or she can be allowed, or enabled to die. Sadly however, the availability of these options is limited and constrained by both social mores and the criminal law. The implications for the patient, her relatives and dependants, the medical carers and for the allocation of scarce resources are profound and emblematic of the experiences of people everywhere. Her dilemma raises legal, social, ethical and medical questions to which there are no easy solutions. Should she be kept alive as long as technology allows? Is it ethical to keep her alive just because we can, or can we morally let her die? Can her family insist that she is kept alive or, conversely, that her life is not maintained? What are the legal rights of the patient and her family? What is the responsibility of the clinicians providing medical care? Is it legal for care to be discontinued? Can the patient herself influence the decisions taken regarding her future medical care?

Questions like these are confronted every day by real people around the world. Those involved may encounter their personal dilemmas due to terminal

---

[6] *Review of National Cancer Registration System*, Series MBI, no. 17 (London, OPCS, 1990).

[7] The level of interest in euthanasia and assisted death in order to avoid prolonged dying is illustrated by the fact that Derek Humphry's book, *Final Exit* (Oregon, Hemlock Society, 1991), was listed as number one in the *New York Times* list of best selling self help books.

[8] Examples of these include *R v. Cox* (1992) 12 BMLR 38, *Airedale NHS Trust v. Bland* [1993] 1 All ER 821, and *Frenchay NHS Trust v. S* [1994] 2 All ER 403.

or incurable disease, the effects of trauma, or simply the degeneration associated with old age. How they came to occupy their present position is often relatively unimportant compared with what happens to them next. Today it is commonplace for people to be kept alive or brought back from the brink of death where in the past they would have died. But what kind of life are they living and how can their carers respond? The answer was considered by the Institute of Medical Ethics Working Party on the Ethics of Prolonging Life and Assisting Death which reported that,

> "The lives of an increasing number of patients, predominantly but by no means all elderly, are now being prolonged by modern medicine in states of coma, severe incapacity, or pain they consider unrelievable and from which they seek release. Doctors in charge of such patients have to decide not only whether they are morally bound to continue with life-prolonging treatment, but also, if no such treatment is being given, whether and in what circumstances it is ethical to hasten their deaths by administration of narcotic drugs".[9]

For these patients, as for the hypothetical patient depicted above, living may amount to little more than survival. Life has been saved, but only because dying has been prolonged, and the quality of that life is questionable. Crucial questions raised by this situation concern exactly how life and death are defined. More specifically, is our understanding of these concepts rigid or must it be flexible in the face of rapid medical and technological advancement? Peter Singer argues persuasively that "the traditional ethic will be unable to accommodate the present demand for control over how we die".[10] The logic of his argument is compelling and suggests that not only must our understandings of life and death be revised, but also that the law should be reshaped in response.

Certainly the ability to preserve life despite trauma and terminal disease, has resulted in more people demanding the right to die with dignity rather than endure the perceived indignity of a dependent existence.[11] Human dignity however is a nebulous concept amenable to a range of interpretations. In the context of the present debate the close association between euthanasia and death with dignity reflects the contemporary emphasis on self-determination as an expression of individual autonomy. In more classical, Kantian, terms, respect for the autonomy of all rational beings demonstrates the intrinsic value of each individual and the esteem and inherent dignity of which each is worthy. Euthanasia in its various forms is one mechanism frequently promoted as a means of maintaining autonomy and achieving death with dignity. However, whether dignity can be achieved through euthanasia depends on the individual circumstances of each case and on how euthanasia is defined.

---

[9] (1990) 336 *The Lancet* 610.

[10] P Singer, *Rethinking Life and Death* (Oxford, Oxford University Press, 1995) at 148.

[11] Opinion polls suggest that, because of fears of prolonged dying, public support for euthanasia has increased from about 50% in the 1960s to approximately 75% in 1992. See, T M Helme, "Euthanasia Around the World" (1992) 304 *British Medical Journal* 717.

Broadly the word euthanasia means "a good death" as derived from the Greek *eu*, meaning well or good, and *thanatos*, meaning death. Contemporary understandings of the term imply the bringing about of a painless and gentle death, particularly in respect of those suffering from painful and incurable disease. Definitions of euthanasia include distinctions between active and passive responses, which are drawn according to the manner in which death is procured and relate closely to the legal understanding of act and omission. Here a positive action constitutes an act and a failure to act amounts to an omission. For example, selective non-treatment, where life-prolonging treatment is withdrawn or withheld is characterised as passive euthanasia because death apparently results from a lack of positive action. The absence of a deliberate positive action where, for example, death is a consequence of the doctrine of double effect[12] means that this too is considered as a form of passive euthanasia. The practical and ethical distinctions between them will be discussed in detail in chapter two alongside similar issues that arise in relation to active euthanasia or mercy killing, described as the intentional killing of a person with benevolent motives. Assisted suicide, where one person offers another the assistance required to bring about her own suicide, is also sometimes described as a form of active euthanasia and is highlighted as such in chapter two.

Euthanasia is sometimes also characterised as voluntary, non-voluntary and involuntary, where voluntary denotes that it is performed with the consent of the recipient. Non-voluntary euthanasia occurs where the person concerned has been unable to express an opinion, usually because she lacks the capacity so to do, but others consider that it is in her best interests to end her life at this time. Within this framework involuntary euthanasia occurs where the recipient has not agreed to the procedure and is an unwilling participant. This application of the word euthanasia is associated with the genocidal activities of the Nazi regime and the heinous crimes committed by Dr Harold Shipman and these associations are often at the root of those objections to euthanasia which regard it as the top of a very slippery slope. Of course this is a fallacious classification since the term euthanasia implies that it is in the person's expressed interests to die and that they are compliant.[13] If the person concerned is unwilling to die it seems reasonable to assume that their preference is to continue living, hence any action to bring about their death would amount to murder or some other form of unlawful killing rather than euthanasia. As the emphasis of this book is on medically assisted voluntary euthanasia as a means of securing death with dignity by the avoidance of futile suffering and the maintenance of personal control, voluntary and non-voluntary euthanasia will represent the primary focus of this analysis in support of a workable proposal for legal reform.

[12] This is the situation which occurs as a recognised side effect of palliative medication. It will be discussed in detail in ch. 2.

[13] For a discussion see Mary Anne Warren, *Moral Status: Obligations to Persons and Other Living Things* (Oxford, Clarendon Press, 1997) at 187.

Several unsuccessful attempts have been made to reform the law and legalise euthanasia in Britain. For example, in 1936 the Euthanasia Bill provided for a system of prior notification whereby adult patients (then classified as persons over twenty-one) suffering from terminal or incurable disease would be permitted to sign a form requesting euthanasia. Two witnesses were required at the signing and the form would then be scrutinised by a referee who was authorised to interview the patient and all other interested parties. After that the matter would be passed to a court which would be authorised to issue a certificate permitting euthanasia to be performed by a doctor in the presence of witnesses. The court was empowered to examine the evidence and decide whether or not the granting of a certificate was appropriate.

The Voluntary Euthanasia Bill 1969 would have allowed euthanasia for patients aged over twenty-one who requested it. Under this Bill a system was proposed whereby if two doctors were satisfied that the patient was suffering from an illness which was serious enough to be "incurable and expected to cause him severe distress or render him incapable of rational existence" they could be authorised to perform euthanasia. Several Bills in the 1970s[14] attempted to provide incurable patients with rights to receive pain relieving drugs in quantities which could induce unconsciousness. Such a right would in practice amount to little short of assisted suicide as the calculation of the dosage necessary to induce loss of consciousness would necessarily be imprecise and death a likely consequence. In 1991 the Euthanasia Bill, which would have allowed doctors to provide active euthanasia to incurable patients who requested it, was introduced. Despite a great deal of publicity and support from a parliamentary euthanasia group, this measure met the same fate as the others and ultimately failed to gain the force of law.

By contrast a Private Members Bill entitled Medical Treatment (Prevention of Euthanasia) Bill was introduced into the House of Commons in December 1999 with the intention of making it unlawful for treatment to be withdrawn or withheld with the intention of causing or hastening death. Its introduction by Ann Winterton MP followed media concerns about reports that some elderly and disabled patients were dying as a result of receiving inadequate care in hospitals and homes. The Bill aimed to address the perceived need of the old and vulnerable to be reassured that they would receive proper medical care at the end of life and followed a flurry of media reports concerning "do not resuscitate orders" apparently imposed upon patients without their knowledge or consent.[15] It failed to progress beyond the second Parliamentary reading.

Until very recently there was no legal right to euthanasia in any western jurisdiction. The Netherlands was frequently quoted as providing an example of legally permissible euthanasia, but until the end of 2000 euthanasia[16] remained

---

[14] Known as the Incurable Patients Bills.

[15] M Hickman, "Tory Proposes Anti-Euthanasia Bill", 9 December 1999, *PA News*.

[16] Euthanasia is defined in the Netherlands as any behaviour carried out with the "victim's" consent, which causes that person's death.

proscribed in the Netherlands and was only permitted subject to strict procedural guidelines and the efficacy of a defence of necessity.[17] This position has
now been regularised. The position is similar in Switzerland and the German
Republic, where assisted suicide is practised but only in extremely limited and
strictly controlled circumstances.[18]

In Australia's Northern Territory legislation was enacted in 1996[19] to permit
medically assisted suicide. Four patients successfully exercised the rights
granted by the Act and were helped to die by their doctor before the legislation
was challenged in the Supreme Court of Australia. The Rights of the Terminally
Ill Act 1996 has now been overruled by the federal Parliament.[20] In the American
state of Oregon legislation was passed in 1994 permitting physician assisted suicide.[21] Though subsequently held to be unconstitutional by a federal court, it
became the subject of various appeals and was eventually narrowly re-enacted.

Away from legislation, the common law position has been extensively
reviewed in Britain and America. The issue of the right to die by assisted suicide
was given comprehensive consideration by the American Supreme Court in the
cases of *State of Washington et al* v. *Glucksberg et al*[22] and *Vacco et al* v. *Quill
et al*.[23] The cases concerned whether or not New York State's ban on assisted
suicide amounted to a violation of the Fourteenth Amendment's Equal
Protection Clause. At first instance it was held not to, but that decision was
reversed on appeal in a judgment based on the fact that different treatment was
being accorded to those seeking to end their lives by self-administering prescription drugs than was available to those who declined therapeutic life support. The respondents argued that there was no relevant distinction between
refusal of life support and assisted suicide and therefore equal treatment ought
to be offered to each group.

The Supreme Court relied upon the well established distinction between on
the one hand, allowing a person to die because they have declined further treatment and on the other, causing them to die by administering drugs.[24] The fact
that the drugs are self-administered is not relevant to this distinction and the
crucial test is one of causation. When a person dies because treatment is not
started or is withdrawn it is the underlying pathology which causes death.

---

[17] See J Keown, "The Law and Practice of Euthanasia in the Netherlands" (1992) 108 *Law
Quarterly Review* 51–78, and J Griffiths, "The Regulation of Euthanasia and Related Medical
Procedures that Shorten Life in the Netherlands" (1994) 1 *Medical Law International* 137–58, for a
full account.

[18] For further detail see, H Nys, "Physician Involvement in a Patient's Death: A Continental
European Perspective", (1999) 7 *Medical Law Review* 208–246.

[19] The Rights of the Terminally Ill Act 1996.

[20] The operation of this legislation is discussed in detail in ch. 2.

[21] The Death with Dignity Act 1994.

[22] *Washington* v. *Glucksberg* S Ct 2258 (1997).

[23] *Vacco* v. *Quill* 117 S Ct 2293 (1997).

[24] See for example, *Matter of Conroy*, 98 NJ 321, 355, 486 A. 2d 1209, 1226 (1985) which held
that, "when feeding tube is removed, death results . . . from [the patient's] underlying medical condition", *Cruzan* v. *Director, Mo. Dept. of Health*, 497 US 261 (1990) at 278–80, *Airedale NHS Trust*
v. *Bland* [1993] 2 WLR 316 at 368, *People* v. *Kevorkian*, 447 (1997) US LEXIS 4038 *3.

However, where death results from the administration of drugs, death is caused by the medication. Therefore the Equal Protection Clause was not violated by upholding this distinction because everyone is allowed to refuse treatment while nobody was at that time permitted to assist suicide, hence New York's prohibition of assisted suicide was not found to be unconstitutional.

In England the common law of homicide is central to the proscription of euthanasia. If the dying process is hastened by one person to limit the suffering of another the criminal law makes no concession for benevolent motives or the wishes of the alleged victim; it steadfastly refuses to "leave the issue in the hands of doctors; it treats euthanasia as murder."[25] John Keown describes the notion that any life may be worthless enough to be discontinued as "alien" to the English criminal law since the principle of the sanctity of human life means that, "because all lives are intrinsically valuable, it is always wrong intentionally to kill an innocent human being".[26] Others have expressed concerns about the potential impact of any relaxation of the prohibition of euthanasia, in all its guises, on the doctor/patient relationship. Capron articulates the point very forcefully, stating:

"I never want to have to wonder whether the physician coming into my hospital room is wearing the white coat . . . of the healer . . . or the black hood of the executioner".[27]

He raises the spectre of doctors practising euthanasia for their own motives, rather than at the voluntary request of their patients.

Despite the obvious validity of such widely held concerns, the words of one woman dying of a brain tumour epitomise the close association between voluntary euthanasia and dignified death in the minds of many when she said:

"If I had my way I could say good-bye . . . I could choose my time and be calm and collected about it. I have had a good life and I would dearly like a good death . . . my last wish is to die with dignity".[28]

In this context voluntary euthanasia offers the opportunity to select the time and manner of one's dying in order to secure a peaceful death, unencumbered by intrusive medical technology. A death such as this, where the person concerned is able to maintain control and exert a similar influence over dying as has been experienced throughout her lifetime, is perceived as inherently dignified. Dignity here represents the capacity to exercise choice and have those choices respected.

Thus if clinicians and carers acceded to requests for voluntary euthanasia they would not do so with malicious intent. They would do so through a compassionate desire to give effect to the autonomous wishes of patients seeking death

---

[25] G Williams, *Textbook of Criminal Law* 2nd edn. (London, Stevens, 1983) at 580.

[26] J Keown, "Courting Euthanasia? Tony Bland and the Law Lords" (1993) 9(3) *Ethics and Medicine* 15.

[27] A M Capron, "Legal and Ethical Problems in Decisions for Death" (1986) 14 *Law Medicine & Health Care* 141.

[28] C Taylor-Watson in Margarette Driscoll "After a Good Life, Why can't we Choose a Good Death?" *The Sunday Times*, 15 January 1995.

with dignity. And, because the fundamental ethical and humanitarian questions raised by voluntary euthanasia are perhaps too complex to facilitate resolution through the criminal justice system, it may be inappropriate to police euthanasia with the blunt instrument of the criminal law of homicide which emphasises sanction, prevention and retribution. A determination of how euthanasia and the law of homicide interact and how they relate to the concept of human dignity is therefore central to this analysis. Before this can be achieved however, it is first necessary to define when life ends and death begins medically, legally and philosophically, since these definitions are central to our social, moral and legal understanding of euthanasia and any criminal culpability that attaches to it.

DEAD OR ALIVE?

There was a time when it was obvious to even the casual observer that a person had died. There would be no respiration or pulse and the body would cease to function finally and irrevocably. This is no longer the case. Even lay people now have the knowledge and ability to resuscitate a person who has suffered a heart attack or respiratory failure and effectively bring them back from the dead. Medical professionals, aided by technology, have the expertise to revive a person who in earlier times would have been considered dead, and to keep a body alive even after the brain has died. As a result, questions of exactly when life ends and how death is defined have been clinically and legally perplexing. Indeed some commentators have regarded the definitions of death available to them as highly ambiguous, such that:

> "at whatever level we choose to call death, it is an arbitrary decision. Death of the heart? The hair still grows. Death of the brain? The heart may still beat".[29]

This being the case, exactly when is somebody medically and legally dead?

Determining the answers to this question with certainty depends upon an understanding of what categorises the distinction between life and death. Currently accepted definitions of life and death are informed by religious,[30] philosophical, cultural and legal perceptions, and are historically specific, having evolved alongside the development of medical science. Modern medicine relies extensively on technology to mechanically support life while diagnostic and therapeutic procedures are undertaken and in some situations diagnosing death has itself become an equally complex process. For example, when a person is warm to touch and rosy to the eye but breathing with the aid of a machine, how can we tell if she is alive or dead?

---

[29] H Beecher, "The New Definition of Death, Some Opposing Viewpoints" (1971) 5 *International Journal of Clinical Pharmacology* 120–1.

[30] Of particular interest here are differing religious explanations of the relationship between body and soul. For example in the Buddhist faith it is accepted that the soul only leaves the body three days after physical death has occurred.

Medically Dead

When the first heart transplant surgery was performed in South Africa in 1967 this question took on a new significance. To transplant a heart successfully the operation must be performed before the organ stops functioning in order to ensure that it is not damaged. But if death is defined in terms of continuing respiration and circulation, the removal of the heart would apparently cause death and could be regarded as murder. If patients are to be offered the benefits of now commonplace techniques such as artificial ventilation and organ transplantation without clinicians being exposed to legal sanction, an accurate and readily understandable definition of death is clearly essential. Similarly, the assessment of potential criminal culpability for euthanasia and assisted death depends upon cognisance of exactly when and how a person has died.

Death does not occur in an instant but is the result of the culmination of the processes of dying. After the cardio-vascular and the respiratory systems have ceased to function, the death of the body tissues at cellular level is a gradual and variable process. Some tissues and organs continue to *live* even after others have died, a phenomenon that was clearly described more than twenty years ago in a report by the Conference of the Medical Royal Colleges, with the words:

> "death is not an event: it is a process, the various organs and systems supporting the continuation of life failing and eventually ceasing altogether to function, successively and at different times".[31]

However, although most body tissues have the capacity to withstand a degree of oxygen starvation and to repair themselves once their oxygen supply is restored all tissues die if they are permanently deprived of oxygen. This, together with the progressive nature of dying, necessitates the identification of those organs which are most vital to the maintenance of life and whose failure effectively defines death.

The cells of the brain and spinal cord are unique in that they do not possess the capacity to regenerate; once brain damage has occurred it is irreversible. But some areas of the brain, most notably the brain stem, are less susceptible to oxygen deficiency than others and can endure longer periods of hypoxia before permanent damage occurs. All the autonomic functions of the body, including respiration, are controlled by the brain stem so if it is damaged breathing will stop. The cessation of spontaneous respiration due to circulatory arrest or "intercranial catastrophe" caused by disease or trauma,[32] will ultimately result in death, although it may be many minutes before cardiac failure finally occurs.[33] At this point modern medical technology can interrupt the natural

---

[31] Editorial, "Diagnosis of Death" (1979) 1 *British Medical Journal* 332.
[32] C Pallis "Return to Elsinore" (1990) 16 *Journal Medical Ethics* 10.
[33] For an interesting discussion of conceptual issues concerned with defining death see E T Bartlett, "Differences Between Death and Dying" (1995) 21 *Journal of Medical Ethics* 270–276.

processes and the patient may be resuscitated and placed on a mechanical respirator. Breathing and circulation will then continue even though the brain stem has ceased to function. Nevertheless a person whose brain stem has been damaged in this way can never regain the ability to function independently.

In the light of the impact of medical advances and authoritative academic and medical comment from around the world,[34] the Report of the Medical Royal Colleges considered how death should be defined in 1976 and recommended that "permanent functional death of the brain constitutes brain death".[35] The following recommendations for the diagnosis of brain stem death were also contained in the 1976 Report:

—the patient should exhibit fixed and dilated pupils (the eyes move with the head and there is no "dolls eye" response),
—there should be no response to touching the eye with a wisp of cotton wool or similar material,
—there should be no eye movement in response to cold water being passed into the ear,
—there should be no gag reflex,
—there should be no response to pain,
—there should be no respiratory response, i.e. the patient will fail to breath spontaneously when the respirator is withdrawn.

This definition of death was affirmed by the Conference of the Medical Royal Colleges in 1979 with the statement that brain death could be diagnosed when brain "functions" had, "permanently and irreversibly ceased".[36] The tests outlined above are designed to determine that brain functions cannot be restored. The use of the word "functions" was carefully chosen to eliminate the possibility of failure to diagnose death in circumstances where continuing metabolic or electrical activity in isolated areas of the brain is demonstrable. Such activity does occasionally occur but if the criteria and tests used to diagnose brain stem death have been satisfied it has no bearing on the patient's prospects of recovery. The medical definition of death is now associated with this kind of irremediable damage to the brain and patients who have sustained such trauma have been variously described as "brain dead" or "brain stem dead". The body remains artificially alive but the brain has died.

Adopting this definition of death has had wide-reaching implications for the law, as well as for the practice of medicine. Once it is recognised that a patient's body can be artificially maintained, beyond the point where brain death is established but that somatic death has not yet occurred, then it must be accepted that a doctor's role is no longer one of merely treating disease and saving life. Indeed the role of the doctor has inevitably been broadened to include the ability to,

---

[34] Perhaps most influential was the Report of the Harvard Brain Death Committee, *Journal of the American Medical Association*, August 1968.
[35] "Diagnosis of Death" (1976) 2 *British Medical Journal* 1187.
[36] "Diagnosis of Death" (1979) 1 *British Medical Journal* 332 at para 7.

"take decisions which may affect the span of human life".[37] Defining death as occurring when the brain ceases to retain the capacity to maintain the bodily functions can also sit uneasily with everyday understandings of life and death. Intuitively a dead person is thought of as inanimate, cold and pale, but the appearance of a person who is "brain dead" and connected to a life support system contradicts this image. While respiration and circulation continue the body appears to be alive, even if the stimulus is inorganic, and this can create false impressions. Those who care for patients maintained in this way habitually refer to them as if they remain alive as do visiting relatives and friends.[38] It is alien to human understanding to relate to a warm "breathing" body as if it were dead; to do so seems disrespectful and destructive of human dignity.

Conversely, some commentators argue that to remain alive but devoid of the ability to function as an independent human being, for example when a diagnosis of permanent vegetative state (PVS) has been made, is an undignified state which ought to be defined as death. A correct diagnosis of PVS or long term coma means that the ability to function as a social human being will never be regained. Spontaneous respiration and circulation can continue but the capacity for cognitive awareness or interaction with the world is permanently absent. Cognitive function is what gives value to human life and when it is permanently lost the unique reasoning character of the human personality disappears with it. Theories of mind/body dualism where the body and the mind are regarded as distinct, help to inform the supposition that a human being amounts to more than just a functioning, breathing body. Here the physical presence of the flesh, bones and organs of the body constitutes the tangible person, but it is the mind that "differentiates a man from other less interesting objects in the world—plants, rocks, and masses of gas, for example".[39] The mind is also regarded as the ultimate repository of the individual human personality so that, "cerebral function is manifested in consciousness, awareness, memory, anticipation, recognition and emotions [and] there is no human life in the absence of these".[40] Therefore, if "the personal, identifiable life of an individual human can be equated to the living function of that part of the brain called the cerebrum"[41] the individual must be considered dead once cognitive or cerebral function has ceased.

A definition of death that centres on the distinctiveness of the entity which is the human being, and provides that once that distinctiveness is lost that person is dead, means that death may be diagnosed when "the medical tests have in fact determined that there is no potential for spontaneous cerebral brain function, even if spontaneous respiration continues".[42] But the implications of adopting

[37] H Beynon, "Doctors as Murderers" [1982] *Crim LR* 17.
[38] Several examples of this phenomenon are offered by Peter Singer in *Rethinking Life and Death* (Oxford, Oxford University Press, 1995) at 32.
[39] K Campbell, *Body and Mind* 2nd edn. (Indiana, Notre Dame Press, 1984) at 2.
[40] S D Olinger, "Medical Death" (1975) 27 *Baylor Law Review* 22.
[41] *Ibid.*
[42] E W Keyserlingk, "Sanctity of Life or Quality of Life" (1979) Law Reform Commission of Canada, Protection of Life Series Study Paper, 62.

these notions about what constitutes death extend beyond the realms of the practical and obvious to the philosophical and religious. Janet Daley eloquently explains the problem:

> "to move from the religious idea that what sanctifies human beings is the possession of an immortal soul, to the rationalist one that the only thing that is sacred—the only thing that gives us a right to live—is a fully functioning mind, is a moral shift of considerable significance".[43]

That moral shift is one that the medical profession appears not to have embraced, since "doctors invariably regard such [PVS] patients as alive"[44] and cognitive death remains peripheral to established medical criteria for defining death and is consequently not definitive. Yet, as will be discussed more fully in chapter two, the treatment of patients in a persistent vegetative state who have suffered cognitive death can be problematic. Frequently the relatives do not wish their loved one to be maintained in such a condition indefinitely, and the demands on scarce medical resources dictate that there is reluctance to persist with costly but futile treatment. The courts have been required to decide whether or not a person must be maintained or may lawfully be allowed to die, and the significance of brain stem death and cognitive death has been assessed in order to establish a legal definition of death.[45]

Legally Alive

There is no statutory definition of death in the United Kingdom, although the merits and demerits of introducing such a definition have been widely discussed.[46] By comparison, in America death has been defined by statute for many years with an early example, Kansas Statutes 1971 including the rather ambiguous statement that:

> "A person will be considered medically and legally dead if, in the opinion of a physician, based on ordinary standards of medical practice, there is the absence of spontaneous brain function".

The situations where a clear legal definition of death can be a significant advantage are many and diverse. It may be necessary to determine exactly when a person died in order to establish who will benefit from the deceased's estate, or to

---

[43] J Daley, "Where's Mercy in Such Killings?" *Daily Telegraph* 16 April 1996.
[44] P D G Skegg, *Law, Ethics and Medicine* (Oxford, Clarendon, 1984) at 215, parenthesis added.
[45] Cases include *Re Quinlan*, 70 NJ 10 353A 2d 647 (1976), *Cruzan* v. *Dept. of Health of Missouri*, 110 S Ct 2841 (1990), *Airedale NHS Trust* v. *Bland*, [1993] 1 All ER 821, and *Re A* [1992] 3 Med LR 303.
[46] Examples of the arguments for and against implementing a statutory definition are included in, I Kennedy, "Alive or Dead" (1969) 22 *Current Legal Problems* 102, P D G Skegg, "The Case for a Statutory Definition of Death", (1976) *Journal of Medical Ethics* 190, and the report of the Criminal Law Revision Committee, *Fourteenth Report: Offences Against the Person*, Cmnd. 7844 (London, HMSO, 1980) at para 37.

allocate criminal responsibility for causing the death, or to absolve professional carers of responsibility by negating any possible duty of care. Each of these situations has featured in cases that have sought to clarify the issue of when a person is legally dead.

Smith v. Smith[47] was an early American case which sought a legal definition of death. Mr and Mrs Smith had died following a road accident. Mr Smith was declared to be dead on arrival at hospital but Mrs Smith was unconscious and remained so until certified dead seventeen days later. The Smiths had no children and each had made a will to the effect that their property should pass to the other in the event of death. At issue was who should inherit the Smith's estate? If Mrs Smith had not died in the accident then Mr Smith's property would pass to her and thence to her beneficiaries on her death. But, under the established law, if they had died simultaneously in the accident then the joint estate would pass to Mr Smith's family.

Reflecting a traditional approach to the issue, the Court held that while a person continued to breathe, even if aided by a machine, he or she remained legally alive. However, as medical technology advanced this approach became increasingly problematic, as is demonstrated by the British case *R v. Potter*.[48]

Here the "victim" was admitted to hospital with severe head injuries following a fight with the defendant in the case. Fourteen hours later he stopped breathing and was placed on a respirator. After twenty-four hours a kidney was removed for transplantation and subsequently the respirator was switched off. He then failed to breath spontaneously and was declared dead. The traditional definition of death dictates that the victim/patient remained alive while respiration and circulation continued, even if this was artificially maintained. Therefore the kidney had been removed while he was still alive, without consent, and for no purpose which was beneficial to him, thus the surgeons had committed a battery. Furthermore, the defendant then argued that the actions of the doctor had broken the chain of causation between the assault, for which he was responsible, and the death of the victim. The court appears to have agreed because the assailant was convicted only of common assault.

The medical definition of death was already clearly in need of refinement when the advent of two important criminal appeal cases made it imperative that the law keep pace with medical developments.[49] In *R v. Steel* the victim was a young woman, Carol Wilkinson, who left her job in a bakery at about 9 a.m. on 10 October 1977 to walk home. At some time between 9 o'clock and 9.30 a.m. she was attacked, stripped of her clothing and beaten about the head with a fifty pound stone that was later found nearby. She was discovered in a field next to the road soon after and taken to hospital where she was found to have

[47] (1958) 317, SW 2d, 275 Supreme Court of Arkansas.

[48] *The Times* 26 July 1963, discussed in D W Myers, *The Human Body and the Law* 2nd edn. (Edinburgh, Edinburgh University Press, 1990) at 190, and I Kennedy, A Grubb, *Medical Law: Text with Materials* 2nd edn. (London, Butterworths, 1994) at 1389.

[49] R v. *Malcherek and Steel* [1981] 2 All ER 422.

suffered multiple skull fractures and concomitant brain damage. Ms Wilkinson was connected to a ventilator but this was disconnected two days later when no electrical brain activity could be detected. The post-mortem examination suggested that decomposition of the brain had already begun. The question was, when did she die?

The same question arose in R v. *Malcherek*, which involved a violent marital dispute between Malcherek and his wife Christina, culminating in her receiving nine stab wounds. One wound penetrated her abdomen necessitating surgery to remove a section of intestine but Mrs Malcherek was initially expected to make a full recovery. Unfortunately she later collapsed and was transferred to another hospital for more specialised treatment. She deteriorated further and was thought to have suffered a massive pulmonary embolism, a recognised complication of major abdominal surgery. Resuscitation and surgery were performed. A large blood clot was removed from her heart which then resumed normal functioning. But, because there had been no circulation for approximately thirty minutes, anoxic brain damage was anticipated. Mrs Malcherek was placed on a ventilator and an electro-encephalogram was performed to determine the level of brain function. The prognosis was poor. She did breathe spontaneously for a while until a further deterioration occurred, which was attributed to a blood clot in the brain. Tests were carried out to confirm that there was irreparable damage to the brain. Consultations then took place with the relatives before the life support system was switched off and she died.

At the trials of both Malcherek and Steel, the juries were advised to consider only the established facts and the intentions of the defendants. Both defendants were convicted but appealed, arguing that the juries should have been invited to consider the issue of causation. They suggested that death had actually been caused by the doctors switching off the machines and not by the actions of the defendants; a view which was consistent with traditional definitions of death.

It was held on appeal that in each case, the medical treatment had been competent and adequate. The wounds inflicted on the victims remained "a continuing and indeed substantial cause of death" such that the defendants must be convicted. Lord Lane said:

> "Where the medical practitioner using generally acceptable methods, came to the conclusion that the patient was, for all practical purposes dead and that such vital functions as remained were being maintained solely by mechanical means and accordingly discontinued treatment, that did not break the chain of causation between the initial injury and death".[50]

The judgment recognised that the action of the doctors was not responsible for the death of the patients and that there could be multiple causes, but it did not explicitly define what constitutes death. Subsequent cases similarly failed to adequately address the issue, despite having the opportunity and the need so

---

[50]   R v. *Malcherek and Steel* [1981] 2 All ER at 430 per Lord Lane.

to do. Amongst these was the case of *Mail Newspapers PLC* v. *Express Newspapers PLC*,[51] concerning who owned the copyright to photographs taken at Mr and Mrs Bell's wedding and published in seven daily newspapers.

Mrs Bell had suffered a brain haemorrhage when she was twenty-four weeks pregnant. She was thought to be clinically dead but was maintained on a life support system in the hope that her baby could be born alive, hence the media interest. Here it would clearly have been appropriate and beneficial for the court to articulate a legal definition of death but none was forthcoming.

The legal ownership of the copyright to the photographs was in doubt because, although Mrs Bell had commissioned them she had acted in consultation with her future husband and it was he that had ultimately paid for them. Mr Bell had signed an agreement with Mail Newspapers PLC, giving them sole rights to future publication but it was questionable whether he had the authority so to do. The court found that the copyright was jointly owned by the couple and that neither co-owner was entitled to grant an exclusive license. According to Millet J there was therefore, "at the very least a serious question to be tried whether Mrs Bell is alive or dead"[52] because only in the event of Mrs Bell's death would Mr Bell be empowered to grant the sole rights to Mail Newspapers PLC. Despite the fact that Mrs Bell's status as dead or alive was recognised as "a serious question" the court avoided the opportunity to define death on this occasion, being content instead to decide the case on the basis of the probability that she was dead.

> "The overwhelming probability must be that, if Mrs Bell is not already dead, she will incontrovertibly be dead immediately or very shortly after the birth of the baby, when it is virtually certain that the life support system, having fulfilled its purpose, will be switched off, so that at that time, if not before, the overwhelming likelihood is that the sole title to the copyright will have vested in Mr Bell".[53]

It is perhaps understandable that a Court convened to hear a case concerning intellectual property rights would be reluctant to propose a legal definition of death. It was then to be another five years before the position was accorded further clarification by Johnson J in *Re A (A Minor)*.[54]

Child A was admitted to hospital via the accident and emergency department following an injury suffered at home. No heart beat could be detected and initial attempts at resuscitation proved unsuccessful until eventually cardiac function was restored. The next day he was transferred to another hospital for assessment and intensive therapy, but still no signs of recovery could be induced. The consultant overseeing A's treatment carried out tests to determine whether the child was in fact, brain stem dead, according to the criteria outlined by the Medical Royal Colleges.[55] When the tests confirmed that he was indeed

---

[51] [1987] FSR 90.
[52] *Ibid* at 94.
[53] [1987] FSR 90 at 95.
[54] [1992] 3 Med L R 303.
[55] "The Diagnosis of Brain Death" (1976) 2 *British Medical Journal* 1187, and "Diagnosis of Death" (1979) 1 *British Medical Journal* 332.

clinically dead they were repeated by a second consultant, a paediatric neurologist, who reached the same conclusion. It was then proposed that Child A be disconnected from the ventilator.

Child A and his siblings were the subject of an emergency protection order under the Children Act 1989. This order decreed that parental responsibility for the children was conferred upon the local authority under section 44(4)(c), but that this was imposed without absolving the parental responsibility of the parents.[56] The parents were hostile to the clinicians and their findings because suspicions had been raised that the child had sustained non-accidental injuries. They refused to give permission for the life support to be withdrawn. Therefore the local authority sought a precise declaration as to the child's status and the legal position should artificial life support be withdrawn. After hearing the evidence Johnson J. declared:

> "*A* is now dead for all legal, as well as medical, purposes, and . . . [I] make a declaration that should the consultant, or other consultants . . . consider it appropriate to disconnect *A* from the ventilator, in so doing they would not be acting contrary to the law . . . I hold too that it would be wholly contrary to the interests of that child, as they may now be, for his body to be subjected to what would seem to me to be the continuing indignity to which it is subject".[57]

This statement effectively incorporates the definition of death adopted by the medical professions in 1976 into the common law by accepting that the legal and medical definitions of death are the same. Brain stem death can now be regarded as definitive of death both medically and legally, provided that the procedures and recommendations of the Report of the Royal Colleges have been strictly adhered to and the brain stem has totally and irreversibly ceased to function.

But it is clear that brain stem death is not universally accepted as the most appropriate method for assessing life's end. Some of the philosophical concerns about distinguishing brain death and cognitive death already discussed were emphasised in the highly publicised case of *Airedale NHS Trust* v. *Bland*.[58] Anthony Bland had been in a PVS for four years when his family and doctors applied to the Court for a declaration that to withdraw nutrition and hydration would be lawful. Advocates of the theory that individuals who have permanently lost cognitive function should be regarded as dead would argue that Anthony Bland had been dead since the accident that resulted in his irreversible coma. Those caring for him regarded him as alive but accepted that there was no prospect of recovery and that treatment withdrawal would lead to his death. In view of these tensions the Law Lords carefully considered the issue of when death occurs.

> "as a result of developments in modern medical technology, doctors no longer associate death exclusively with breathing and heartbeat, and it has come to be accepted that death occurs when the brain, and in particular the brain stem, has been destroyed".[59]

---

[56] s.2(b) Children Act 1989.
[57] [1992] 3 Med LR 303, at 305.
[58] [1993] 1 All ER 821, [1993] 2 WLR 316.
[59] *Ibid* per Lord Goff at 366.

The Law Lords concluded that:

> "in law, Anthony is still alive. It is true that his condition is such that it can be described as a living death; but he is nevertheless still alive . . . The evidence is that Anthony's brain stem is still alive and functioning and it follows that, in the present state of medical science, he is still alive and should be so regarded as a matter of law".[60]

Cognitive death is not therefore a state presently recognised as death by medicine or the law. Were it to be so it would raise serious problems concerning the cause of death in trauma victims and the victims of crime, as well as for the care of brain damaged infants and adults. These issues will be discussed in greater detail in chapter two.

EUTHANASIA AS HOMICIDE

These medical and legal definitions of death have been outlined in order to facilitate this discussion of the ethical and legal implications of euthanasia and assisted death. It is also necessary to consider the relationship between euthanasia and homicide which dictates criminal culpability where euthanasia and assisted death are at issue. Homicide includes murder and manslaughter[61] both of which are common law offences, without statutory definition. Murder is classically defined as, "when a man of sound memory, and the age of discretion unlawfully killeth within the country of the realm any reasonable creature . . . under the Kings peace, with malice aforethought".[62] Modern language therefore describes murder as the intentional, unlawful killing of one human being by another and it is clear that euthanasia will tend to fall within this definition.

Yet the criminalisation of voluntary euthanasia is increasingly at odds with our libertarian society's definition of morally wrong behaviour and conduct which is harmful to others. Harm itself is a concept susceptible to a variety of moral interpretations and Ashworth correctly states that, "one cannot proceed far without adopting a definition of harm".[63] John Stuart Mill's liberal philosophy declares that individual autonomy should be respected and that the state should criminalise only conduct which is harmful to others.[64] Voluntary euthanasia falls outside the scope of criminal behaviour in this model since the harm is not inflicted on others and is performed at the volition of the "victim". Against this, Feinberg has argued that the criminal law should be invoked to prevent or reduce *any* conduct that *may* prove harmful to others,[65] of which

---

[60] [1993] 2 WLR 316, per Lord Goff at 368.

[61] Infanticide is also defined as homicide but, under the Infanticide Act 1938, it applies only where a woman causes the death of her own child before that child reaches the age of twelve months.

[62] Coke, 3 Inst 47.

[63] A Ashworth, *Principles of Criminal Law* 2nd edn. (Oxford, Clarendon Press, 1995) at 30.

[64] J S Mill, *On Liberty* (London, Parker, 1859).

[65] J Feinberg, *Harm to Others* (Oxford, Oxford University Press, 1984), J Feinberg, *Harmless Wrongdoing* (Oxford, Oxford University Press, 1988).

voluntary euthanasia is clearly an example. Voluntary euthanasia therefore remains contrary to the criminal law but does not, in practice, sit easily with the principles that underpin it. The following cases demonstrate that as a consequence, people (doctors, patients and carers) who confront a choice between protracted, undignified, suffering, and quick release, are not well served by a criminal justice system which rests upon such uncertainty and inconsistency. As a result of criminalisation dignity in dying may be achieved at the expense of the dignity of a caring medical practitioner, family member or compassionate friend.

In 1957 Dr John Bodkin Adams was tried for the murder of an eighty-four year old woman in his care, who had named him as a beneficiary in her will.[66] The patient was terminally ill and succumbed following the administration of large doses of narcotics prescribed by Dr Adams. Other, similar cases were also suspected in his practice. Devlin J advised the jury that, regardless of the health of the victim and the motive of the accused, the law would treat as murder any action which intended to kill and did in fact kill. Despite this he also ruled that,

> "If the first purpose of medicine, the restoration of health, can no longer be achieved there is still much for a doctor to do, and he is entitled to do all that is proper and necessary to relieve pain and suffering, even if the measures he takes may incidentally shorten human life".[67]

After a seventeen day trial the jury declined to convict. They deliberated for only forty-five minutes before finding Dr Adams not guilty.

Acquittal was also the outcome of the trial of Dr Leonard Arthur, a paediatrician who was charged with the murder of a neonate with Down's Syndrome.[68] The child had been rejected by his parents who instructed Dr Arthur that they did not wish the baby to survive. Subsequently a note was entered in the medical records that the baby should receive "nursing care only". The infant was not fed but received strong pain killing drugs, allegedly to ease his distress. He died three days later. The doctor argued that the child died of natural causes due to Down's Syndrome, and when evidence was revealed that other significant congenital abnormalities were also present, the charge was reduced to attempted murder. Despite being advised that doctors, like everyone else, must practise within the law, and that benevolent motives are irrelevant in determining intention, the jury failed to convict Dr Arthur.

The pattern was repeated in the trial of Dr Carr who was charged with attempted murder when his patient died after he injected him with a huge dose of phenobarbitone (a barbiturate).[69] Compelling evidence was presented that the

---

[66] H Palmer, "Dr Adams on Trial for Murder", R v. *Adams* [1957] Crim LR 365.

[67] *Ibid*, at 375.

[68] R v. *Arthur, The Times*, 6 November 1981, 1, and (1993) 12 BMLR 1. This case remained officially unreported for many years but many accounts are available, see for example, Poole, "Arthur's Case: A Comment" [1986] *Crim LR*. 383.

[69] R v. *Carr, The Sunday Times*, 30 November 1986, 1.

patient had been suffering terribly with inoperable lung cancer and had repeatedly requested that his inevitable death be hastened. Dr Carr was acquitted.

A different outcome occurred in *R v. Cox*.[70] Here the clinician carried out the wishes of his distressed and dying patient and deliberately injected her with strong potassium chloride, a drug which causes death but had no therapeutic value. She died soon afterwards and Dr Cox was charged with attempted murder. The jury was given no choice but to convict in this instance since the death had resulted from deliberate unlawful killing and was therefore categorised as homicide in spite of the apparently benevolent motive. There was no legal alternative to finding Dr Cox guilty as charged, even though the patient's family considered that he had enabled their elderly relative to secure a merciful release from the terrible pain and distress she was enduring so that she could die with dignity. That, and subsequent cases[71] generated considerable public debate and concern for the doctor, the patient, her family and others who may find themselves in a similar situation.

These cases stand as authority for the basic premise that deliberately to take the life of another is a crime. They are also testimony to the hesitance of juries to disregard the compelling motives of the individuals concerned, unless the evidence is incontrovertible. Against this background, *Airedale NHS Trust* v. *Bland*,[72] was presented to the courts to obtain a declaration that withdrawal of "treatment"[73] leading to death was lawful, so that the medical attendants could avoid criminal prosecution. Those caring for Anthony Bland faced an ethical dilemma if they continued to treat him and a legal one if they did not. His condition offered no prospect of recovery or improvement, so to maintain a regime of burdensome and invasive treatment was medically futile. Yet to discontinue treatment would cause his death and give rise to criminal culpability. Withholding nutrition and hydration from Tony Bland would inevitably result in his death; this was clearly understood, even desired, by those responsible for his care, and would therefore signal the imposition of murder charges.

Similar issues were graphically depicted by the harrowing experiences of Thomas Creedon and his family.[74] This child was born so severely brain damaged that he could never interact with the world around him or those in it. He could only sustain nourishment through intrusive tube feeding and was often inconsolable. The paediatrician responsible for Thomas's initial care dismissed his parents' pleas for their son's life to be brought to a peaceful and dignified conclusion, arguing that to do so would contravene the criminal law. Feeding,

---

[70] *R v. Cox* (1992) 12 BMLR 38.

[71] Most notably amongst these is the case brought by Annie Lindsell, who sought a right to die with dignity in 1997, and the later criminal case brought against Dr David Moore, who was acquitted of murder in 1999.

[72] [1993] 1 All ER 821.

[73] The emphasis on "treatment" is intended to demonstrate the unease with which many commentators have approached the fact that the provision of nutrition and hydration was described as such.

[74] K Toolis, "A Death for Thomas", *The Guardian Weekend*, 3 February 1996, 18–23.

he stated, was a basic right and he had a duty to provide it. Perhaps fortunately for all the Creedons, Thomas died before it became necessary to determine through the courts whether allowing Thomas to die, at his parents' request, would constitute homicide.

The issues raised by these cases characterise the medico-legal dilemma generated by voluntary euthanasia. Good medical practice requires that patients do not experience unnecessary and unwelcome suffering but the criminal law is inconsistent in its response to practitioners who take life-limiting decisions. Clinicians like Nigel Cox, who openly end their patients' lives out of compassion, are sanctioned,[75] while euthanasia through the subterfuge of selective non-treatment,[76] and double effect, where beneficial medication is given in the certain knowledge that death will occur as a side effect,[77] has been permitted.[78] Some authors have suggested that if Dr Cox had used pain relieving medication, instead of strong potassium chloride, he would have been shielded from conviction by the doctrine of double effect.[79] Such an approach would have placed Cox's conduct firmly within Devlin J.'s contention that, "the doctor is entitled to relieve pain and suffering even if the measures he takes may incidentally shorten life",[80] but would not have avoided the simple truth that it was his intention to kill the patient, albeit for benevolent motives. Within the law as it stands Dr Cox was criminally culpable because he had foresight of the consequences of his actions,[81] and those actions were a probable cause of the patient's death. The consent of the deceased and the approval of her relatives is irrelevant in this context, providing no effective defence for the clinician.

The allocation of criminal responsibility in cases involving euthanasia and assisted death are, as in all criminal cases, dependent upon determining the *actus reus* and *mens rea* of the crime involved, namely homicide. The requisite *mens rea* is apparent in *Bland* in that the purpose of withdrawing treatment is to bring about death. The *actus reus* is less clear cut, depending on whether treatment withdrawal is properly described as an act or an omission, whether the cessation of treatment is a demonstrable cause of death and, if treatment withdrawal constitutes an omission, was there a duty of care? Ann Winterton's Medical Treatment (Prevention of Euthanasia) Bill, presented to the House of Commons in December 1999, had at its core the intention to remove such distinctions. It aimed to prohibit the withdrawal and withholding of medical treatment and sustenance from a patient where the intention is to cause death. Its enactment would have effectively prevented cases similar to Tony Bland's achieving similar resolution.

---

[75] R v. *Cox* (1992) 12 BMLR 38.

[76] *Airedale NHS Trust* v. *Bland* [1993] 1 All ER 821, *Frenchay NHS Trust* v. *S* [1994] 2 All ER 403.

[77] H Palmer, "Dr Adams on Trial for Murder", R v. *Adams* [1957] Crim LR 365.

[78] These issues will be discussed in detail in ch. 2.

[79] C Wells, "Patients, Consent and Criminal Law" (1994) 1 *Journal of Social Welfare and Family Law* 65, at 73.

[80] H Palmer, "Dr Adams on Trial for Murder", R v. *Adams* [1957] Crim LR 365.

[81] R v. *Moloney* [1985] AC 905, R v. *Nedrick* [1986] 3 All ER 1.

Chapter two will analyse the legal and ethical issues raised by the withdrawal of nutrition and hydration in detail alongside those related to other forms of euthanasia such as assisted suicide, double effect and mercy killing. The fine distinctions between killing and caring will be examined by exposing the tensions that are inevitably generated by end of life treatment decisions. Killing is a crime and generally the criminal law distinguishes conduct which society considers harmful as worthy of criminal sanction. Therefore in most instances of homicide, death is the harm caused by the conduct of the accused who has killed the victim. With euthanasia, it is the indignity of enduring the kind of *living death*, associated with the protracted dying process associated with terminal disease, or surviving in a persistent vegetative state, that can appear more harmful than death itself. So ending the harm by bringing the life of the victim to a dignified end can be considered caring. As a result great significance is attached to the perceived need for dignity in dying by those who advocate euthanasia, but there are fundamental questions which need to be addressed before a valid case can be made for euthanasia as a mechanism for providing dignity in dying.

EUTHANASIA AS DEATH WITH DIGNITY

Human dignity is a descriptive and value-laden quality encompassing self-determination and the ability to make autonomous choices, and implies a quality of life consistent with the ability to exercise self-determined choices. It is a concept that is gaining currency with modern political philosophers. Ronald Dworkin, for example, describes belief in individual human dignity as the most important feature of Western political culture giving people the moral right "to confront the most fundamental questions about the meaning and value of their own lives".[82] People who examine the meaning and value of their lives in the face of imminent death often express concerns that their dignity may be compromised if the dying process is prolonged and involves becoming incapacitated and dependent. The ability to retain a similar level of control over dying as one has exercised during life is widely regarded as a way of achieving death with dignity. Madan argues that this is because:

> "dignity does not come to the dying from immortality fantasies, or compensatory ideas, such as reincarnation and paradise, nor does it come from empowerment through modern medicine. It comes from the affirmation of values, not only up to the boundaries of death . . . but in a manner that encompasses dying under living and does not oppose the two in a stern dualistic logic".[83]

In line with this view advocates of euthanasia as death with dignity believe that respect for individual autonomy should allow patients the opportunity to choose euthanasia as an alternative to becoming dependent upon medical carers

---

[82] R Dworkin, *Life's Dominion* (London, Harper-Collins, 1993) at 166.
[83] T N Madan, "Dying with Dignity" (1992) 35 *Social Science and Medicine* 425–32.

and burdensome to family and society.[84] Patient autonomy, self-determination and control are given legal expression through the law of consent which theoretically offers every person the right to "determine what shall be done with his own body"[85] and ensures that anyone who imposes medical treatment, involving physical contact or harm upon another, in the absence of valid consent, will be criminally culpable. Any patient with the mental capacity to give consent is also entitled to withhold consent,[86] "even if a refusal may risk personal injury to his health or even lead to premature death".[87] Established exceptions to this general rule allow for treatment to be administered in the absence of consent if there is a duty to act,[88] or necessity.[89] And failure to obtain consent where these exceptions are not present can amount to criminal assault and battery. The law pertaining to consent and issues relating to it are therefore pivotal to an analysis of euthanasia and death with dignity. Chapters three and four offer a detailed analysis of these issues and demonstrate that in practice an individual's right autonomously to determine what is done with her body is often limited.

The law of consent gives individuals the ability to choose whether or not to accept whatever treatment is offered; it does not confer any right to demand that particular forms of treatment be provided, even in the quest for death with dignity. Voluntary passive euthanasia, where death results from selective non-treatment because consent is withheld, is therefore legally permissible while active euthanasia is prohibited. In this way people with the capacity might be able to orchestrate the timing of their own deaths, in an attempt to achieve dignity in dying. However, many of those who may become the potential subjects of concerns about euthanasia are lacking in the mental capacity to give or withhold consent to medical treatment. Their rights to have their wishes and interests respected through autonomy and advance decision-making, and those of their carers and clinical decision-makers will also be considered.

At first glance living wills appear to provide an opportunity to take and maintain control of ones life throughout its entirety. They are frequently promoted as a means of achieving dignity in dying because they provide a mechanism whereby a person's wishes can be recognised and acted upon even after the capacity to consent is lost. Their usefulness to people who are no longer able to participate in medical decision-making will be carefully assessed in chapter five's assessment of their relevance to euthanasia and death with dignity, but it seems likely that their greatest significance may lie in their promise rather than in their practical effect.

---

[84] M Kelner, I Bourgeault, "Patient Control Over Dying: Responses of Health Care Professionals" (1993) 36 *Social Science and Medicine* 757–765, C Seale, J Addington-Hall, "Euthanasia: Why People Want to Die Earlier" (1994) 39 *Social Science and Medicine* 647–54.

[85] *Schloendorf* v. *Society of New York Hospital* (1914) 105 NE 92, 93, (NY) per Cardozo J.

[86] *Re C (Adult Refusal of Treatment)* [1994] 1 All ER 819, [1994] 1 WLR 290.

[87] *Re T (An Adult) (Consent to Medical Treatment)* [1992] 2 FLR 458, per Lord Donaldson MR at 473C.

[88] *R* v. *Stone* [1977] QB 354, *R* v. *Wilkinson, The Times*, 19 April 1978, 5, *R* v. *Smith* [1979] Crim LR 251.

[89] *Murray* v. *McMurchy* [1949] 2 DLR 442, *Re F* [1990] 2 AC 1.

In jurisdictions other than Britain people have brought cases based upon claims of a constitutional right to die with dignity.[90] These examples focus on the right to selective non-treatment and assisted suicide as an alternative to a perceived life of indignity. They do not adequately address the fundamental question of whether this kind of death constitutes dignified dying. British law does not explicitly recognise any right to die with dignity, although both *Airedale NHS Trust* v. *Bland*[91] and *Frenchay NHS Trust* v. *S*[92], amongst others, referred to the importance of dignity and the *indignity* of being maintained in a living death. Non-treatment though could in some circumstances only accomplish a death that has little to do with dignity. Death will result from slow starvation, for those like Bland who have been diagnosed as PVS; untreated infection, for handicapped infants like Thomas Creedon, or perhaps AIDS sufferers; or suffocation due to the discontinuation of artificial respiration for those inflicted with Guillain-Barre syndrome or similar pathology. In each case the dying person can be supported by palliative therapy to lessen any suffering associated with the dying process but few observers would describe such deterioration and decline as dignified.

Moreover, in the broader context of active voluntary euthanasia, death may be caused by drug overdose, asphyxiation, or lethal injection.[93] Such conduct promotes patient autonomy but may not be inherently dignified because the dignity of others may be compromised. Over-emphasising individual autonomy can cause other concepts of private and public good, which might permit greater recognition of the potential effects on people other than the patient, to be overlooked.[94] In particular it is questionable whether the ability to choose and practise euthanasia can actually promote dignity in dying while it remains unlawful and exposes practitioners to the prospect of criminal and professional sanction.

R v. *Cox*,[95] where the doctor exercised absolute respect for his patient's autonomy by responding to her appeals that he curtail her suffering by killing her, illustrates the dilemma. The patient allegedly achieved her dignified death but the doctor who assisted her was subjected to the indignity of a criminal trial. He was convicted of attempted murder and as a consequence faced a professional disciplinary hearing to assess his proficiency and moral integrity. Dr Cox received a suspended jail sentence and a supervision order regarding his clinical conduct. *His* dignity was jeopardised because he acceded to his patient's request for a dignified death.

---

[90] *Rodriguez* v. *A-G of British Columbia* [1993] 3 WWR 553, *B(Nancy)* v. *Hotel-Dieu de Quebec* (1992) 86 DLR (4th) 385, (Quebec Supreme Court), *Cruzan* v. *Missouri Department of Health* 110 S Ct 2841 (1990), and *Re Quinlan* (1976) NJ 355 A 2d 647.

[91] [1993] 1 All ER 821.

[92] *Frenchay NHS Trust* v. *S* [1994] 2 All ER 403.

[93] It is interesting to note that in the context of execution, lethal injection is considered more humane, and therefore perhaps more dignified, than hanging or gassing.

[94] S Jinnet-Sack, "Autonomy in the Company of Others", in A Grubb (ed.), *Choices and Decisions in Health Care* (Chichester, Wiley, 1993) at 97.

[95] *R* v. *Cox* (1992) 12 BMLR 38.

The methods adopted by other health care professionals, who have been acknowledged as instrumental in the premature deaths of others, also demonstrate that euthanasia does not necessarily impart dignity. For example the Dutch doctor, Boudewijn Chabot, was subjected to the indignity of several court and disciplinary procedures after he assisted in the suicide of a physically healthy but depressed patient. Chabot was steadfast in his defence of his actions, believing that his response had been humane, but the court refused to accept his plea that he had acted out of the recognised defence of necessity. It is interesting to ponder on the impact of the court cases and media attention on the dignity of his patient's family.

The practices of the American doctor Jack Kevorkian, alias "Dr Death", also suggest that enabling people to fulfil their desire for death with dignity may simultaneously be destructive of the dignity of others. The former pathologist used the media to promote the commercial use of his suicide machines to people seeking assisted death. One highly publicised criminal case in Michigan involved Janet Adkins, who was suffering from the initial stages of Alzheimer's disease and was anxious to avoid the debilitating progression of the condition. She and her husband met and dined with the doctor and two days later she used Kevorkian's specially converted Volkswagen van to kill herself in a public park. Mrs Adkin's motivation may be wholly understandable as may the doctor's respect for her wish to escape the undignified death she anticipated, but "Dr Death's" methods do little to advance the cause of death with dignity. Of concern here is whether respect for human dignity extends beyond the dignity of the individual involved in a particular enterprise, namely suicide and assisted suicide, to the wider community, in this instance other users of the public park. The dignity of one may be achieved by compromising the dignity of others. Despite this however, for years juries repeatedly declined to convict Dr Kevorkian of homicide or assisting suicide.[96] His techniques may have been undignified and contrary to the letter of the criminal law but they satisfied the morality of a significant proportion of American society.

Euthanasia can offer the opportunity to select the time and manner of one's dying in order to secure a peaceful death, unencumbered by intrusive medical technology, and such a death is perceived by many as inherently dignified. However it is important to identify the precise nature of dignity in this context. Human dignity is a quality with different connotations for different people and in the context of dying many consider it more dignified to take the opportunity to experience every second that life has to offer. The complex arguments around dignity and the way it relates to euthanasia will be expanded in chapter six which will discuss the similarities and differences between perceptions of dignity in dying in different cultures. It will also consider the alternative to euthanasia

---

[96] Reporting from New York for the *Daily Mail* on "Dr Death's" involvement in the death of Briton Austin Barnstable in Michigan on 10 May 1996, 25, Tony Gallagher quotes Jack Kevorkian as stating that this was "the 28th time he had assisted a suicide"; he was on bail following an earlier case of assisted suicide on this occasion.

offered by the hospice movement which regards palliative medicine and good terminal care to be a more dignified option than euthanasia.

Whether a perceived need for death with dignity can be met through euthanasia and whether this should be achieved by legal reform to give people the legal right to opt for euthanasia and assisted death is the central theme of this work. The conclusion will draw together the threads of the argument and review the possibilities for legal reform which might provide individuals with the opportunity to select euthanasia. It will also describe some of the uncertainties that surround the outcome of the possible introduction of legislation permitting euthanasia, particularly for people who may subsequently discover that euthanasia has become a duty rather than a right.

2

Euthanasia and Clinically Assisted Death: From Caring to Killing?[1]

INTRODUCTION

Questions about the relationship between killing and caring are inevitable in a climate where popular perceptions of the infallibility of advanced medical technology and its apparently relentless ability to prolong living and dying have increased awareness of voluntary euthanasia and assisted death. Clinical situations that might permit patients or doctors to select a course of medical treatment that has potentially life-limiting consequences, raise profound legal and ethical concerns. As a result, doctors confronted by distressed patients or relatives seeking interventions that may be construed as euthanasia can experience the killing/caring dichotomy as a moral dilemma emanating from a tension between their ethical duty to relieve suffering and the responsibilities imposed upon them by the law.

In Britain, medical decision-making at the end of life has never been subject to greater scrutiny than in the post-Harold Shipman era. The distinction between caring and killing has become highly contentious. Greater public awareness of patient's rights has developed through the publicity surrounding a number of high profile cases,[2] and the passage through Parliament of The Medical Treatment [Prevention of Euthanasia] Bill 1999. Current political ideology has promoted consumerism through *The Patients Charter*,[3] accompanied by an expansion of doctors' public accountability. Together these have emphasised the practical role of individual patient autonomy in the provision of health care, especially at the end of life. Yet the absolute endorsement of the patient's right to autonomy in the pursuit of choice may compromise the clinician's professional and ethical integrity if it results in euthanasia.

This chapter defines and describes medical environments presently associated with end of life decisions, and the legal response to them. It examines the medical circumstances in which clinically assisted death sometimes seems appropriate to patients seeking death with dignity, and the methods by which that might

---

[1] This chapter formed the basis of an article published under the title "Decisions and Responsibilities at the End of Life: Euthanasia and Clinically Assisted Death" (1996) 2 *Medical Law International* 229–245.

[2] Examples include, R v. Cox (1992) 12 BMLR 38, and *Airedale NHS Trust v. Bland* [1993] 1 All ER 821.

[3] *The Patients Charter* (London, HMSO, 1991).

be achieved. The ability to exercise choice, patient autonomy, the practical treatment options available, and the role of the criminal law inevitably provide the axes around which this legal and ethical analysis will turn.

Respect for individual autonomy is central to modern medical practice, dictating that all patients have the right to exercise self-determination in respect of their medical care. The law of consent gives legal expression to individual autonomy[4] and permits a competent adult absolute sovereignty to give or withhold consent even if death will be the result.[5] And regard for individual autonomy and autonomously made decisions can endure even after a patient loses the mental capacity to participate in medical decision-making.[6] However, the right to give or withhold consent, either contemporaneously or in advance, does not extend to requesting that a physician assist a patient to die by performing an act that is contrary to professional ethics or could lead to criminal prosecution. Indeed, Kennedy and Grubb argue that a reasonable clinical judgement cannot be overridden by the patient or the law[7] and case law supports their view that the principle of respect for patient autonomy does not entitle patients to demand treatments regarded as not clinically indicated.[8]

There might however be circumstances where a doctor feels an ethical compulsion to comply with such a request. Arguably Dr Nigel Cox felt such a responsibility when he responded to the repeated pleas of his long-term patient Lillian Boyes to be released from pain by hastening her death.[9] Similarly with the Dutch doctor Boudewijn Chabot who controversially assisted a physically healthy but clinically depressed patient to commit suicide.[10] The doctor's legal and ethical duty is always to provide treatment in the patient's "best interests", but the patient's understanding of "best interests" may be at odds with conventional medical wisdom and the law,[11] especially if the patient, or her relatives, are convinced that only the immediate ending of suffering through death represents the best interests. A request for deliberate life shortening action or a refusal to consent to treatment are the probable consequences, and here clinicians may find themselves being pressed to take decisions that are contrary to their ethical

---

[4] Numerous cases endorse this right, see for example, *Schloendorf* v. *Society of New York Hospital* (1914) 105 NE 92, (NY), *Sidaway* v. *Bethlem Royal Hospital Governors* [1985] 1 All ER 643 at 666, *Re T* [1992] 4 All ER 649 at 652–3. A full discussion of consent in the context of end of life decisions follows in ch. 3.

[5] This right was reiterated in *Airedale NHS Trust* v. *Bland* [1993] 1 All ER 821 at 860 per Lord Keith, and in *Re C (Adult: Refusal of Treatment)* [1994] 1 WLR 290.

[6] *Re T (Adult: Refusal of Treatment)* [1992] 4 All ER 649, endorsed the patient's right to refuse medical treatment in advance of that treatment becoming necessary, and *Re C (Adult: Refusal of Treatment)* [1994] 1 WLR 290, held that this right persists even in the event of supervening incapacity. See also ch. 5.

[7] I Kennedy, A Grubb, *Medical Law: Text with Materials* 2nd. edn. (London, Butterworths, 1994) at 1278.

[8] See for example *Re J (A Minor)* [1992] 4 All ER 614 CA.

[9] *R* v. *Cox* (1992) 12 BMLR 38.

[10] Supreme Court of the Netherlands, Criminal Chamber, 21 June 1994, nr 96.972, and the following discussion of assisted suicide.

[11] A full discussion of the concept of *best interests* is included in ch. 3.

or clinical judgements. Tensions are most likely to occur in clinical situations where the clinician believes it to be in the patient's best interests to discontinue therapy but the patient or relatives disagree, or where the relatives or patient wish the treatment to be discontinued against the advice of the doctor. Hence when a caring physician is confronted by the disturbing realisation that conventional medicine is unable to assuage a patient's distress and symptoms the pleas of patients and relatives for an end to suffering may be compelling.

Where a patient is unable to speak for herself or express her preferences the problems are exacerbated. Good medical practice dictates that the views of relatives should be considered, but medical ethics and legal precedents suggest that these views should not be decisive.[12] Families may be understandably anxious for treatment to be either continued or terminated in opposition to the beliefs of the clinician responsible for the decision. Whether the decision is to cease or continue medical treatment, doctors may need to be "tactfully resistant" in order to avoid sacrificing the interests of the patient "to the emotional distress of the relatives".[13] The dilemma for the doctor lies in attempting to respect the wishes of patient and family while maintaining legal and ethical standards of care.

But should patients and their relatives be entitled to expect compliance with their requests for a humane and dignified, but permanent, resolution? Or, should they exhibit a greater degree of moral responsibility by not placing the doctor in the position of being forced to choose between legal and professional suicide, and the ultimate act of compassion? If the exercise of patient's rights compromises the professional integrity of those responsible for the provision of medical care the advancement of those rights becomes problematic. Celia Wells identified the issues precisely when she argued that "refusal of life-saving treatment cannot always be an individual prerogative".[14] The impact of such a refusal on others must always be considered, especially where the demands of patient autonomy may place the doctor in a position almost as intolerable as that occupied by the patient.

Despite this, patients, and their relatives, continue to seek clinically assisted death in order to curtail what they perceive as the futile suffering associated with protracted dying. But doctors and other health care professionals who comply with requests to hasten death expose themselves to criminal and professional

---

[12] *Re G* [1995] 3 Med LR 80, [1995] 2 FLR 528, and *Practice Note (persistent vegetative state: withdrawal of treatment)* [1996] 4 All ER 766 at 767–8 provide authority for this point. In the USA however, the principle of substituted judgement has been recognised and used, for example, in *Cruzan* v. *Dept of Health of Missouri* 110 S Ct 2841 (1990). *Airedale NHS Trust* v. *Bland* [1993] 1 All ER 821 per Lord Goff at 872 considered substituted judgement and dismissed it as having no part to play in English law. Some of the problems associated with placing too great an emphasis on the opinions of family members are highlighted in B Winter, S Cohen, "ABC of Intensive Care: Withdrawal of Treatment" (1999) 319 *BMJ* 306.

[13] E Wilkes, "On Withholding Nutrition and Hydration in the Terminally Ill: Has Palliative Medicine Gone Too Far? A Commentary" (1994) 20 *Journal of Medical Ethics* 144–5 at 145.

[14] C Wells, "Patients, Consent and Criminal Law" (1994) 1 *Journal of Social Welfare and Family Law* 65, at 65.

sanction. In practice compromises are frequently necessary to maximise the right of the individual to choice, autonomy and bodily integrity, within the defined responsibilities of the doctor in respect of that right. Thus the present legal position concerning life-limiting treatment decisions often fails to afford either group the degree of protection to which they should be entitled, with a consequent loss of dignity for both.

In clinical situations where the continued provision of medical treatment represents little more than a prolongation of the dying process the dilemma, and the caring or killing dichotomy, is particularly acute. Here the possible treatment options include, the indefinite continuation of palliative treatment, withholding or withdrawing treatment, the administration of increasing doses of pain relieving medication until respiratory suppression occurs (the principle of *double effect*), the provision of drugs to assist the patient to cause her own death (physician-assisted suicide) and mercy killing. These options will be scrutinised in turn to assess the medical, legal, ethical, and social implications of each, as well as their potential impact on individual choice and the death with dignity debate. A detailed analysis of the legal aspects of causation, acts and omissions and the duty to provide care will provide a backdrop to the investigation of selective non-treatment, while criminal intention and its relationship with motive will be scrutinised alongside the discussion of the principle of *double effect*.

THE INDEFINITE CONTINUATION OF PALLIATIVE TREATMENT

The terms "palliative care" and "palliative medicine" describe a treatment regime that recognises cure as impossible but aims to alleviate suffering wherever practicable. The World Health Organisation (WHO) definition of palliative care describes the discipline as:

> "the active, total care of patients whose disease is not responsive to curative treatment. Control of pain, other symptoms and psychological, social and spiritual problems is paramount. The goal of palliative care is the achievement of the best quality of life for patients and families".[15]

Within this framework, palliative medicine uniquely regards the holistic needs of the patient and her family as virtually indistinguishable and quality of life as central.[16] Many believe that this is an ideal mechanism for promoting dignity in dying.

For some patients indefinite palliative treatment is the only available therapy. In these circumstances, maintaining the patient in as comfortable and pain free

---

[15] World Health Organisation, cited in B Farsides, "Palliative Care—a Euthanasia Free Zone?", (1998) 24 *Journal of Medical Ethics* 149.

[16] Further discussion of the concept of palliative care as embodied in the hospice movement is detailed in ch. 6.

condition as possible and complying, wherever feasible, with the patient's wishes regarding the administration of treatment, are the aims of palliative medicine. Where the patient has the capacity to participate in the decision-making process patient autonomy can usually be upheld and patients may exercise their right to accept or refuse the offered treatment according to their own preferences. The indefinite continuation of palliative care can become contentious however if patients, or their carers, consider it to be a futile prolongation of life.

Palliative care is generally associated with patients who are terminally ill and most frequently with those receiving care in a hospice environment. Here it is unlikely that the indefinite continuation of palliative care will be a realistic option or become problematic since life span is inevitably limited by disease. More compelling dilemmas concerning the indefinite continuation of palliative treatment can perhaps be illustrated by considering the rather desperate position of patients who live in a permanent vegetative state (PVS).[17] Clearly these patients are not typical of those one would usually expect to be receiving palliative care because they are incapacitated and may be expected to survive for some considerable time. Many commentators regard continuing to maintain patients in PVS as unethical because it is futile and cannot benefit the patient.[18] However, hard decisions are born of difficult cases so, not surprisingly, such an analysis may be resisted in favour of arguments contending that human life has value in and of itself, which dictate that treatment should be continued indefinitely.[19] Hence the range and severity of issues concerning the treatment of patients in PVS provides an extreme example of those relating to the indefinite continuation of palliative care in general.

PVS was first legally defined in the American case *Re Karen Quinlan*[20] where the court recognised that this condition dictates that the brain "no longer has any cognitive function" but retains "the capacity to maintain the vegetative parts of neurological function".[21] Because cognitive function and social interaction have been irretrievably lost, patients in this condition are devoid of many, if not most, of the attributes which define each of us as distinct human personalities. The unique reasoning character of the individual has been destroyed

---

[17] This condition was first described by B Jennet and F Plum, "Persistent Vegetative State After Brain Damage" (1972) 1 *The Lancet* 734–7, and has been distinguished from other medical conditions in R Cranford, H Smith "Some Critical Distinctions Between Brain Death and Persistent Vegetative State" (1979) 6 *Ethics in Science and Medicine* 199. The term "permanent" is now regarded as more appropriate than "persistent" since it denotes no prospect of recovery or improvement. A persistent vegetative state is one which may become permanent or may improve with time.

[18] See for example B Jennet, "Letting Vegetative Patients Die" in J Keown, (ed.) *Euthanasia Examined: Ethical, Clinical and Legal Perspectives* (Cambridge, Cambridge University Press, 1997) at 169.

[19] J Boyle, "A Case for Sometimes Feeding Patients in PVS" in J Keown, (ed.) *Euthanasia Examined: Ethical, Clinical and Legal Perspectives* (Cambridge, Cambridge University Press, 1997) at 189, offers one such argument.

[20] (1976) 70, NJ10, 355 A 2nd 647.

[21] *Ibid*, at 650.

together with all capacity for awareness and memory. PVS patients have periods when they appear to be awake, though unaware, and others when they seem to be sleeping. There is no observable cognitive perception of pain or discomfort although they do exhibit local reaction to painful stimuli. They survive as purely physical beings,[22] a condition which many regard as undignified.

In Britain it is established medical practice not to confirm the diagnosis of PVS until one year after the onset of brain damage.[23] There are no wholly definitive criteria for defining or diagnosing PVS, with some professional bodies drawing distinctions according to criteria like the age of the patient and whether or not the PVS is the result of trauma.[24] The evidence base for diagnosing permanence is reputed to be poor,[25] and clinically the features of PVS are variable such that patients may exhibit some limited awareness but still meet the criteria for PVS. Diagnosis therefore remains contentious.

An early Japanese study of one hundred and ten PVS patients, reported that approximately half the patients died within the first year, while more than a quarter survived for over three years. Four patients continued to live for ten years or more, but generally the possibility of recovery remained slight:

> "Vegetative patients have a consistently poor prognosis. During the three year follow up period, more than 60 per cent of the patients died, despite attentive medical care. On the other hand, some patients regained awareness and were able to speak a little but were unable to resume activity as a social human being. Persistent recovery has been attained in three cases . . . only one patient regained nearly normal brain function".[26]

The criteria adopted by this study for the diagnosis of PVS are questionable since true PVS offers no scope for recovery, though long term survival is possible. Perhaps the term "recovery" used in this context simply expresses survival or maybe differentiating more precisely between persistence and permanence would aid clarity?

Later research by Keith Andrews has suggested that the incidence of true PVS is lower than previously thought and that some level of actual recovery may indeed be possible even after considerable periods of time have elapsed.[27] The methods adopted by this research team are themselves open to critique however. The research results were based on a retrospective study of forty patients admitted to a specialist unit who had been referred with a diagnosis of PVS. Of these forty patients it was claimed that seventeen had been incorrectly diagnosed

[22] J Fletcher, "Medicine and the Nature of Man" (1973) 1 *Science, Medicine and Man* 93.

[23] See BMA Committee for Medical Ethics discussion paper *The Treatment of Patients in PVS* September 1992.

[24] B Jennet, "Letting Vegetative Patients Die" in J Keown, (ed) *Euthanasia Examined: Ethical, Clinical and Legal Perspectives* (Cambridge, Cambridge University Press, 1997) 169–188 at 174–5.

[25] According to Professor Derick Wade in a lecture entitled "Permanent Vegetative State" presented at The City of Westminster Law Society, 13 April 2000.

[26] Higashi, Sakato, Hatano "Epidemiological Studies on Patients with a Persistent Vegetative State", (1977) 40 *Journal of Neurology, Neurosurgery, and Psychiatry* 876.

[27] K Andrews, L Murphy, R Munday, C Littlewood, "Misdiagnosis of the Vegetative State: Retrospective Study in a Rehabilitation Unit" (1996) 313 *BMJ* 13–16.

because they later exhibited signs of awareness. Yet ten of the seventeen were admitted to the unit less than twelve months after their initial injury and hence failed to meet the established criteria for diagnosing PVS to begin with.[28] Nevertheless, it has been estimated that at any one time there are at least fifteen hundred PVS patients in the United Kingdom who have been diagnosed using established diagnostic criteria.[29] Also, contrary to Andrews work, which suggests high levels of false positive diagnoses, earlier studies cautioned that due to inaccurate underdiagnosis there are potentially many more.[30]

Patients survive in a PVS without the assistance of artificial life support systems and do not conform to criteria for diagnosing brain stem death. As was discussed in chapter one, they remain clinically and legally alive, although concerns have been expressed as to what kind of life they live.

"What is meant by 'life' in the moral precept which requires respect for sanctity of human life? If the quality of life of a person . . . is non-existent since he is unaware of anything that happens to him, has he a right to be sustained in that state of *living death* and are his family and medical attendants under a duty to maintain it".[31]

Similar views about degenerating quality of life are sometimes expressed by those suffering from terminal and incurable illnesses, and their carers. Though PVS patients will never be able to express a view again, it must be recognised, that they are in many respects inseparable from the people who existed before they entered PVS. No patient exists in a vacuum. They all have a social history that persists beyond the hospital bed and the body occupied by the victim of illness. Treatment decisions cannot be taken in isolation or without regard to prior lifestyle and opinions because this "is not simply a technical medical issue",[32] and to fail to continue with treatment may be regarded as a devaluation of the worth of that patient.[33] Decisions to continue with palliative care indefinitely also have implications beyond those associated with the individual patient however. "The burden is great on patients . . . on their families, on the hospitals, and on those in need of hospital beds already occupied".[34] The impact of the indefinite continuation of palliative care upon each of these groups and the options available to them is worthy of further scrutiny.

[28] R Cranford, "Misdiagnosing the Persistent Vegetative State" (1996) 313 *BMJ* 5. The Royal College of Physicians have developed guidelines for the diagnosis of PVS but these have sometimes, as in *Re H (adult: incompetent)* (1997) 38 BMLR 11, been found imprecise. For an overview of the issues see Adam Nicolson, "Caught Between Life and Death", *Sunday Telegraph Review*, 26 May 1996 1–2.

[29] "Institute of Medical Ethics Working Party on the Ethics of Prolonging Life and Assisting Death. Withdrawal of Life Support from Patients in PVS" (1991) 337 *The Lancet* 96–98.

[30] K R Mitchell, I H Kerridge, T J Lovat, "Medical Futility, Treatment Withdrawal and the Persistent Vegetative State" (1993) 19 *Journal of Medical Ethics* 71.

[31] *Airedale NHS Trust* v. *Bland* [1993] 2 WLR 316, per Lord Browne-Wilkinson.

[32] P D G Skegg, *Law, Ethics and Medicine* (Oxford, Clarendon Press, 1988) at 144.

[33] J M Finnis, "*Bland*: Crossing the Rubicon?" (1993) 109 *Law Quarterly Review* 329, at 334.

[34] H K Beecher, "A Definition of Irreversible Coma" (1968) 205 *Journal of the American Medical Association* 337–340 at 338.

A regime of continuing palliative care can involve carers in many months, or years, of burdensome and stressful toil performed in the knowledge that it can never improve the prognosis of the patient. Therefore a decision to continue indefinitely with palliative care carries with it social and emotional costs, particularly to the carers and family. Observing the steady decline of a person for whom medicine offers no hope is demanding for professional and emotional carers alike and inevitably exacts a heavy toll. As time passes, requests to discontinue treatment become more likely but these requests carry costs in themselves since relatives who have loyally cared for a patient over a protracted period may feel uneasy about advocating a decision to curtail treatment knowing that the consequence will be death. Equally significant is the impact upon others who require hospital care, particularly if the continuation of futile palliative care effectively denies them treatment.

Determining which patients, or which conditions, have the most worthy or most just claim to any particular facility is a complex process, especially where the funding for medical care is centrally distributed. The provision of scarce resources is readily conceived of in terms of competing claims to be assessed according to a variety of preordained criteria,[35] especially as most methods of resource allocation include a comparative assessment. Many are controversial both conceptually and in their application.[36]

For example the allocation could be made by assessing the patient according to a test that calculates the probable medical benefit that will result from treatment. Clearly the prognosis for a patient diagnosed as terminally ill or incurable is poor by comparison with other patients whose conditions are either temporary or allow scope for recovery,[37] in which case the claims of a patient receiving only long term palliative care are always likely to be less favourably assessed. Another method involves making a comparison on the basis of the individual patient's value to society. This calculation is also highly subjective, resulting at best in inconsistency and at worst in discrimination. How, for example, is it possible to distinguish between the value to society of any two different individuals? Consider the situation where a gifted doctor has a confirmed diagnosis of PVS and a convicted murderer has recently sustained a severe head injury from which she may or may not recover. Which is in greater need of treatment? Which is likely to be of the most, or least, value to society? And, what if one has several children in need of support and guidance while the other has none? These rhetorical questions serve to emphasise the competing claims that

---

[35] C Newdick, *Who Should We Treat?* (Oxford, Oxford University Press, 1996), examines the issue in terms of the legal response to the competing claims of patients, doctors, and managers to NHS resources.

[36] The issues are clearly outlined and discussed in, P A Lewis and M Charney, "Which of Two Individuals Do You Treat When Only Their Ages are Different and You Can't Treat Them Both?" (1989) 15 *Journal of Medical Ethics* 28.

[37] Higashi, Sakato, Hatano "Epidemiological Studies on Patients with a Persistent Vegetative State" (1977) 40 *Journal of Neurology, Neurosurgery, and Psychiatry* 876, demonstrated a recovery rate of below 3%.

might be made based on justice but fail intrinsically to address the problems as they relate to individual cases.

The concept of *quality adjusted life years* (QALYs), essentially an economic indicator, is one mechanism developed to help resolve some of these issues.[38] Though now largely disregarded, QALYs represent a numerical calculation of life expectancy and quality. Scores are attained on a scale which values each year of healthy life as one, death as zero, and each year of unhealthy life as less than one. The scale allows for the degree of the reduction in quality of life to be accounted for in the extent to which the score falls below one. Therefore, "a life considered to be worse than death can be afforded a minus score".[39] QALYs are dependent upon medical personnel judging the potential quality of life of other people. Such assessments are inherently value laden and subjective. Patients may themselves value some aspects of their lives more than others and the opinions of those who are responsible for allocating resources may run counter to those values. A stereotypical example presents the scenario where the patient relishes and would deliberately choose to sit and smoke all day while watching television, while the clinician making the assessment might be appalled by the prospect. Moreover, QALYs are inherently disadvantageous to certain groups of patients, specifically the elderly and those whose prognosis is poor. If the treatment concerned is purely palliative and the patient has no prospect of recovery, decisions made by applying the quality adjusted life years standard can never be beneficial.

Other methods of determining how resources should be allocated have been suggested,[40] but most frequently, medical treatment decisions are still taken on the basis of the clinical assessment of the individual patient's medical condition and its prognosis. Describing treatment as "not clinically indicated" where it is the only treatment maintaining life is inevitably contentious. A decision to discontinue palliative treatment may easily be construed as euthanasia through the back door, especially where concerns about rationing and resource allocation are raised.[41]

However, if an individual patient's condition dictates that the prospect of improvement is minimal or non-existent even with sustained medical intervention, all the costs of indefinitely continuing to provide treatment must be weighed against the remoteness of securing a beneficial outcome. Dan W Brock offers a useful analogy here stating that:

---

[38] See A Williams, "The Economic Role of 'Health Indicators'", in G Teeling-Smith (ed.) *Measuring the Social Benefits of Medicine* (Oxford, Oxford University Press, 1983).

[39] J K Mason & R A McCall Smith, *Law and Medical Ethics* 5th edn. (London, Butterworths, 1999) at 303.

[40] Examples include, E Nord, "An Alternative to QALYs: The Saved Young Life Equivalent (SAVE)" (1992) 305 *British Medical Journal* 875, and R Klein, "Dimensions of Rationing: Who Should Do What?" (1993) 307 *British Medical Journal* 93.

[41] T Hope, D Springings and D Crisp, "Not Clinically Indicated: Patients Interests or Resource Allocation?" (1993) 306 *BMJ* 379.

"it is *not* considered any requirement of justice to continue to search for those lost at sea or trapped in mines so long as there is any possibility of saving them, no matter how small".[42]

Applying Brock's reasoning to decisions to discontinue the treatment in appropriate clinical circumstances suggests that they are not inherently unjust. Consequently selectively withholding or withdrawing treatment may be the most ethical and dignified response.

WITHHOLDING OR WITHDRAWING TREATMENT

The implications of withholding or withdrawing treatment may be the same where the result will be the end of a patient's life, but the process of making such decisions differs. Withholding treatment implies that the therapy in question has never been started, while a decision to withdraw treatment suggests that a regime previously considered beneficial will be discontinued. The individual patient's medical condition will determine whether and when a medical decision might be taken to withhold or withdraw treatment. Usually these decisions will only be taken in relation to patients who are terminally ill or incurable, though occasionally a rare clinical situation dictates that a competent and sensate patient is receiving only basic life sustaining treatment.[43] Here it is possible that the patient herself will take a life-limiting decision by refusing to consent to continued treatment,[44] and all mentally competent patients have an absolute legal right to make such a decision, and to have it upheld, as long as the implications of that decision have been explained and understood.[45] Lord Keith reiterated this right in *Bland*, when he said that, ". . . a person is completely at liberty to decline to undergo treatment, even if the result of his doing so will be that he will die".[46] In practice, the endorsement of patients' rights to autonomy in decisions to withdraw life-sustaining treatment may give rise to tensions within the doctor-patient relationship, particularly where death will be the inevitable outcome.[47] However, if a competent patient seeks to retain control over the dying process by selecting this option as an expression of personal autonomy, no liability will normally attach to the clinician who does not intervene.

[42]   D W Brock, *Life and Death* (Cambridge, Cambridge University Press, 1993) at 240, emphasis added.

[43]   Paraplegia and motor neurone disease amongst them.

[44]   Patients who are able to decide for themselves are entitled to decline to consent to any treatment at will, see *Re T (adult: refusal of treatment)* [1992] 4 All ER 649, [1992] 3 WLR 782.

[45]   There are exceptions to this general rule, one of which concerns the competent minor, see for example *Re W (a minor)(Medical treatment)* [1992] 4 All ER 627 CA and further discussion in chs. 3 and 5.

[46]   [1993] 1 All ER 821, at 860.

[47]   These tensions were graphically illustrated in Brian Clark's dramatic play, *Whose Life is it Anyway?* (New York, Dodd Mead, 1979), wherein the fictional character Ken Harrison requests to be discharged from hospital so that all treatment will be withdrawn. Further discussion of these issues is contained in ch. 4.

Even where the patient does not or cannot request treatment withdrawal, therapy can be legitimately terminated if its futility denotes that to continue with it would be contrary to the best interests of the patient.[48] If there is no demonstrable clinical benefit, therapies, such as antibiotics to fight infection and artificially administered nutrition and hydration,[49] may be selectively withdrawn to allow the patient to die peacefully and with dignity. Control of symptomatic pain and distress is fundamental to good palliative care in these circumstances and should be maintained as part of basic medical care.[50] However, because withholding or discontinuing these types of treatment will result in death regardless of the underlying pathology, treatment decisions taken in the expectation that death will result must always be carefully considered. Where there are doubts about its efficacy or disputes between professional and emotional carers a High Court declaration may be required to ensure that this may be lawfully accomplished.[51]

Potential criminal liability is assessed according to the nature of the conduct involved. The extent of liability will depend upon an analysis of what was the cause of death; whether the conduct which resulted in death is properly categorised as an act or an omission; and, whether a duty of care demands that treatment should have been continued in the particular circumstance.[52] The following discussion considers the legal and ethical principles involved and explains how the courts will apply established criminal law principles in order to determine the lawfulness of withdrawing treatment.

Causing Death

Verification of the actual cause of the patient's death is central to the determination of culpability in any case where a clinician may be criminally liable for a

---

[48] In *Airedale NHS Trust* v. *Bland* [1993] 1 All ER 821, Lord Goff stated that, ". . . in a case such as the present, it is the futility of the treatment which justifies its termination", at 870. However in some situations these decisions give rise to frequent controversy, see for example J Sanders, "Medical Futility: CPR" in R Lee and D Morgan, *Death Rites: Law and Ethics at the End of Life* (London, Routledge, 1996) 72–90, which discusses issues concerning "do not resuscitate orders". Ch. 3 offers a detailed analysis of the concept of best interests, its application and assessment.

[49] Innumerable medical conditions can render a patient incapable of sustaining nutrition and hydration without active medical intervention. Included here are PVS, anorexia nervosa and terminal cancer complicated by intestinal obstruction, amongst others. It is also possible for a patient to be rendered incapable of maintaining her own nourishment and hydration through the imposition of medical treatment, especially where a patient who is terminally ill requires heavy sedation.

[50] *Basic care* is defined as the therapy required to keep an individual comfortable; generally this will include the provision of general hygiene and pain relief. The Law Commission has reaffirmed the view of the BMA and nursing professional bodies, that no patient should have the right to refuse *basic care* because of the distress that such a refusal would be likely to cause carers and other patients, see Law Commission Report 231, *Mental Incapacity, Item 9 of the Fourth Programme of Law Reform: Mentally Incapacitated Adults* (London, HMSO, 1995) at para. 5.34.

[51] *Airedale NHS Trust* v. *Bland* [1993] 1 All ER 821, Practice Note [1994] 2 All ER 413.

[52] The *mens rea* or intentions of the clinician are also relevant but will be analysed in detail in the following discussion of double effect.

patient's death. Where death occurs following treatment withdrawal, the cause of death seems obvious in the light of earlier comments about the certainty of death resulting from lack of nutrition and hydration, but sometimes the apparently obvious cause of death is not the actual or legal cause.

R v. *White*,[53] where Mrs White's son decided to kill his elderly mother by placing poison in her bedtime drink, is a case in point. White prepared a hot beverage, took it to his mother at bedtime and in the morning the old lady was found dead in her chair, but the drink was only partially consumed. She had not ingested sufficient of the poison to kill her and her death was attributed to a heart attack. White clearly intended to kill his mother and had taken steps so to do, but had not actually caused her death. He was convicted of attempted murder.

Similarly, the circumstances surrounding a patient's death may suggest that a particular feature of the treatment has directly resulted in death, but before criminal liability can be attached the factual and legal cause of death must be established. Arguably if a patient dies because treatment is not administered, it is not the failure to treat that has caused death but the condition that generated the need for treatment in the first place.[54] In which case it is tempting to conclude that this indicates that medical intervention will not break the chain of causation between the onset of the condition and the patient's eventual demise, although legal precedents do not wholly support this contention.

In *R* v. *Jordan*[55] the defendant was convicted of murder after his victim died from serious stab wounds he had inflicted. Whilst in hospital however, a doctor had administered the antibiotic terramycin even though the victim was known to be allergic to it. Further negligent treatment resulted in a fluid imbalance, which culminated in the patient's lungs becoming water-logged. In the Court of Appeal it was held that the original wound was virtually healed when the victim died and that death was caused by the grossly negligent and "palpably wrong" treatment that resulted in pneumonia. It was also recognised that ordinarily, ". . . death resulting from any normal treatment employed to deal with a felonious injury may be regarded as caused by the felonious injury", but that because, ". . . this was not normal treatment",[56] the causal link was broken.[57] Jordan's conviction was quashed. But *Jordan* is an exceptional case in British law and a series of subsequent cases have adopted a contrary stance.[58]

R v. *Smith*[59] concerned the administration of "thoroughly bad" treatment to the victim of a barrack room brawl. Despite the role played by the poor quality

---

[53] [1910] 2 KB 124.

[54] Of course this contention is dependant on the absence of a duty to treat the patient. Where such a duty exists and is neglected criminal or tortious liability will attach.

[55] (1956) 40 Crim App Rep 152.

[56] *Ibid.*

[57] H L A Hart and A M Honoré, *Causation and the Law* 2nd edn. (Oxford, Clarendon Press, 1985) at 355.

[58] See *R* v. *Smith* [1959] 2 All ER 193, *R* v. *Blaue* [1975] 3 All ER 446 and *R* v. *Cheshire* [1991] 3 All ER 670.

[59] [1959] 2 All ER 193.

of the treatment, the chain of causation between the victim and his assailant was held to have remained in tact. Lord Parker CJ explained that:

> "if at the time of death the original wound is still an operating cause and a substantial cause, then the death can properly be said to be the result of the wound, albeit that some other cause is also operating. Only if it can be said that the original wound is merely the setting in which another cause operates can it be said that the death does not result from the wound . . . only if the second cause is so overwhelming as to make the original wound merely part of the history can it be said that the death does not flow from the wound".[60]

R v. *Cheshire*[61] further negates *Jordan*'s suggestion that the chain of causation may be disrupted by the intervention of medical treatment. Here the victim died of asphyxiation following the negligent management of a tracheotomy performed in the initial stages of treating gunshot wounds inflicted by the defendant. At the time of death the bullet wounds were themselves no longer life threatening but still the court held that, "even though negligence in the treatment of the victim was the immediate cause of his death, the jury should not regard it as excluding the responsibility of the accused unless the negligent treatment was so independent of his acts, and in itself so potent in causing death, that they regard the contribution made by his acts as insignificant".[62]

Regardless of the fact that the treatment administered to this patient was clearly negligent, the Court of Appeal regarded the narrowing of the trachea,[63] as not only a "rare complication" but also ". . . a direct consequence of the appellants acts, which remained a significant cause of his death".[64] Unlike *Smith*, which can be distinguished on its facts, *Cheshire* and *Jordan* are factually similar. Both concern negligent medical treatment of patients whose injuries were substantially remedied, yet the judgments differ in emphasis and outcome. Of course causation is conceptually complex and requires recognition of the possibility of multiple causes, but these judgments may also reflect an inherent reluctance in the courts to acquit obviously implicated defendants at the risk of incriminating doctors.[65] Where the actions of a defendant can be shown, however unsatisfactorily, to remain operative, substantial or significant causes of death, the intervention of medical treatment is unlikely to damage the chain of causation. The issues are often further complicated by the fact the alleged victim has refused to consent to treatment rather than any suggestion that the medical response has been inappropriate. Here the possibility exists for death to be attributed to more than one cause.

---

[60] *Ibid* at 198.
[61] [1991] 3 All ER 670.
[62] *Ibid* at 678.
[63] A recognised but unusual side effect of tracheotomy.
[64] [1991] 3 All ER 670, at 678.
[65] David W Meyers also promulgates this view in *The Human Body and the Law* (Edinburgh, Edinburgh University Press, 1990) at 98.

Such was the situation in *R v. Holland*[66] where the victim sustained cuts to one of his fingers when assaulted by the defendant. His refusal of medical treatment meant that he subsequently died of tetanus. The defendant was found to have caused his death, despite the treatment refusal, because the original wound remained an operating and substantial cause of death. Medical treatment would have been unnecessary *but for* the action of the defendant in assaulting his victim. Similarly, in *R v. Blaue*[67] where the victim suffered four serious stab wounds, one of which punctured a lung. In hospital she was advised that the nature and severity of her injuries meant that she required a blood transfusion in order to save her life, but being a Jehovah's Witness, she declined to consent to a blood transfusion and ultimately died from internal bleeding. On appeal the defendant argued unsuccessfully that it was the lack of medical treatment that had caused her death. His conviction was upheld because:

> "the physical cause of death in this case was the bleeding into the pleural cavity arising from penetration of the lung. This was not brought about by any decision made by the deceased girl but by the stab wound".[68]

The reasonableness of the victim's refusal of treatment, and its impact upon the chain of causation and therefore on the defendant's culpability, was also questioned but Lawton LJ denied its relevance:

> "It has long been the policy of the law that those who use violence on other people must take their victims as they find them. This in our judgement means the whole man, not just the physical man. It does not lie in the mouth of the assailant to say that his victim's religious beliefs which inhibited him from accepting certain kinds of treatment were unreasonable. The question for decision is what caused the death? The answer is the stab wound".[69]

The physical cause of death was the bleeding caused by the stab wound inflicted by Blaue. The fact that the victim chose to decline medical treatment was clearly also a cause of her death, but it was held to be subordinate to the factual cause of her death. Where a patient dies after declining to accept medical treatment death would be caused by the underlying medical condition combined with the treatment refusal, but where a doctor decides not to provide treatment the legal position is less clear cut.

Similarly in *R v. McKechnie and Others*[70] the victim died in hospital more than four weeks after being assaulted when the defendants broke into his home. On admission to hospital he was found to be unconscious, having sustained acute head injuries as a result of a severe beating and being hit over the head with a television set. While undergoing treatment a bleeding duodenal ulcer was also diagnosed which would require surgical intervention. However, the severity of

---

[66]   [1841] 2 Mood & R 351.
[67]   [1975] 3 All ER 446.
[68]   *Ibid*, per Lawton LJ at 450.
[69]   *Ibid.*
[70]   (1992) 94 Crim App Rep 51.

the head injuries was such that the risk of administering a general anaesthetic was too great and no operation was performed. The victim died when the duodenal ulcer perforated. At issue was whether McKechnie had caused the victim's death since the injuries he inflicted were remote from the ulcer that ultimately killed him. At first instance the jury were directed that, in order to convict, they must be satisfied that the head injuries had significantly contributed to the death; they were. On appeal the direction to the jury and the verdict were endorsed because the decision not to operate was regarded as reasonable in the circumstances and the defendant's actions were more than a minimal cause of death. If the victim's anaesthetic tolerance had not been reduced by the beating he received from McKechnie, his ulcer could have been treated and he would not have died. The head injury was not the only cause of death but it was a significant one without which death could have been avoided.

In each of these cases defendants attempted to define medical intervention as an intervening act with the capacity to break the chain of causation between the injury and the death. With the notable exception of *Jordan*, the courts have consistently rejected an argument which would clearly absolve a culpable assailant from responsibility. This rejection has not however excluded the possibility of medical treatment or non-treatment being *a* causative factor in the death of a patient, which could result in criminal culpability. What if the victim is a patient suffering from disease or accidental injury where there is no culpable defendant, and the clinicians decline to treat or commence treatment and subsequently withdraw treatment? The case of Tony Bland,[71] the innocent victim of the Hillsborough Football Stadium disaster, is a prime example.

Tony Bland never recovered from the trauma he received in the Hillsborough stadium in April 1989. He remained in a PVS with no prospect of improvement or recovery for more than three years during which time his parents and the clinicians caring for him resolved to allow him to die by withdrawing nutrition and hydration. What would be the cause of death if Tony Bland was allowed to die in this way? Would it be the conduct of the clinician in withholding treatment or would it be the injuries sustained at the football match?

The situation is not analogous to one where mechanical life support is withdrawn from a patient who is subsequently declared dead. There criminal liability does not ordinarily flow as a result of cessation of life support because a patient who is wholly maintained by a mechanical life support system, and is incapable of life independent of the machine is, according to established criteria for the diagnosis of brain stem death, already medically and legally dead prior to the disconnection of the ventilator. As long as the patient has been diagnosed as brain stem dead before the treatment is discontinued the clinician will not be responsible for causing death; a point which was emphasised by Lord Lane in *R v. Malcherek*.[72]

---

[71] [1993] 1 All ER 821, at 870.
[72] [1981] 2 All ER 422.

> "Where a medical practitioner, using generally acceptable methods, came to the conclusion that the patient was for all practical purposes dead and that such vital functions as remained were being maintained solely by mechanical means, and accordingly discontinued treatment, that did not break the chain of causation between the initial injury and the death".[73]

Hence, a doctor who follows this course of action, "would simply be allowing the original injury to operate to cause death and would thus be protected from criminal liability".[74]

Following *Holland, Blaue* and *McKechnie*, where the victims were not treated and the wounds inflicted by their assailants were deemed to have caused their deaths, it might be plausible to conclude that failure to treat would not constitute the cause of death in Tony Bland's case. However, in those cases treatment was never instigated, it was withheld rather than withdrawn. Therefore to attribute the cause of death to medical intervention would be unsatisfactory unless there was a clear duty to provide the treatment in the circumstances.[75] In *Bland*, the treatment had been provided for over three years so it was not a case of failing to treat but of deliberately ceasing to treat. So the withdrawal of treatment must surely constitute *a* cause of death even if other causes, such as the original injury, co-existed because Tony Bland would not have died at that time had treatment been continued.

Lord Goff avoided reaching this conclusion by suggesting that as long as the withdrawal of treatment from Tony Bland was lawful, it would not constitute the cause of death. Accordingly death would have been caused by the injuries sustained in the Hillsborough football stadium.

> "The established rule [is] that a doctor may, when caring for a patient who is, for example, dying of cancer, lawfully administer painkilling drugs despite the fact that he knows that an incidental effect of that application will be to abbreviate the patient's life. Such a decision may properly be made as part of the care of the living patient, in his best interests; and, on this basis the treatment will be lawful. Moreover, where the doctor's treatment of his patient is lawful, the patient's death will be regarded in law as exclusively caused by the injury or disease to which his condition is attributable".[76]

But cause is an objective phenomenon; a matter of fact. As such, causing death may or may not attract criminal liability depending on the presence or absence of the other elements of the crime and it is these which denote the lawfulness or otherwise of the conduct concerned. Lord Mustill offered an interpretation of the relevance of causation that conforms to this model,

> "the argument presented to the House asserts that for the purpose of both civil and criminal liability the cause of Anthony Bland's death . . . will be the Hillsborough

---

[73] [1981] 2 All ER 422, at 428–9.

[74] R Cooper, Comment "Withdrawal of Life Support—Lawful?" [1993] *Journal of Criminal Law* 283 at 286.

[75] See below for a discussion of the when and where a duty to act will arise.

[76] [1993] 1 All ER 821, at 868.

disaster. As a matter of the criminal law of causation, this may well be right, once it is assumed that the conduct is lawful . . . It does not perhaps follow that the conduct of the doctors is not also causative, but this is of no interest since if the conduct is lawful the doctors have nothing to worry about. If on the other hand the conduct is unlawful, then it is in the same case as active euthanasia or any other unlawful act by doctors or laymen. In common sense they must all be causative or none; and it must be all, for otherwise euthanasia would never be murder".[77]

Doctors may effectively cause the death but in so doing they will not attract criminal liability if the causative conduct is considered lawful. Assessing the lawfulness or otherwise of a course of conduct is reliant upon the characterisation of the conduct as an act or an omission and the existence, or otherwise, of a duty of care.

Act or Omission?

Where an action causes death, the commission of that act can be defined as the *actus reus* of homicide. Ordinarily the *actus reus* of murder will be a positive action which results in death and criminal liability will arise where the *actus reus* coincides with the intention to kill (the *mens rea* of murder). Where there is a failure to act rather than a positive action, that failure is described as an omission. An omission causing death will generally give rise to criminal liability only where the person who failed to act was under a duty to act in the particular circumstances of the case as is illustrated by *R v. Gibbins and Proctor*.[78] The facts were that Gibbins and his common-law wife omitted to provide food for his child who died as a consequence. Gibbins had given Proctor money to buy food but she had neglected to do so, and he failed to ensure that the child was fed. The Court of Appeal held that the judge at first instance was correct in directing that they were guilty of murder if their intention in withholding food was to cause grievous bodily harm.[79] The father had a duty towards his child and his mistress had assumed a similar duty, hence, even though the child's death was caused by an omission, the couple could be criminally responsible for murder.

To assess the potential criminal liability of those withdrawing medical treatment, including hydration and nutrition from a patient, it is first necessary to determine whether such conduct is properly categorised as an act or an omission. In Tony Bland's case the Law Lords decided that the withdrawal of artificial feeding by the removal of the naso-gastric tube constituted not an act but a mere omission, in spite of protestations to the contrary by the Official Solicitor. Bland's feeding was administered via a naso-gastric tube delivering liquid food

[77] *Ibid*, at 892.
[78] (1918) 13 Crim App Rep 134.
[79] The required *mens rea* for the offence of murder is the intention to kill or cause grievous bodily harm.

directly into his stomach. Failure to introduce nutrients through the tube would clearly constitute an omission that would ultimately result in death. However, causing death by physically removing the tube so that food could no longer be administered in this way could equally be described as a positive act resulting in criminal liability. This apparently arbitrary distinction between act and omission would determine the extent of criminal liability flowing from this situation. Helen Beynon considered these issues in depth and concluded that:

> "perhaps the distinction in this context is that if the doctor's course of conduct made the patient's condition worse, it should be described as an 'act'; whereas if it failed to make the patient's condition any better, it should be described as an 'omission' ".[80]

The distinction between making a patient's condition worse and failing to make it better is unhelpful when the ultimate consequence of either is death. In relation to this discussion of the withdrawal of nutrition and hydration perhaps it is more germane to assess whether criminal culpability is appropriate in the circumstances. In which case the potential liability of those who withhold or withdraw medical treatment will hinge upon the duty of care owed.

The Duty to Provide Medical Care

No criminal liability arises for omissions to act unless the relationship or the situation is one that gives rise to a legal duty of care. An obvious example of such a situation exists where a duty to act is imposed upon an individual via contractual obligations.[81] However, a duty of care can also arise in the absence of a contractual duty if an appropriate relationship exists between the people involved. Family relationships, close domestic proximity, and situations where there has been a voluntary assumption of a duty of care, as in *R v. Instan*,[82] are all examples.

The defendant in *Instan* was the plaintiff's niece who lived in her aunt's house and consumed food provided by her aunt. The aunt was ill and eventually became immobile and died when Instan failed to supply food. The court held that the niece owed a duty to her aunt since she had voluntarily undertaken to care for her and had received board and lodging in return. In *R v. Stone and Dobinson*,[83] Stone's elderly sister who lived with the couple, refused nourishment and medical care and died. It was held that the couple had voluntarily assumed a legal duty to care for the sister. Their failure to discharge their duty meant that the victim died as a result of their neglect and they were criminally liable for her manslaughter. Stone and Dobinson were convicted despite the fact

---

[80]   H Benyon, "Doctors as Murderers" (1982) *Crim LR* 17.
[81]   *R v. Pittwood* (1902) 19 TLR 37.
[82]   [1893] 1 QB 450.
[83]   [1977] QB 354, [1977] 2 All ER 341.

that Stone was described as being of below average intelligence, almost blind and partially deaf, while his mistress, Dobinson, was "inadequate", calling into question their capacity to assume such a responsibility in the first place.

A legal duty of care also arises by virtue of a person's position in society and her, or his, relationships with others. Those who hold public office or occupy a position of trust as a consequence of their profession inevitably owe a duty of care to those for whom they are responsible. Doctors, nurses and other health care professionals fall within this category. Lord Nathan explains that

> "the medical man's duty arises then quite independently of any contract with his patient. It is based simply upon the fact that the medical man has undertaken the care and treatment of the patient".[84]

Thus all doctors owe a duty of care to their patients and in each case the duty arises by virtue of the fact that the doctor has undertaken to treat the patient concerned. In the performance of that duty a doctor must act

> "in accordance with a practice accepted at the time as proper by a reasonable body of medical opinion even though other doctors adopt a different practice. In short, the law imposes the duty of care; but the standard of care is a matter of medical judgement".[85]

Essentially, under this *Bolam* principle, a doctor will not be in neglect of her duty of care if it is demonstrable that other doctors would treat patients with the same condition and prognosis in the same way.[86] In *Bland* therefore the extent of the doctor's duty of care became the central issue in determining criminal liability. Their Lordships were in complete agreement that a doctor is under no duty to provide or continue treatment which is not in the patient's best interests and that Tony Bland's persistent vegetative state was irreversible, rendering the continuation of treatment "futile". Accordingly, continuing to administer the invasive and burdensome treatment would provide no benefit to the patient and was contrary to his best interests. The doctor's duty to provide sustenance was therefore negated.[87]

In general clinicians have a duty to make treatment decisions according to an assessment of the "best interests" of the patient, particularly if the patient lacks the capacity to participate in the decision-making process. *Bland*,[88] and subsequent cases involving patients in PVS[89] concerned the withdrawal of hydration

---

[84] Lord Nathan, *Medical Negligence* (Oxford, Oxford University Press, 1957) at 8.

[85] *Sidaway* v. *Bethlem Royal Hospital Governors* [1985] 1 All ER 643, per Lord Scarman at 649, reiterating the *Bolam* principle as articulated in *Bolam* v. *Friern Hospital Management Committee* [1957] 2 All ER 118.

[86] *Bolam* v. *Friern Hospital Management Committee* [1957] 2 All ER 118, [1957] 1 WLR 582.

[87] Lord Mustill qualified this contention however by arguing that in fact this particular patient had no interests by virtue of his medical condition.

[88] [1993] 1 All ER 821.

[89] Inter alia, *Frenchay Healthcare NHS Trust* v. *S* [1994] 2 All ER 403; *Re G (Persistent Vegetative State)* [1995] 2 FLR 528; *Swindon and Marlborough NHS Trust* v. *S* [1995] 3 Med LR 84; *Re C (adult patient: restriction of publicity after death)* [1996] 2 FLR 251; *Re D* (1997) 38 BMLR 1; *Re H (adult: incompetent)* (1997) 38 BMLR 11.

and nutrition from incompetent patients; a course of action which is endorsed by the courts as representing the individual patient's "best interests".[90] These judgements are necessarily reliant upon the efficacy of the medical evidence presented to the court by doctors. Yet it has been observed that "no doctor's judgement is infallible when it comes to predicting how close a patient is to death".[91] Indeed patients in PVS or similar conditions are usually not close to death and there is still sometimes controversy over their exact diagnosis.[92] In the light of these factors, and concerns about the gravity of the outcome, the House of Lords Select Committee on Medical Ethics[93] endorsed the proposition in *Bland* that all cases concerning the withdrawal of nutrition and hydration should be referred to the courts so that doctors would not be taking life-limiting decisions in isolation. This requirement has now been relaxed, following a number of authoritative cases and the publication of detailed guidance by the British Medical Association.[94]

For those seeking relief from the rigours of terminal disease the withdrawal of nutrition and hydration or medication is not always the most appropriate or dignified option. More often than not patients are receiving medication to control pain and other distressing symptoms alongside nutrition and hydration. Simply discontinuing artificial hydration and nutrition, or neglecting to treat an infection in these circumstances, could exacerbate existing pain and suffering. In which case, the principle of *double effect*, whereby increasing doses of pain relieving medication are administered until respiratory suppression occurs is in practice more likely to provide a final solution.

THE PRINCIPLE OF DOUBLE EFFECT

The principle of *double effect* refers to the fact some conduct has simultaneous intentional and unintentional consequences. In general terms, *double effect* suggests that while it is wrong to perform a bad act for the sake of the good consequences that may follow, it may be permissible to perform a good act even if some bad consequences can be anticipated. A graphic illustration of the ambiguities involved in the application of *double effect* is offered by Hart's example concerning the case of a man trapped inside a burning vehicle who implores

---

[90] Other examples of court decisions based on similar reasoning include, *In the Matter of a Ward of Court* [1995] 2 IRLM 401, and *Law Hospital NHS Trust* v. *Lord Advocate* [1996] 1 *Scots Law Times* 869.

[91] G M Craig, "On Withholding Nutrition and Hydration in the Terminally Ill: Has Palliative Medicine Gone too Far?" (1994) 20 *Journal of Medical Ethics* 139–143, at 140.

[92] In *Re H (adult: incompetent)* (1997) 38 BMLR, the condition of the patient concerned failed to accord completely with the criteria of the Royal College of Physicians for the diagnosis of PVS. Experts involved in the case were nonetheless convinced that her vegetative state was permanent.

[93] Select Committee on Medical Ethics (1993–4) HL 21–II.

[94] *Practice Note(Persistent Vegetative State: Withdrawal of Treatment)* [1996] 4 All ER 766, BMA, *BMA Guidelines on Treatment Decisions for Patients in Persistent Vegetative State* (London, BMA Publications, 1996).

a passer by to shoot him dead and relieve him of further pain and suffering.[95] Clearly the bystander can foresee that if he does nothing the trapped man will burn to death in agony. Yet if he acts as requested and shoots the man dead he will be criminally liable for causing the man's death. Death is inevitable; the only choice is how it occurs. Which would be the *good* act, shooting the man or allowing him to die in the fire? The criminal law dictates that deliberately hastening the death of another is conduct that attracts criminal liability, regardless of the circumstances because:

"however gravely ill a man may be . . . he is entitled in our law to every hour . . . that God has granted him. That hour or hours may be the most precious and most important hours of a man's life".[96]

An alternative for the passer-by might be to simply knock out the trapped man, thereby sparing him from further conscious appreciation of his agony while allowing the fire to inevitably kill him. This can be seen as analogous to the situation where a doctor uses strong pain-killing medication to relieve the pain that is frequently symptomatic of terminal disease knowing that the patient will inevitably die of the disease.

Terminal pain can usually be controlled by the administration of narcotic drugs, but the effectiveness of the drugs gradually decreases as the body becomes accustomed to them. Simultaneously, the disease process tends to lead to ever more severe symptoms, requiring that the dosage is incrementally increased to ensure adequate pain relief throughout a prolonged period of terminal care. Alongside their beneficial, palliative effects, these drugs can produce harmful side-effects which, in high doses can dull the responses, cause drowsiness, and suppress appetite and respiration, ultimately causing death. Controlling pain in terminal care thereby presents a clinical setting where *double effect* may readily occur. Narcotics may be used both to relieve symptoms and avoid further suffering but might also hasten death, raising complex legal and ethical issues. Medicine takes as its central aims the preservation of life and the relief of suffering. In the context of *double effect* these objectives are apparently contradictory since the relief of suffering may bring life to an end. The tension between these principles, and the legitimacy of *double effect*, were central to the notorious case of Dr Bodkin Adams.[97]

Dr Adams was tried for murder following the death of an eighty-four year old patient in his care. The patient had named him as a beneficiary in her will and there was evidence that large doses of heroine and morphine had been instrumental in her death. The drugs were prescribed and administered by Dr Adams who claimed that they were required for symptomatic relief. At issue was the right of the doctor to give such medication in circumstances where it might have a detrimental effect on the patient's longevity. Confronting the situation the

---

[95] H L A Hart, "Intention and Punishment" (1967) *The Oxford Review*.
[96] R v. *Carr*, *The Sunday Times*, 30 November 1986, per Mars-Jones J, at 1.
[97] R v. *Adams*, *The Times*, 9 April 1957.

judgement stated that a doctor "is entitled to do all that is proper and necessary to relieve pain and suffering, even if the measures he takes may incidentally shorten human life".[98] Hence it does appear to be legally permissible for a doctor to use whatever measures she deems appropriate to keep the patient comfortable and pain free, even if death may be hastened as an indirect or even inevitable consequence. More contemporary cases indicate that the courts, and public opinion, are prepared to allow doctors to exercise their considerable discretion in this area, though this approach may be at odds with criminal law dicta.

The tension is revealed in the trial of Dr Cox, where Ognall J stated that:

"if a doctor genuinely believes that a certain course is beneficial to his patient, either therapeutically or analgesically, then even though he recognises that that course carries with it a risk to life, he is fully entitled nonetheless to pursue it".[99]

By implication, while it would be *bad* to give a lethal dose of medication with the intention of killing, it is permissible to perform the *good* act of administering high doses of analgesia to relieve suffering, even if the patient dies as a result. From the perspective of the criminal law the crucial factor is the intention of the actor, so that:

"if the acts done are intended to kill and do, in fact, kill, it does not matter if a life is cut short by weeks or months, it is just as much murder as if it were cut short by years".[100]

Accordingly, the intention, or *mens rea*, of the practitioner of double effect must be clearly identified before legal responsibility can be established. For murder the *mens rea* is the intention unlawfully to kill or do serious bodily harm to another person. Giving pain relieving medication with the sole intention of alleviating symptoms is beyond reproach. However the medication may also have unintentional but foreseen consequences, that are problematic for criminal law because the law of homicide extends the concept of intention to include foresight of the consequences of one's actions.[101] If it is possible to extrapolate that the drug was given because of its side effects as well as for its therapeutic value, the subjective intention of the clinician is ambiguous and the action may be unlawful. Where the use of *double effect* in terminal care is concerned, the recognition, or foresight, that one consequence of administering high doses of analgesics is death must surely always be there.

Fried has analysed the relevance of foresight in this context, and suggested that it can be permissible to follow a course of action which will foreseeably lead to a person's death, so long as death is not the intended result.[102] Criminal law would certainly find this an acceptable argument since proof of intention is an

[98] H Palmer, "Dr Adams' Trial for Murder" (1957) *Crim LR* 365, at 375.
[99] R v. *Cox* (1992) 12 BMLR 38, at 39.
[100] H Palmer, "Dr Adams' Trial for Murder" (1957) *Crim LR* 365, at 375.
[101] *R v. Nedrick* [1986] 3 All ER 1.
[102] C Fried, *Right and Wrong* (Harvard, Harvard University Press, 1978).

essential requirement in the successful prosecution of any homicide case. Where death has occurred but was not the intended consequence, the position regarding *mens rea* was clarified in *R* v. *Nedrick* which held that:

"When determining whether the defendant had the necessary intent, it may be helpful for a jury to ask themselves two questions. (1) How probable was the consequence which resulted from the defendant's voluntary act? (2) Did he foresee that consequence?

If he did not appreciate that death or serious harm was likely to result from his act, he cannot have intended to bring it about. If he did, but thought that the risk to which he was exposing the person killed was only slight, then it may be easy for the jury to conclude that he did not intend to bring about that result. On the other hand, if the jury are satisfied that at the material time the defendant recognised that death or serious harm would be virtually certain . . . to result from his voluntary act, then that is a fact from which they may find it easy to infer that he intended to kill or do serious harm, even though he may not have had any desire to achieve that result".[103]

Norman echoes this opinion when he argues that if analgesics are administered specifically to relieve pain, and simultaneously to hasten death, life has indeed been *intentionally* terminated and that, if the doctor "says that she is not intentionally ending the patient's life, she is deceiving either herself or others".[104] This may well be true but to endorse that sentiment in the arena of terminal care leaves doctors vulnerable to the rigours of the criminal law.

Yet if the control of symptomatic pain is the only available treatment, it is essential that it be provided without reservation, even though death is a recognised side effect. Failure to do so would be more harmful and therefore unethical. Ordinarily the assessment of whether a specific treatment will be beneficial to a patient incorporates a judgement that it would be in the patient's "best interests". For the terminal or incurable patient determining whether a course of treatment is in the best interests of a particular patient can be problematic. The patient may consider that her best interests lie in alleviating pain and suffering by ending her life, while her professional and emotional carers favour symptomatic relief. In this context "best interests" has been described as a "pious fiction" which disguises the fact that the patient's interests cannot be easily divorced from those of the carers,[105] calling into question the intentions of the clinician and raising doubts about the efficacy of a particular treatment.[106] Should those doubts include concerns about the cause of a patient's death and lead to criminal proceedings a genuinely held belief that the actions taken were in the patient's best interests will not alone absolve the clinician from responsibility.

The distinction between subjective intention and acting in the patients best interests is, in many respects, analogous to that between intention and motive in

---

[103] *R* v. *Nedrick* [1986] 3 All ER 1, at 3–4.
[104] R Norman, *Ethics, Killing and War* (Cambridge, Cambridge University Press, 1995) at 87.
[105] M Brazier, *Medicine, Patients and the Law* (London, Penguin, 1992) at 109.
[106] Further analysis of the concept of best interest follows in ch. 3.

criminal law. Motive can be described as the reason why a person commits an act which is intellectually distinct from whether the consequences of the act were intended or foreseen. The attitude of the law to this distinction was succinctly enunciated by Farquharson J in R v. *Arthur* when he advised the jury that, "however noble his *(the doctor's)* motives were . . . is irrelevant to the question of your deciding what his intent was" (parenthesis added).[107] A rather different emphasis is offered by the case of R v. *Steane*[108] however.

During the second World War, Steane was alleged to have assisted the Germans by making radio broadcasts. He argued in his defence that his intention in so doing had been to protect his family from the threat of harm, rather than to assist the enemy. Steane was convicted at first instance but appealed, and on appeal it was noted that:

> "While, no doubt, the motive of a man's act and his intention in doing the act are in law different things, it is none the less true that in many offences a specific intention is a necessary ingredient and the jury have to be satisfied that a particular act was done with that specific intent, although the natural consequences might, if nothing else was proved, be said to show the intent for which it was done".[109]

The judgement recognised that some actions may be "equally consistent with an innocent intent as with a criminal intent" and accordingly it was held that Steane did not possess the specific intention to assist the enemy as was required for the offence with which he was charged.[110]

A different construction of these events suggests that in fact although Steane's intention was to help his family he did so by intentionally assisting the Germans. Complying with the enemy's demands was the only way he could save his family therefore it was his intention so to do,[111] even though he did not make the broadcast with the purpose of assisting the enemy.[112] Thus revealing that in criminal law "the concept of 'intention' has a chameleon-like character and changes its meaning according to its context".[113]

Following the dicta in *Nedrick*, doctors who use *double effect* and are "virtually certain" that death will result have the *mens rea* of murder. Adopting the reasoning employed in *Steane* would provide an acquittal due to the lack of "specific" intent and *Mohan*[114] suggests that juries should regard criminal intention within the common-sense and ordinary meaning of the word, as, "a decision to

---

[107] *The Times*, 6 November 1981, [1986] *Crim LR* 383.

[108] [1947] 1 All ER 813.

[109] *Ibid*, at 820.

[110] Today it is widely believed that *Steane* is been better categorised as a case of duress of circumstance, see C Clarkson and H Keating, *Criminal Law: Text and Materials* 4th edn. (London, Sweet & Maxwell, 1998) at 147.

[111] A Halpin, "Intended Consequences and Unintentional Fallacies" (1987) 7 *Oxford Journal of Legal Studies* 104, G Williams, "Oblique Intention" [1987] CLJ 417.

[112] A Duff, "Intentions Legal and Philosophical" (1989) 9 *Oxford Journal of Legal Studies* 76.

[113] C Clarkson and H Keating, *Criminal Law: Text and Materials* 4th edn. (London, Sweet & Maxwell, 1998) at 141.

[114] [1976] 1 QB 1.

bring about a certain consequence". Price argues that, because of the inconsistency it promotes in the law, the doctrine of double effect is "the prime catalyst for jurisprudential distortion"[115] in the context of medical decisions at the end of life. He asserts that "life-shortening pain relieving measures are justified but *intentional* killings. . ." and suggests that a new defence justifying killing in these circumstances would be a more appropriate way for the law to legitimate the proper use of these techniques.[116]

In accord with Price's argument, John Harris offers an ethical perspective whereby he contends that the actual intention to produce a consequence is of lesser significance than being responsible for causing that consequence.

> "If you know that as a result of what you deliberately choose to do, the patient will die, then that death is your responsibility. The question you must address is: ought this patient to die in these circumstances? If they should, then it doesn't matter whether you intend it or not, if they shouldn't you should neither intend it nor allow it to happen as a second effect".[117]

Under Harris's interpretation the most important aspect of a case like Dr Arthurs[118] is not whether he performed the act without intending for the patient to die, but whether or not he was actually responsible for the action that caused the death of the patient.[119] The moral intent of the actor is as significant as the consequences of the action and the circumstances within which the act is carried out. It is then not just consequential harm that denotes criminal intent but also the fact that the harm caused resulted from an evil intent.[120]

The differences between these legal and ethical responses to the use of *double effect* may explain the tension in the relationship between those who wish doctors to use it to end a life of suffering (patients and relatives), and those who must perform it (doctors). Medication may be justifiably administered, even if it has the side effect of causing death, so long as the intention of the doctor prescribing and giving the drug is therapeutic and beneficial, but morally the practice is less easily justified. Distinctions must surely also be drawn between the unintentional use of *double effect* which results in death, and its deliberate application, which is a manipulation of its current legal status. Where a patient specifically asks the doctor to prescribe drugs for the express purpose of causing death and promoting dignity, the practice cannot be easily legitimated and may be better defined as assisted suicide or even active euthanasia.

---

[115] D Price, "Euthanasia, Pain Relief and Double Effect" (1997) 17 (2) *Legal Studies* 323, at 324.
[116] *Ibid*, at 341–2.
[117] Professor John Harris speaking during *Hypotheticals: Kill or Cure?* broadcast on BBC 2 television, July 1994, transcript published by Broadcasting Support Services.
[118] *R v. Arthur* (1993) 12 BMLR 1, *The Times*, 6 November 1981, 1.
[119] Similar views were expressed by The British Humanist Society in evidence presented for the *Report of the Select Committee on Medical Ethics* HL Paper 21-I (London, HMSO, 1994) at para 76.
[120] See R A Duff, *Intention, Agency and Criminal Law* (London, Blackstone Press, 1990) at 112 for a fuller explanation.

PHYSICIAN ASSISTED SUICIDE

Physician assisted suicide usually involves a patient taking her own life with the help of a doctor. Assistance is often necessary because the patient is practically or contextually prevented from ending her own life. She may be physically incapacitated, either because illness limits her mobility or because she is confined to home or hospital. Access to the means to take her own life is then denied in circumstances where the doctor is often regarded as the person best able to assist. A request to collaborate in suicide, usually by prescribing the appropriate drugs and advising on their use, may be the result.

Assisted suicide is distinguishable from mercy killing because it is the patient who acts to bring about her own death, rather than the doctor or other carer. The person who provides a patient with the means to secure her own demise will not therefore be guilty of homicide or unlawful killing. Neither will the patient, should she survive, be liable for prosecution as it has not been an offence to attempt to commit suicide since the enactment of the Suicide Act 1961. However, in Britain a deliberate action performed with the intention of helping another person to kill herself is a criminal offence, even if the act is unsuccessful.[121] Accordingly, even if the suicidant acts with clearly motivated self-determination, anybody who intentionally provides the means to enable that person to commit suicide will be culpable.

Despite this, a doctor suspected of assisting in a suicide will be liable to prosecution only if sufficient clear and unequivocal evidence is available to establish that an offence has been committed. Some of the difficulties of obtaining evidence to this effect are demonstrated by *Attorney-General* v. *Able*[122] where a court declaration was sought that it was an offence for the Voluntary Euthanasia Society to sell a booklet detailing various methods of committing suicide. Evidence suggested that fifteen cases of suicide were associated with the booklet, which detailed various ways and means of securing personal "deliverance". The Society claimed that, in the absence of legislation allowing euthanasia, it had no alternative but to provide its members with information, but in order to convict the prosecution had to demonstrate that the booklet was distributed with the intention of assisting the particular recipient to commit suicide using that information. Furthermore, the individual victim must have actually committed suicide as a consequence of reading the booklet. A lack of evidence of a clear causal link between the reading of the booklet and the suicides prevented conviction in this instance. However, where evidence is available the courts will reflect the gravity of the offence in the sentence.[123]

---

[121] s.2 (1) Suicide Act 1961 makes it an offence to aid, abet, counsel or procure the suicide or attempted suicide of another.

[122] [1984] QB 795.

[123] In *R* v. *Beecham*, reported in the *Daily Telegraph*, 18 February 1988, a father assisted his daughter, who suffered with persistent pain from cancer and multiple sclerosis, to commit suicide

Nevertheless it has been argued that in some instances it can be morally acceptable for a physician to assist a patient to commit suicide, as long as it is done with an entirely compassionate motive.[124] Some doctors have openly assisted their patients to kill themselves and defended their actions by arguing that this was a compassionate and caring response to the situation.[125] Assisting suicide will in these circumstances be regarded as a means with which to enable a person to exercise her own choices and thereby maintain dignity until the point of death. As such it is questionable why it should be a crime to help those who wish to pursue this course of action but are prevented from so doing by the consequences of disease when it is not a crime for people to take their own lives if they can. Dr. Timothy Quill carefully considered these issues in respect of his patient known as Diane:

> "It was extraordinarily important to Diane to maintain control of herself and her own dignity during the time remaining to her. When this was no longer possible, she clearly wanted to die . . . When the time came, she wanted to take her life in the least painful way possible. Knowing of her desire for independence and her decision to stay in control, I thought this request made perfect sense".[126]

Diane was dying from incurable leukaemia and sought help in committing suicide so that she could be certain that she would die when she decided the time was right. In reviewing her case, Peter Singer supported Quill's response stating that "not all patients are fortunate enough to have a doctor like Timothy Quill".[127] In a similar vein, Dr Jack Kevorkian, who is thought to have used a home made suicide machine to help at least one hundred people to commit suicide[128] has been hailed as "a medical hero":

> "No one has demonstrated any discernible motives from him except that he believes his work is right. Greed for money is absent because he has charged no fees. Greed for fame, too, seems unlikely because he has shunned the media except to explain his position. And no one has accused him of sadism in ending the lives and, according to him, the suffering of his patients".[129]

Dr Kevorkian's conduct was unlawful and not universally admired however, and he was repeatedly tried for assisting suicide. Until 1999 juries persistently declined to convict him when he persuasively defended his actions as being purely compassionate. Eventually though, following a debacle about a case

---

and was given a twelve month suspended sentence. The judge said that "offences of this nature must in all circumstances be met with a term of imprisonment". See J Horder, "Mercy Killings—Some Reflections on Beecham's Case", (1988) 52 *Journal of Criminal Law* 309.

[124] R Weir, "The Morality of Physician-Assisted Suicide" (1992) 20 *Law Medicine and Health Care* 116.

[125] Timothy E Quill, "Death and Dignity: A Case of Individualized Decision-Making" (1991) 324 (10) *New England Journal of Medicine* 691–4.

[126] *Ibid.*

[127] P Singer, *Practical Ethics* 2nd edn. (Cambridge, Cambridge University Press, 1993) at 198.

[128] H Brody, "Kevorkian and Assisted Death in the United States" (1999) 318 *BMJ* 953.

[129] J Roberts, C Kjellstrand, "Jack Kevorkian: A Medical Hero" (1996) 312 *BMJ* 1434.

where he claimed to have removed a kidney from one of his 'victims' and a television screening of his involvement in the death of Thomas Youk, he was convicted of second degree murder. He was sentenced to serve between ten and twenty five years in prison. The Dutch doctor Boudewijn Chabot has also been widely criticised for his part in the assisted suicide of a patient who suffered only from depression.[130] Indeed he was criminally convicted but, despite the fact that assisting suicide could at that time attract a three year prison sentence in the Netherlands, no criminal sanction was imposed. Despite the public and professional misgivings about cases like these debate about the efficacy of assisted suicide continues and has been intensified in recent years with the introduction of permissive legislation in Australia and America.

In 1995 Australia's Northern Territory enacted legislation permitting doctors to provide assistance for terminally ill patients who wish to end their own lives. The Rights of the Terminally Ill Act 1996 became effective on 1 July 1996. In February 1996, prior to its introduction, it was amended to include stricter eligibility requirements.[131] The Federal Parliament overturned the legislation in March 1997 but not before four patients took the opportunity to end their lives with the aid of their doctors.

On 22 September 1996, Bob Dent became the first person in the world to die by "legal" assisted suicide when he used specially designed computer software to kill himself. The computer program, called "Final Exit", was developed by Dr Philip Nitschke to enable patients to end their own lives in a clinical and reliable manner. The process was designed to take a minimum of nine days and involved the participation of up to six medical professionals including a GP and a psychiatrist. The patient was required to respond to a series of twenty two questions prompted by the computer program beginning with "does the medical practitioner wish to give assistance?". All questions were to be answered in the affirmative for the "countdown" to continue. Once the final stages of the program were reached a doctor would need to fit a cannula which would facilitate the injection of lethal intravenous drugs. The final communication stated baldly, "If you press 'YES', you will cause a lethal injection to be given within 30 seconds and you will die". A positive response would result in the administration of a lethal cocktail of drugs inducing unconsciousness and then death.

Predictably the Northern Territories legislation and the computer assisted process received both support and condemnation from groups on either side of the euthanasia lobby. A clear consensus emerged amongst people who welcomed the opportunity to use the computer programme to deliver legal physician assisted suicide however and many were prepared to travel to

---

[130] *Nederlands Juristenblad* (1994) 26: 893–5, T Sheldon "Judges make Historic Ruling on Euthanasia" (1994) 309 *BMJ* 7. H Biggs and K Diesfeld, "Assisted Suicide for People with Depression: An Advocate's Perspective", (1995) 2 (1) *Medical Law International* 23.

[131] Instead of requiring the agreement of one psychiatrist and one doctor a patient wishing to use the Act would need the agreement of four doctors: a psychiatrist, the medical practitioner who would assist the patient to die, a palliative care expert who must have explained the palliative options, and an independent clinician with expertise in the patients terminal condition.

Northern Australia to take advantage of it.[132] When the Act was overturned two people, having obtained the necessary signatures, were waiting to use its provisions. In view of their peculiar position it was proposed that a special amendment could be passed to permit them to receive the help they sought in their own time, even though such action was no longer legally permitted. The Federal Parliament denied their request.

Similar legislative twists and turns have been experienced in Oregon, the only American State to permit legal physician assisted suicide. Oregon's Death with Dignity Act 1994 was initially passed after a citizen initiated referendum. Immediately after its introduction it became the subject of a legal challenge that labelled it as potentially discriminatory and contrary to a number of constitutional protections. In 1995 it was held to be in violation of the Equal Protection Clause of the Fourteenth Amendment of the American Constitution and therefore unconstitutional.[133] This ruling was subsequently challenged and rechallenged until the Oregon legislature decided to hold a second referendum in November 1997. An increased majority in favour meant that the Act became law, allowing doctors to prescribe lethal medication on request to adult patients who have the capacity to "make and communicate" health care decisions and are terminally ill.[134] The Act specifies the format of the written request, including the requirement for at least two witnesses, one of whom must be entirely independent of the patient. The patient's own doctor is specifically excluded from being a witness. The patient must request the drugs both orally, twice, and in writing. At least fifteen days must elapse between the time of the first request and the delivery of the prescription, which may also not occur until at least forty eight hours after the written request is made.[135]

According to the Oregon Health Division, twenty nine prescriptions for lethal medication were written for patients requesting death with dignity between December 1997 and August 1999.[136] The reasons given by the patients concerned for selecting physician assisted suicide ranged from "non-existent quality of life", through "loss of control of bodily functions" resulting in loss of autonomy, to being "determined to have control".[137] It seems therefore as though the Oregon Death with Dignity Act was meeting the expressed needs of people seeking to achieve dignity in dying by retaining control and using medication deliberately prescribed for the purpose to end their own lives. However, like the Australian Northern Territories legislation, opposition to the Act

---

[132] C Zinn and S Potts, "Australians to log on for the Final Exit" *The Observer* 9 June 1996 at 23.

[133] *Lee* v. *Oregon* 891 F Supp 1239 (D Or 1995).

[134] The Act defines terminal disease as disease that has been medically confirmed as incurable and irreversible and which reasonable medical judgement expects to produce death within six months.

[135] For further detail on the scope and operation of the Oregon Death with Dignity Act 1994 see M Otlowski, *Voluntary Euthanasia and the Common Law* (Clarendon, Oxford, 1997) particularly 368–374.

[136] Oregon Health Division, "Oregon's Death with Dignity Act Annual Report 1999" at <http://www.ohd.hr.state.or.us/chs/pas/ar-dosc/htm>.

[137] *Ibid.*

remains so strong that it was reported in November 1999 that the Death with Dignity Act would be overturned by the Pain Relief Promotion Act passed by the US House of Representatives,[138] prohibiting the use of federally controlled substances, like morphine and similar narcotics, being prescribed "for the purpose of causing death" and effectively outlawing physician assisted suicide in Oregon.

So the legalisation of assisted suicide remains contentious even though a patient's request for assisted suicide may be wholly understandable in the rare cases where orthodox medical techniques are unable to alleviate the anguish imposed by intolerable illness.[139] In the face of intolerable and ultimately unrelievable suffering the act of enabling a patient to commit suicide can be readily viewed as the supreme act of compassion. Particularly where a patient articulates a desire to maintain autonomy over her living and dying which will be denied by the inevitable progress of disease, and when conventional medical therapy has been exhausted.[140] But to assist suicide is clearly contrary to the ethos of the medical profession and exposes the clinician to the potential of criminal and professional sanctions. Furthermore, a doctor who decides not to comply with a request for assistance may come to feel that her inability to provide such ultimate care is a failure of her moral responsibility as a clinician. Respect for individual autonomy does not include the right to place another in a position where they feel morally obliged to perform such an act. That would surely be an affront to the practitioner's dignity. And inevitably, those who are prepared to comply with a request to assist suicide may be perceived as exploiting the vulnerable[141] and sliding down the slippery slope towards mercy killing.

MERCY KILLING

The term *mercy killing* describes the situation where a person (in practice this will often be a medical professional) deliberately takes the life of another in order to alleviate suffering. In Britain and all other Western jurisdictions, anybody who intentionally terminates the life of another is morally and criminally culpable, whether or not the "victim" complies. The law takes no account of

---

[138] F Charatan, "New US Act Overturns Legality of Doctor Assisted Suicide in Oregon" (1999) 319 *BMJ* 1312.

[139] The public and professional sympathy provoked by Annie Lindsell's unreported and aborted application for a Court declaration that her GP would not be the subject of criminal prosecution if he complied with her request for potentially lethal medication is evidence of this point. See E Wilkins, "Dying Woman Granted Wish for Dignified End" (1997) *The Times*, 29 October, 3.

[140] New York internist Dr Timothy Quill received much public and media sympathy after publishing an account of how he came to assist his patient "Diane" to commit suicide in 1991.

[141] Doctors Chabot and Kevorkian have been placed in this category by some commentators, see for example, A D Ogilvie, S G Potts, "Assisted Suicide for Depression: the Slippery Slope in Action?" (1994) 309 *BMJ* 492, H Biggs, K Diesfeld, "Assisted Suicide for People with Depression: an Advocate's Perspective" (1995) 2 (1) *Medical Law International*, 23, and, S Gutmann, "Dr Kevorkian's Woman Problem: Death and the Maiden" 24 June 1996, *New Republic* 1.

compassionate motives or of the status or profession of the individual concerned, "it always treats mercy killing as murder".[142] As has been shown, the
doctrine of *double effect* means that if a patient dies as a result of the administration of medication which was vital for symptomatic relief, a prosecution for
homicide would probably be unsustainable. But, if the drug given has no therapeutic value, as in the case of Dr Cox,[143] criminal responsibility is irrefutable
because, "if he injected her with potassium chloride with the primary purpose
of killing her, of hastening her death, he is guilty of the offence charged".[144]
Accordingly, Dr Cox was tried and ultimately convicted of attempted murder.
The fact that his patient had been cremated before the criminal investigation
began, and that she was dying anyway, made it impossible to determine the
cause of her death with any certainty. Even though Dr Cox had recorded that he
had administered the lethal drug there was no evidence to establish whether the
drug or the disease had killed her.[145] It has been suggested that had Cox given
his patient an overdose of narcotics, in the guise of relieving pain, he would
have safeguarded himself against criminal responsibility.[146] Resting upon
the assumption that *double effect* can be used to shorten life this proposition is
correct, so long as the only motive is pain relief.[147] However, Dr Cox made a
conscious decision to end his patient's suffering and her life, at her request, and
acted upon it. Furthermore he took full responsibility for his actions by chroni-
cling his conduct in the patient's medical records. As a consequence he was subjected to the full force of the criminal law and the scrutiny of the doctor's
professional body, the General Medical Council.

The case provoked an emotional response from those who were involved.
Many of the jury members wept openly when the guilty verdict was delivered.
And, after convicting Cox of attempted murder, Ognall J went on to temper
justice with mercy by imposing a sentence of twelve months imprisonment, suspended for twelve months, apparently in recognition of the dilemma the doctor
had experienced. This benevolence was reflected in the subsequent disciplinary
hearing of the General Medical Council, which declined to remove his name
from the professional register, the usual sanction for a doctor convicted of a
serious crime. Instead it compelled Dr Cox to attend a training course on pain
management and then to work under supervision for a specified period. The
GMC's formal judgement expressed sympathy for the predicament faced by
doctor and patient, echoing the perception of a significant section of public
opinion. The patient's son, who gave supportive evidence on the doctor's behalf
at the disciplinary hearing, revered the outcome as entirely just.

---

[142] G Williams *Textbook on Criminal Law* 2nd edn. (London, Stevens, 1983) at 580.
[143] *R v. Cox* (1992) 12 BMLR 38.
[144] *Ibid* at 39, parenthesis added.
[145] Compare with *R v. White* [1910] 2 KB 124.
[146] C Wells, "Patients, Consent and Criminal Law" (1994) 1 *Journal of Social Welfare and Family Law* 65, at 74.
[147] P Devlin, *Easing the Passing* (London, Bodley Head, 1985).

Mason and McCall-Smith state that "there is an innate reluctance on the part of the courts to convict the genuine 'mercy-killer' of an offence which carries a mandatory sentence of life imprisonment".[148] The Cox case and several subsequent cases that have seen lay people treated even more generously by the criminal justice system seem to bear this out.

For example, in March 1996 care worker Rachel Heath appeared before Winchester Crown Court charged with the murder of a seventy-one year old woman who had been suffering from cancer and was in Rachel's care. Her trial was abandoned after Ognall J reviewed evidence of her compassionate motives and declared that prosecution in such a case was not in the public interest. The Crown Prosecution Service reconsidered its position and offered no evidence.[149] In the High Court in Glasgow Paul Brady was charged with murder for killing of his brother who suffered from Huntingdon's disease and had repeatedly appealed to his family to help him die.[150] This charge was reduced to culpable homicide because, as Lord McFadyen explained, the Court's reduction of the charge to culpable homicide allowed for the exercise of discretion in sentencing and a custodial sentence was regarded as inappropriate.[151] These cases are illustrative of the gradually changing public and judicial attitude towards mercy killing, which are typified by inconsistency between what the law says and the way it is applied. Such cases and the legal uncertainty their outcomes generate are, at least in part, responsible for the apparently increasing public support for permissive legal reform.

CONCLUSIONS

Within the present legal system and the definitions it upholds, those who care might be compelled to kill in order to relieve suffering. All decisions concerning terminal medical care bring into sharp focus the divergence between the rights of patients and the responsibilities of doctors, and the fine distinctions between killing and caring are emphasised in this context. The demands now commonly made by patients and their relatives for death with dignity and the constraints imposed by the law diverge at the point where continuing medical care simply prolongs the dying process but doctors cannot lawfully participate in actions that curtail life. In practice it may not be possible to provide the kind of care required by a terminal or incurably ill patient without straying into territory policed by the criminal law, which means that doctors often have to deny patients the choice they seek.

[148] Mason and McCall-Smith, *Law and Medical Ethics* 5th edn. (London, Butterworths, 1999) at 416.

[149] A Mollard, "Nurse Cleared of Mercy Killing" 28 March 1996, *Daily Mail*, 1, unreported elsewhere.

[150] *HM Advocate v. Brady* (1996) unreported.

[151] See B Christie, "Man Walks Free in Scottish Euthanasia Case" (1996) 313 *BMJ* 961.

In recent years patients have been afforded greater involvement in treatment decisions through the development of the concepts of consent and patient autonomy. But, regardless of these advances, legal and ethical constraints prevent doctors from complying with requests for treatment options that will deliberately hasten death. Autonomy may be retained until the very end of life but, because the law dictates the circumstances in which life-limiting treatment decisions are taken, choice is necessarily limited. Requests for terminal treatment options, other than where this can be achieved by refusing consent to life prolonging interventions, are not presently legitimate. Yet, if a patient wants the opportunity to end her own life at a time of her own choosing and is able to make an autonomous decision, why should the law prevent her simply because she is constrained by geography or physical disability? And if a person is able to express a confirmed desire but physically unable to carry it out perhaps it would be more dignified for her to be permitted to die quickly and painlessly, if that is her choice, rather than enduring the protracted dying process associated with treatment refusal?

Ethical medical practice encourages health care professionals to protect people from experiencing intolerable distress and suffering against their wishes but few doctors would seek the power to actively terminate a patient's life. The certainty and consistency demanded by patients and required by health care professions is presently limited by the application of strict legal criteria to terminal care decisions. Clinically assisted death is possible and legally permissible in some forms, but, as this chapter demonstrates, its availability is largely determined by the medical circumstances relating to each specific patient and their relationship with the criminal law.

Those who are able to exercise their autonomy by refusing to accept life prolonging treatment may opt for death while those who are dependant upon institutional or emotional carers are denied choice. Here justice is denied to the patient who is prevented, by disease and the law, from exercising choice, as it may be to the practitioner or carer who flouts the law in order to compassionately comply with a person's legitimate dying wishes. Greater use and recognition of advance directives would be valuable in the promotion of patients rights and choices at the end of life. Their usefulness can only be fully assessed however, through the careful analysis of individual consent, legal capacity and autonomy conducted in the following chapters where close attention is paid to defining the precise nature of death with dignity in relation to the legal and ethical responsibilities held by medical practitioners. In this environment care must be taken to avoid criminalising those whose motives are benevolent, particularly when they have simply responded to a request for mercy. This too is undignified.

3

Consent to Treatment but Not to Death

INTRODUCTION—WHY CONSENT?

For the hypothetical patient described in chapter one, confined to her hospital bed, clinging to life but with little prospect of recovery, the outlook is bleak. Respect for autonomy and the law of consent theoretically allow her an absolute right to give, or withhold, consent to medical treatment and may enable her to influence the way in which events unfold, but whether or not she can depends largely on the individual circumstances of her case. More particularly, it will depend upon whether she has the legal capacity to participate in the medical decision-making process, and the fortitude to ensure that her wishes are upheld.

In a case like this consent is central to understanding the relationship between medicine, the law and the choice to die with dignity. Based on respect for individual autonomy, the law of consent enables people to decide whether or not to accept the medical treatments offered to them and thereby exert some control over their clinical management. Alongside this function, consent can also legitimate many practices that would otherwise be regarded as crimes. It is also central to the exercise of autonomy, choice and the maintenance of control over medical decisions at the end of life, which are widely regarded as essential for achieving dignity in dying. At present, the law of consent permits only limited success in the pursuit of dignity in dying, largely because the major method by which control can be exercised is where death results from withdrawing or withholding consent, and such a death may not be inherently dignified. Any proposals to revise law in favour of voluntary euthanasia would of course need to be firmly grounded on mechanisms for ensuring that consent is freely given, informed and valid within the context of an enduring decision to die. Before this can be achieved a sound understanding of the law of consent and current restrictions on its application is required. This chapter will outline the background to the law of consent and its application in respect of euthanasia and life-limiting medical decisions in order to ascertain its value in the pursuit of dignity in dying.

The legal foundation of consent in relation to medical treatment is precisely articulated in Cardozo J's statement that "every human being of adult years and sound mind has the right to determine what shall be done with his own body".[1] It requires that no person should be touched by another without

---

[1] *Schloendorff* v. *Society of New York Hospital* (1914) 105 NE 92, 93 (NY) per Cardozo J.

express authorisation, which, when applied to the context of medical care, means that no treatment should be given in the absence of valid consent. Consent is required regardless of whether the contact occurs in everyday life or during examination by a medical professional intent on diagnosis or treatment,[2] and generally ensures the protection of personal bodily integrity and individual autonomy. As such there are various heads of liability that attach to unauthorised touching, medical or otherwise, as well as various mechanisms available to legitimate treatment without consent in appropriate circumstances. The ability of consent to safeguard a patients interests and wishes at the end of life depends on the complex relationship between liabilities imposed for treatment in the absence of valid consent, and the mechanisms through which treatment without consent can be legitimated. These will form the substance of this chapter. Attention will be paid to the situations where consent is specifically refused in the discussion of living wills in chapter five.

WITHOUT CONSENT

Liability arising from unauthorised contact may be civil or criminal. In civil law the tort of battery derives from the right of an individual to autonomously dictate what is done to her body and provides a remedy for a form of trespass that results from intentionally causing offensive or harmful contact with another. As such it:

> "serves the dual purpose of affording protection to the individual not only against bodily harm but also against any interference with his person which is offensive to a reasonable sense of honour and dignity. The insult of being touched is traditionally regarded as sufficient, even though the interference is only trivial and not attended with actual physical harm".[3]

Tortious battery requires no evidence of consequential physical harm, merely an insult to bodily integrity,[4] but successful cases of this kind are rare in the British courts.[5] Only a handful have been brought and most have failed on the basis that there can be no battery once consent is given for some kind of physical contact. Indeed one case went significantly further, suggesting that the touching

---

[2] *Schloendorff* v. *Society of New York Hospital* (1914) 105 NE 92, 93 (NY), *Sidaway* v. *Bethlem Royal Hospital Governors* [1985] 1 All ER 643 at 666, and *Airedale NHS* v. *Bland* [1993] 1 All ER 821, provide examples of prominent cases that include statements emphasising this right. It is also endorsed in the Government policy document *"A Guide to Consent for Examination and Treatment"* issued by Dept. of Health and the Welsh Office, and *The Patient's Charter*.

[3] Fleming, *Law of Torts* 8th edn. (Sydney, Law Book Company, 1992) at 24.

[4] *Allan* v. *Mount Sinai Hospital* (1980) 109 DLR (3d) 536, a Canadian case in which a patient successfully sued when she was injected in her left arm, after giving explicit instructions that she wished to be injected only in the right arm. Consent was required to be specific to the treatment or procedure involved.

[5] See for example, *Cull* v. *Royal Surrey County Hospital* (1932) 1 BMJ 1195, and *Hamilton* v. *Birmingham RHB* (1969) 2 BMJ 456.

must be hostile in order to impose tortious liability for battery.[6] That judgment has subsequently been discredited:

"In the old days it used to be said that, for a touching of another's person to amount to a battery, it had to be a touching 'in anger' . . . and it has recently been said that the touching must be 'hostile' to have that effect (see *Wilson* v. *Pringle*). I respectfully doubt whether that is correct".[7]

The judgment in *Wilson* v. *Pringle* was indicative of the stringent efforts typically made by courts to avoid finding in favour of battery, particularly if the factual situation presents the possibility of liability in negligence where the availability of damages is restricted to foreseeable harms.[8] Successful claims for battery allow damages to be recovered for all direct consequences of the tort whether or not they were foreseeable, while the level of damages available in negligence is more restricted because awards are limited to reasonably foreseeable consequences. Moreover, successful actions in negligence also require the plaintiff to demonstrate that the injury or harm for which damages are sought was *caused* by the negligent action of the tortfeasor.

Away from the medical arena, harms "including any hurt or injury calculated to interfere with the health or comfort of the prosecutor"[9] resulting from physical contact can rarely be legitimated by the giving of consent and will usually attract criminal sanction, but there are some notable exceptions. Ordinarily, "if an act is unlawful in the sense of being in itself a criminal act, it is plain that it cannot be rendered lawful simply because the person to whose detriment it is done consents to it. No person can license another to commit a crime".[10] Yet in some circumstances,

"activities carried on with consent by or on behalf of the injured person have been accepted as lawful, not withstanding that they involve actual bodily harm or may cause serious bodily harm".[11]

Therefore, "ritual circumcision, tattooing, ear piercing and violent sports including boxing are lawful activities"[12] and it is accepted that when a person actively seeks any of these types of action she does so in anticipation of the hurt that will inevitably result and often welcomes its effect. These activities are condoned because society respects freely given consent and tolerates the resulting harm.

Medical treatment provides numerous examples of foreseeable physical harms, which would not usually be legitimated by consent. The "more than trifling"[13]

---

[6] *Wilson* v. *Pringle* [1986] 2 All ER 440.

[7] *Re F (A Mental Patient: Sterilisation)* [1990] 2 AC 1, [1989] 2 All ER 545 (HL), per Lord Goff.

[8] See M Brazier, *Medicine, Patients and the Law* (London, Penguin, 1992) at 74 for further discussion.

[9] *R* v. *Donovan* [1934] 2 KB 498, at 507, per Swift J.

[10] *A-G's Reference (No.6 of 1980)* [1981] 2 All ER 1057 at 1059.

[11] *R* v. *Brown* [1993] 2 WLR 558, per Lord Templeman.

[12] *Ibid.*

[13] *R* v. *Donovan* [1934] 2 KB 498, at 507, per Swift J.

harms that might result from medical diagnosis and treatment, such as venepuncture, incisions and strenuous palpation of parts of the body, would certainly fall within the description of "any hurt or injury calculated to interfere with the health or comfort of the prosecutor",[14] which would ordinarily attract criminal liability. There is however a presumption that any physical contact occurring in the course of medical treatment will be for the benefit of the recipient and is therefore, ultimately in the public interest and can be sanctioned by valid consent.[15] Hence even though medical treatment may involve contact which in another context could constitute bodily harm, it is not usually regarded as criminal behaviour.

Criminal responsibility for bodily contact causing non-fatal bodily harm will usually be determined according to the Offences Against the Person Act 1861. The offences range from assault and battery, through actual bodily harm to grievous bodily harm and, if death results, murder or manslaughter charges may be brought. In terms of general criminal liability the words assault and battery are frequently used interchangeably although they are distinct statutory offences with separate common law definitions.[16] Assault does not require physical contact with the victim,[17] while battery involves intentional or reckless infliction of unlawful physical contact, both could apply to very many diagnostic and therapeutic procedures. Clearly therefore, criminal liability can flow from medical misconduct, albeit rarely. The types of physical contact involved in the provision of medical care will frequently fall within the definitions contained in the Offences Against the Person Act 1861,[18] which cannot generally be legitimated by reference to the victim's consent. However, the 1861 Act does not provide that the commission of grievous bodily harm will automatically be unlawful, implying that if grievous, or serious, bodily harm is caused unintentionally or lawfully it will not be an offence. In *R* v. *Hogan*,[19] Lawton J construed "unlawfully" in section 18 as meaning "without lawful excuse",[20] hence any harm resulting from proper medical treatment will be lawful as long as the treatment is performed with valid consent. As such legitimate medical treatment is considered an exception to the general rules on non-fatal offences so that anyone performing it legitimately will not normally attract criminal sanction.[21]

---

[14] R v. *Donovan* [1934] 2 KB 498, at 507, per Swift J.

[15] It should be noted however that some medical procedures appear to provide little or no physical benefit to the individual patient concerned. The removal of organs for transplantation or the extraction of bodily tissues or fluids for donation are obvious examples but, *A-G's Reference (No. 6 of 1980)*, [1981] QB 715, refers at 719D to the removal of kidneys from living donors for transplantation as being done for "good reason" and therefore legitimate.

[16] *Taylor* v. *Little* (1992) 95 Crim App R 28.

[17] R v. *Mansfield Justices (ex parte Sharkey)* [1985] QB 613, [1985] 1 All ER 193, per Lord Lane.

[18] Offences Against the Person Act 1861, s.18, s.20, and s.47, define the offences of causing grievous bodily harm, inflicting grievous bodily harm and, assault occasioning actual bodily harm, respectively.

[19] (1973) 59 Crim App R 174.

[20] *Ibid* at 176.

[21] See *R* v. *Brown* [1993] 2 WLR 558, especially the dissenting judgments of Lord Mustill and Lord Slynn. I Kennedy, A Grubb, also suggest that where medicine is practised in good faith there

Where the conduct concerned is not legitimate consent will be negated by the nature of the harm involved or by issues which question the validity of the consent, such as fraud, or mistaken identity. *R v. Flattery*,[22] is a case in point. Here the doctor made the false representation to his patient that sexual intercourse was a legitimate method of medical examination and she permitted him to proceed. Consent was apparently given but was invalidated by the doctor's misrepresentation of the facts. Dr Flattery was convicted of rape because he had sexual intercourse with this patient without obtaining her valid consent. Medicine was obviously not being practised in good faith and criminal prosecution was appropriate.

KILLING AND CONSENT

Criminal prosecution can also be appropriate in circumstances where poor medical practice results in breach of a professional duty leading to the death of a patient. The patient will of course have consented to the treatment in the expectation that it will be performed to an established and safe standard, which will not be the case where negligence occurs. Although the *mens rea* for murder will be absent, where the performance of a duty of care falls so far below an accepted standard a manslaughter conviction can result from grossly negligent medical practice.[23] More generally, any deliberate action by one person which causes the death of another is categorised as homicide, murder or manslaughter, under the common law, even if the perpetrator is a medical professional, as in the notorious case of Harold Shipman.

The relationship between homicide and euthanasia was discussed in chapter one and is encapsulated in Lord Goff's statement in *Bland* that:

"it is not lawful for a doctor to administer a drug to his patient to bring about his death, even though that course is prompted by a humanitarian desire to end suffering".[24]

So it is of no consequence that such an action was performed by a medical professional, neither is it relevant that the act was performed with the consent of the "victim". But the insignificance of consent may be problematic here, particularly because it can sometimes be difficult to determine exactly what kind of conduct can be justified by giving valid consent. Why, for example, can consent legitimate participation in dangerous contact sports like boxing where serious physical damage may be intentionally caused, when the same conduct outside a bar

is in reality no likelihood of criminal prosecution *Medical Law: Text with Materials* 2nd edn. (London, Butterworths, 1994) at 90.

[22] (1877) 2 QBD 410, *R v. Williams* [1923] 1 KB 340, provides a similar example where a music teacher persuaded his student that sexual intercourse was an exercise to improve her breathing.

[23] *R v. Adomako* [1994] Crim LR 757, [1993] 4 All ER 935.

[24] *Airedale NHS Trust v. Bland* [1993] 1 All ER 812, per Lord Goff.

is considered criminal? Two consultation papers published by the Law Commission,[25] have specifically addressed the exceptions and perceived inconsistencies in the law of consent, one of which contained the following summary of the law of consent:

> "In short, the consent of the injured person does not normally provide a defence to charges of assault occasioning actual bodily harm or more serious injury. On to this basic principle the common law has grafted a number of exceptions to legitimise the infliction of such injury in the course of properly conducted sports and games, lawful correction, surgery, rough and undisciplined horseplay, dangerous exhibitions, male circumcision, religious flagellation, tattooing and ear piercing".[26]

There is no discernible logical reason why these practices should be exceptions, other than that they represent behaviour upon which custom and practice have had a normalising effect. Equally, the list itself is by no means comprehensive. Other permanently body altering practices such as nipple and navel piercing are today commonplace and many types of medical procedure other than surgery fall within the definitions of the 1861 Act but do not ordinarily attract legal sanction. Every year thousands of patients validly consent to treatments, operations and clinical trials knowing that they might suffer more harm than good, or even die as a result. If all of these practices are accepted as legitimate because they are consensual, commonplace and carry known and accepted risks, why should euthanasia and assisted death remain excluded from the list if there is significant public support for it? Certainly consent would have to be demonstrably freely given and fully informed but mechanisms already exist to ensure these protections in other contexts, so why not here? Perhaps the answer lies firstly in concerns about professional accountability that have already been mentioned, and secondly in issues surrounding the adequacy of consent procedures?

VALID CONSENT, FREELY GIVEN?

To avoid civil or criminal liability, and in order to maintain respect for patient autonomy, medical professionals are charged with the duty to obtain valid consent before commencing treatment. But how is a doctor's duty to a patient defined with respect to obtaining consent and the provision of medical services, and how far does that duty extend?

Bolam v. Friern Hospital Management Committee[27] is the seminal case defining negligence and the duty clinicians owe to their patients generally. Mr Bolam was a voluntary patient in a mental hospital who suffered severe fractures during

---

[25] *Consent and Offences Against the Person*, Law Commission Report, No. 134 (London, HMSO, 1993), and *Consent in the Criminal Law*, Law Commission Report, No. 139 (London, HMSO, 1995).

[26] *Consent in the Criminal Law*, Law Commission Report, No. 139, (London, HMSO, 1995) at para 1.11.

[27] [1957] 1 WLR 582, [1957] 2 All ER 118.

electro-convulsive therapy (ECT). He claimed that his doctor had been negligent in the performance of his professional duty by failing to ensure that the therapy was performed safely. In defining the nature of the doctor's obligations in the performance of his professional duty the judgment drew on ancient and informative dicta which decreed that:

"every person who enters a profession undertakes to bring to the exercise of it a reasonable degree of care and skill. He does not undertake . . . that he will perform a cure; nor does he undertake to use the highest possible degree of skill".[28]

Furthermore, *Bolam* determined that the standard of skill exercised by a member of a professional body must simply be "the standard of the ordinary skilled man exercising and professing to have that special skill",[29] and need not be the highest possible level of expertise.

Whether or not there had been negligence depended on the precise extent of the doctors duty, and this would be assessed by analysing the details of the case. Factually it was established that two approaches to the administration of ECT were commonly used at the time. One body of expert opinion regarded it as crucial that muscle relaxing anaesthesia be used while the other considered that additional risks might be imposed by so doing. The court held that doctors would not be negligent so long as they acted "in accordance with the practice accepted at the time as proper by a responsible body of medical men skilled in that particular art".[30] If therefore there were opposing professional opinions about what was the most correct procedure to adopt there would be no negligence as long as the doctor adhered to one of those established practices. The courts would not be concerned to challenge the scientific integrity of one approach over another, it would be sufficient that a responsible body of professional opinion regarded it as a proper practice. Hence the standard weighs the professional competence of doctors against the practices of their peer group, rather than imposing a minimum standard of professional practice or providing any expectations as to the level of care that should be incorporated into the performance of a professional duty.

Negligence liability is of particular relevance to the law of consent because in recent years, it has been recognised that it is germane not only to the physical provision of diagnostic, surgical, or medical skills, but also to the provision of information prior to obtaining consent. Valid and effective consent is founded on the provision of sufficient information upon which patients can base decisions about whether to accept or decline the treatments offered. Accordingly the law of negligence has developed towards defining the concept of informed consent in many jurisdictions. Cases discussed here[31] question the validity of consent given

---

[28] *Lamphier* v. *Phipos* (1838) 8 C & P 475, per Tindall CJ, at 478.
[29] *Bolam* [1957] 2 All ER 118, at 121.
[30] *Ibid*, per McNair J at 122.
[31] R v. *Flattery* (1877) 2 QBD 410, R v. *Adomako* [1993] 4 All ER 935, and *Sidaway* v. *Bethlem Royal Hospital Governors* [1985] 1 All ER 643.

by a patient who is not aware of the full implications of a particular course of treatment. In relation to treatment decisions at the end of life, full and frank exchanges of information between doctor and patient are essential. Patients need to know complete details about their diagnosis and prognosis if they are to have the opportunity to reflect upon the potential consequences of their decisions and be enabled to make informed choices concerning treatment options at the end of life. Nobody can take an informed decision to consent, to refuse treatment, or construct a valid advance directive, without being adequately appraised of the medical facts, and ethically, a competent patient should be given every opportunity to fully reflect upon the consequences of giving or refusing consent.

Initially the concept of informed consent grew out of a perceived need to protect patients engaged in clinical research and was first mentioned in the American case of *Salgo* v. *Leland Stanford Junior University Board of Trustees*.[32] Here it was held that a doctor has a duty to inform her patient of, ". . . any facts that are necessary to form the basis of an intelligent consent . . . to the proposed treatment".[33] In England the concept was first alluded to in *Chatterson* v. *Gerson*[34] and later became the focus of the action brought in *Sidaway* v. *Bethlem Royal Hospital Governors*,[35] where a patient alleged that her surgeon was negligent for failing to inform her of the possible side effects of an operation to relieve pressure on a nerve root in her neck.

Mrs Sidaway suffered partial paralysis and became severely disabled after the surgery. The damage she suffered was caused by a known complication of the operation, of which the patient claimed she had not been informed. She claimed that she would not have consented to the surgery if she been aware of the potential risk of this particular outcome and sued in both battery and negligence.

Evidential problems arose during the case because Mrs Sidaway's neuro-surgeon died before the court action commenced. The case went ahead based on the assumption that Mr Falconer (the neuro-surgeon) would have given general warnings about the kind of damage that might occur, but not about the specific damage that did result since the operation carried a less than one per cent risk of causing this injury. In line with earlier judgments the claim in battery failed at first instance, where it was affirmed that providing a patient is cognisant of the nature of the surgery in general it will not constitute a battery. The negligence claim also failed both at first instance and in the Court of Appeal, but a further appeal was made to the House of Lords.

The Law Lords confirmed that the *Bolam* test is equally applicable to diagnosis[36] and treatment,[37] and that it applies similarly to the provision of advice and information. The case failed. However, the *Bolam* test was not endorsed

[32] 317 P 2d 170 (Cal, 1957).
[33] *Ibid* at 172.
[34] [1981] All ER 257.
[35] [1985] 1 All ER 643.
[36] *Maynard* v. *West Midlands Health Authority* [1984] 1 WLR 634.
[37] *Whitehouse* v. *Jordan* [1981] 1 WLR 246.

without reservation. Lord Bridge, supported by Lord Keith, considered that there are some situations where the courts might intervene even though accepted medical practice suggests there is no necessity to disclose specific information. He remarked:

"I am of the opinion that the judge might in certain circumstances come to the conclusion that disclosure of a particular risk was so obviously necessary to an informed choice on the part of the patient that no reasonably prudent medical man would fail to make it".[38]

But his comments were somewhat diluted in the light of his earlier statement that:

"when questioned specifically by a patient of apparently sound mind about risks involved in a particular treatment proposed, the doctor's duty must, in my opinion, be to answer both truthfully and as fully as the questioner requires".[39]

The way was left open for the exercise of clinical judgement in determining exactly how detailed an answer the patient needs. Lord Diplock's judgment reflects these sentiments in its support for the use of the *Bolam* test:

"To decide what risks of the existence of which a patient should be voluntarily warned . . . is as much an exercise of professional skill and judgement as any other part of the doctor's comprehensive duty of care to the individual patient, and expert medical evidence on this matter should be treated in just the same way. The *Bolam* test should be applied".[40]

Questions about the adequacy of consent procedures, coupled with concerns about professional accountability are unavoidable when faced with the endorsement of such wide clinical discretion in an area as fundamental as the provision of information prior to gaining patients consent to treatment. Allowing too much latitude in the exercise of clinical discretion can enhance the existing paternalism in many medical relationships, and may be destructive of patient autonomy.[41] It will be especially problematic where potentially life-limiting decisions are to be made by doctors and patients. Lord Bridge's comments above[42] recognised the importance of enabling patients to make informed choices and opened up the potential to develop the concept of informed consent, but the courts have been slow to respond. In *Gold* v. *Haringey Health Authority*,[43] for example, it was argued that, on the facts of the case, the *Bolam* test did not apply to the provision of contraceptive advice. Mrs Gold had undergone a sterilisation operation and subsequently become pregnant. She had not been warned that the operation could fail, that the consequences of failure could be that she would become pregnant, or that there were alternative forms of contraception available, namely that her husband could have undergone a

[38] [1985] 1 All ER 643 per Lord Bridge at 663.
[39] *Ibid* at 662.
[40] [1985] 1 All ER 643 per Lord Diplock at 658.
[41] See ch. 4 for a detailed discussion on medical paternalism, autonomy and the validity of consent.
[42] [1985] 1 All ER 643 per Lord Bridge at 663.
[43] *The Times* 17 June 1986.

vasectomy. At first instance it was held that the *Bolam* test did not apply to information given in non-therapeutic medical situations such as the provision of contraceptive advice. This meant that the surgeon was found to be negligent even though there was evidence that a significant body of doctors, one witness said fifty per cent, would also not have issued a warning. But, in the Court of Appeal, Lord Lloyd held that the *Bolam* test is equally applicable to this kind of clinical environment as any other so the doctor had not been negligent.[44]

The patient in *Blyth* v. *Bloomsbury Area Health Authority*[45] was a qualified nurse. She sued the health authority in negligence, arguing that it was in breach of a duty owed to her by failing to inform her of all the known potential consequences of the treatment she received. Ms Blyth had asked numerous detailed questions concerning potential side effects before she was injected with the contraceptive Depo-Provera. After beginning the treatment she experienced prolonged vaginal bleeding, a potential side effect of which she had not been informed and was unprepared. At first instance the trial judge found in her favour, but in the Court of Appeal it was held that the doctor had not been negligent because the amount of information given to a patient is a matter of clinical judgement, even where the patient specifically requests it. Any suggestion that *Sidaway* implied that patients should be given *all* available information on a particular form of treatment was rejected[46] and the *Bolam* test was endorsed as being generally applicable to the provision of information, even if the patient makes specific enquiries.[47] This is perhaps the kind of reasoning that has led to recent debacles like that associated with the unauthorised removal and retention of organs from dead babies at Alder Hay Hospital.[48]

The judgment in *Blyth* was just one in a line of similar decisions that received criticism from both the medical fraternity and academic lawyers.[49] Subsequently the case of *Smith* v. *Tunbridge Wells Health Authority*[50] has demonstrated that a more patient centred approach can be adopted in cases involving negligence, consent and the provision of full information. Here a twenty-eight year old married man had undergone a surgical operation intended to correct a rectal prolapse. Bladder dysfunction and impotence were recognised complications of this particular operation and Mr Smith was afflicted with both after his operation. He brought an action in negligence against his surgeon, claiming that no warning of the risks inherent in the operation had been issued and that had he known of them he would not have consented to the procedure.

---

[44] *Gold* v. *Haringey Health Authority* [1987] 3 WLR 649, at 656–7.

[45] [1993] 4 Med LR 151.

[46] *Ibid*, per Neill LJ.

[47] [1993] 4 Med LR 151, per Neill LJ and Kerr LJ.

[48] *The Royal Liverpool Children's Inquiry Report: House of Commons Papers 2000–01 12–II* (London: HMSO, 2001)

[49] See for example, I Kennedy, "The Patient on the Clapham Omnibus" in *Treat Me Right: Essays in Medical Law and Ethics* (Oxford, Clarendon, 1991) 210–212, and S McLean, *A Patient's Right to Know* (Aldershot, Dartmouth, 1989).

[50] [1994] 5 Med LR 334.

Evidence was presented that although the side effects Mr Smith suffered were recognised they were not mentioned in the leading text book on this type of surgery at the time. Professor Golligher, the author of the book, gave evidence to this effect but also claimed that he considered the non-inclusion to be an oversight which may have misled many surgeons. The surgeon, Mr Cook, himself said in evidence that he could not remember warning the patient of these particular risks, and had not noted that he did so, but he considered that he would have been in breach of his duty to the patient had he failed to.

Morland J accepted that a young man like Mr Smith was unlikely to have consented to the operation without further enquiry or information about alternative treatments, had he been aware of the risk of impotence, and held:

"In my judgement Mr Cook, in stating that he considered that he owed a duty to warn, was reflecting not only the generally accepted standard practice, but also the only reasonable and responsible standard of care to be expected from a consultant in Mr Cook's position faced with the plaintiff's situation. On this issue the plaintiff succeeds applying the *Bolam* test as elucidated in *Sidaway*".[51]

This judgment, in combination with others[52] goes some way towards demonstrating that the law has begun to question the traditional and paternalistic attitudes to medical negligence reflected in *Bolam* and *Sidaway*. Yet the impact of the decision in *Smith* may, as a first instance judgment, be limited if its relevance is confined to its particular facts.

Nevertheless, there is evidence of growing concern amongst health care professionals that patients should be supplied with full information. The wording of the Department of Health's standard consent form for routine surgery, investigation, or treatment now emphasises the patient's right to know and to demand explanations. The trend towards greater openness by practitioners and the need for improved patient awareness is gradually becoming established, but still needs firmer foundations. Ultimately perhaps this will amount to a body of responsible medical opinion that considers the provision of full information a necessity. The judgment in *Smith* certainly appears to represent a departure from decisions in previous English cases while reflecting decisions reached in many other jurisdictions. Some commentators have therefore suggested that a move towards a fully evolved legal concept of informed consent is inevitable,[53] but it seems to be a long time coming.

The present debate concerning voluntary euthanasia end of life decision-making requires consent issues to be approached with certainty and consistency. Patients who might wish to select life-limiting treatment options within the current legal environment need to be in possession of all the facts and know that

---

[51] *Ibid*, at 338.

[52] *Bolitho v. City and Hackney Health Authority* [1998] AC 232, [1997] 4 All ER 771.

[53] See *Rogers v. Whitaker* (1992) 67 ALJR 47 (High Court of Australia), K Tickner, "*Rogers v. Whitaker*—Giving Patients a Meaningful Choice" (1995) 15 (1) *Oxford Journal of Legal Studies* 110 at 118, and C Newdick, *Who Should We Treat? Law, Patients and Resources in the NHS* (Oxford, Oxford University Press, 1995) at 297.

they have received good advice so that they can participate fully in the decision-making process. It may be difficult for lay people, especially once they have become patients,[54] to comprehend the full ramifications of a complex medical situation, but thoughtful and sensitive explanations should enhance autonomy and promote understanding. Information must be provided, not only about the therapeutic options available but also about the implications for themselves and their carers if dignity in dying is to be achieved.

However, some patients are unable to influence decisions about their medical care even if they could have been given full information. These are the groups who are excluded from Cardozo Js description of those who have a right to determine what shall be done with their bodies, notably, children,[55] who are not of "adult years", and those who are not "of sound mind" and lack full mental capacity. Despite their inability to consent in the usual way, various legal mechanisms exist to legitimate the provision of treatment, giving rise to situations that are influential in the discussion of end of life decision-making, hence it is germane to briefly consider them here.

OLD ENOUGH TO CONSENT

Generally children can be regarded as equivalent to incompetent adults because they lack the capacity to make their own treatment decisions. The practical situation is rather more complex than that however, since a parent will usually have parental responsibility by virtue of their relationship with the child.[56] Where a child has no parent or legal guardian who can authorise treatment, Wardship proceedings can be instituted to enable the courts to decide. Similarly, in situations where the efficacy of a proposed treatment is questionable or is not demonstrably in the child's best interests, the Family Courts are empowered to give or withhold consent. In the alternative, the court possesses the constitutional prerogative of *parens patriae* which provides it with the authority to consent to treatment on the child's behalf.

Under The Family Law Reform Act 1969,[57] a person reaches maturity for the purposes of consent to medical treatment at the age of sixteen. However, the ability to give legally valid consent to medical treatment is not determined solely according to chronological age, it also depends on an individual's demonstration

---

[54] Ch. 4 explores further the detrimental effects to autonomy that can result when a person is redefined as a patient.

[55] Ordinarily minors, below the age of majority, which in Britain is 18 years of age, have limited legal rights and are deemed not competent to consent to medical treatment because they are not sufficiently mature. However, under the Family Law Reform Act 1969, s.8 (1), (2), and (3), a person between the ages of 16 and 18 years may consent to medical treatment.

[56] Exceptionally, the natural father of a child who was not married to the mother at the time of birth will not automatically acquire parental responsibility. Under s.4 of The Childrens Act 1989 such a father may obtain parental responsibility by agreement with the mother or by court order.

[57] s.8 (1), (2), and (3).

that she has the capacity to decide for herself. A child below sixteen years of age may be regarded as competent to consent to treatment if she has attained a level of maturity which her doctor considers enables her to make an informed decision. In this situation the minor may be described as *Gillick competent*, a term derived from the name of the case brought by Mrs Victoria Gillick that was ultimately decided in the House of Lords in 1985.[58]

The case turned upon the legal status of advice and guidance issued to doctors by the Department of Health and Social Security (DHSS) in 1974 and revised in 1980. Following the collation of statistics revealing a high incidence of teenage pregnancy and abortion a need was identified for contraceptive services to be made more accessible to this group. The DHSS issued circulars to doctors concerning the provision of contraceptive advice to teenagers, including those under sixteen, explaining that not only could contraception be provided but also that confidentiality should be respected if the girl preferred not to inform her parents.[59] Mrs. Gillick, a devout Catholic and, at that time, mother of four daughters under sixteen, found the advice unacceptable and disputed the assumption that medical treatment of children under sixteen could be lawful in the absence of parental consent. She also argued that, since it is a criminal offence for a man to have sexual intercourse with a girl below the age of consent, providing contraceptive advice to children of this age would signify that a crime was being condoned.

Rejecting her argument, the House of Lords held that the guidance to doctors was not unlawful. Children under sixteen can lawfully receive medical advice and treatment in the absence of parental consent, provided that the particular minor has achieved a degree of maturity that enables her to comprehend fully the implications of the treatment being proposed. The judgment recognised that people mature at different rates so that flexibility in the application of legal principles is essential to uphold the autonomy of those who attain maturity at a younger age. In Lord Scarman's words:

> "if the law should impose upon the process of growing up fixed limits where nature knew only a continuous process, the price would be artificiality and a lack of realism in an area where the law must be sensitive to human development and social change".[60]

Yet the principles upheld in *Gillick* are not absolute and have been seriously undermined in subsequent cases by both medical and legal paternalism in ways

---

[58] *Gillick* v. *West Norfolk and Wisbech AHA* [1985] 3 All ER 402, HL.

[59] s.8 (3) of The Family Law Reform Act 1969 makes provision for situations such as this, stating as it does that "Nothing in this section shall be construed as making ineffective any consent which would have been effective if this section had not been enacted". This is a reference to the assumption which had existed before the Act that individuals between 16 and 18 could consent in particular circumstances, and was considered pertinent to those under 16 once the legal position regarding the over 16s was clarified.

[60] *Gillick* v. *West Norfolk and Wisbech AHA* [1985] 3 All ER 402, HL.

which may also have implications for the ability of adults of questionable competence to refuse consent to treatment.[61]

Re W,[62] involving a girl of sixteen who was transferred to a psychiatric hospital against her will to undergo treatment for anorexia nervosa, provides a graphic demonstration. Here the court relied on the interpretation of *Gillick* put forward in *Re R*[63] as deciding that, while minors under sixteen could consent to treatment, their refusal could be overridden by others with the authority to consent for them. *Re W* extended that principle further by including minors over the age of sixteen, even though their rights to give or withhold consent had been apparently firmly established by the Family Law Reform Act 1969.[64] The judgments turn upon the minor's capacity to consent and the distinction between giving and withholding consent, especially when death will be the likely result of treatment refusal. Further analysis of this type of judicial reasoning will be included in chapter five's discussions of living wills and anticipatory decisions, especially in relation to adults who lack capacity and cannot decide for themselves.

DECIDING FOR OTHERS

A legal presumption exists that every adult has the capacity to consent, unless the contrary has been demonstrated. Once attaining adult status, a patient is the only person who can give legally valid consent for a medical procedure on herself.

That some patients lack capacity is abundantly clear, few doubts arise in relation to those who are very young or unconscious.[65] For others though the assessment of capacity is more ambiguous. A person may have sustained an injury that has interfered with her intellectual ability to process and respond to information, such an injury may be traumatic or the result of degenerative disease. The ability to engage in competent decision-making may be disrupted by temporary, permanent, or fluctuating mental illness, or by emotional upset. Diagnosis of incapacity is further complicated by the fact that, regardless of cause, competence is specific to the particular decision and relative to the context within which the decision must be made. In other words a person may be competent to make one decision but not another, depending on the type and gravity of the decision and on her general understanding of its impact in the circumstances. To give an extreme example, a person who refuses a necessary life-saving treatment only because she wants to avoid the food on the supper menu the next day is

---

[61] J Murphy, "W(h)ither Adolescent Autonomy?" (1992) *Journal of Social Welfare and Family Law* 529.

[62] [1992] 4 All ER 627.

[63] (1992) Fam 11.

[64] s.8.

[65] Clearly however medical decision-making in the context of permanent unconsciousness due to trauma or disease is distinguishable from that provoked by temporary anaesthesia.

likely to be considered incompetent because she lacks insight of the full implications of the decision. Not only will she avoid the dreaded meal but she will also be dead. By contrast, a person who has considered all of her treatment options and arrived at a decision that it would be more dignified for her to die, rather than live a totally dependent existence, may be making a legally valid choice, as long as she is competent.

Two issues arise. How is capacity assessed and, once incapacity is determined, how can treatment decisions be taken? Ultimately the assessment of an individual's capacity is a legal question for a court to decide,[66] but in practice the assessment of an adult's capacity to give or withhold consent is more often a matter of clinical judgement.[67] So when an incompetent adult requires medical treatment for which she cannot consent clinicians appear to face an uncomfortable choice; either administer the treatment without consent, or don't give the treatment. In circumstances where the patient is mentally ill and requires treatment for that specific illness special provision is made under the Mental Health Act 1983. However, these measures are of little application to this analysis of the role of consent to treatment in respect of euthanasia and death with dignity so only scant reference will be made to them. Otherwise treatment without consent is usually legitimated in ways that depend upon the circumstances in which the need for treatment arises. Medical emergency, where doctors are permitted to act out of necessity, is one example while if treatment is clinically indicated but no emergency or urgency exists, best interests criteria will be employed. Each of these instances is particularly relevant to end of life decision-making where non-treatment decisions resulting in death are taken for people who cannot participate in the decision-making process. Underpinning such decisions are principles developed to enable treatment to be provided for those who cannot consent so the methods by which this is achieved form an important element of this discussion.

Necessity and Emergency

The popular perception of an emergency medical situation is one where a person is admitted to a hospital accident and emergency department in a condition that prevents communication with the medical staff. In order to legitimate treatment in the absence of consent the situation must be one of authentic emergency, where ". . . it would be unreasonable, as opposed to merely inconvenient, to postpone until consent could be sought".[68] The emergency itself does not

---

[66] *Richmond* v. *Richmond* (1914) 111 LT 273. *Re MB (an adult: medical treatment)* [1997] 8 Med LR 217, 38 BMLR 175, gives the definitive legal assessment of incapacity.

[67] The BMA with the Law Society, *Assessment of Mental Capacity: Guidance for Doctors and Lawyers* (London, BMA, 1995) at 66.

[68] P D G Skegg "Justifications for Medical Procedure Performed without Consent" (1974) 90 LQR 512, also the Canadian case of *Murray* v. *McMurchy* [1949] 2 DLR 442, and *Devi* v. *West Midlands Regional Health Authority* [1981] (CA Transcript 491) both reiterate this point.

sanction treatment in the absence of consent, rather it is the urgency of the need for treatment that is decisive. However, the emergency is relevant because, "it gives rise to a necessity to act in the interests of the assisted person, without first obtaining his consent".[69] Failure to treat in these circumstances, with potentially deleterious consequences, is contrary to the ethic of medicine,[70] and may constitute a breach of a professional obligation.

Accordingly, wherever a patient is in urgent need of medical treatment, the attendant doctors usually have little hesitation in defining the situation as one of clinical emergency and the law is sympathetic to the notion that an emergency obviates the need to obtain consent.

> "if a patient is unconscious and therefore unable to give or to withhold his consent, emergency medical treatment, which may include surgical procedures, can lawfully be carried out . . . The treatment which can be so given, however, is, within broad limits, confined to such treatment as is necessary to meet the emergency and such as needs to be carried out at once".[71]

Administering treatment without consent, even in a genuine emergency, amounts to invading a person's bodily integrity in neglect of her autonomy. It is therefore something that should always be approached with caution, particularly in clinical situations that do not fit easily into this understanding of an emergency but whose circumstances nevertheless apparently suggest that doctors have a duty to act. These situations are both rare, controversial and often subject to reinterpretation in the light of changing historical or cultural mores, as *Leigh* v. *Gladstone*,[72] illustrates.

Marie Leigh was a member of the Suffragette movement who went on hunger strike while detained in prison. She brought an action for damages against Gladstone *et al* claiming that the forcible feeding she had been subjected to amounted to an assault because it had been against her wishes. It was argued that only minimal force was used, and that the action was necessary to save the woman's life. In a judgment that appears to disregard the principle that a person's bodily integrity should not be violated without express or implied consent, the court held that, ". . . it was the duty . . . of the officials to preserve the lives and health of the prisoners, who were in the custody of the Crown".[73] Such an approach would not be advocated in the UK today where, on the basis of present day attitudes towards autonomy and self-determination, this judgment is no longer regarded as good law and it is now accepted that the existence of a duty of care does not allow the imposition of treatment upon a non-compliant competent person simply to maintain good health. As long as the individual

---

[69] *Re F (A Mental Patient: Sterilisation)* [1990] 2 AC 1, [1989] 2 All ER 545 (HL), per Lord Goff.
[70] See C Wells, "Patients, Consent, and Criminal Law" (1994) 1 *Journal of Social, Welfare and Family Law* 65 at 69, for a graphic illustration of the dilemma.
[71] *Re F (A Mental Patient: Sterilisation)* [1990] 2 AC 1, [1989] 2 All ER 545 (HL), per Lord Goff.
[72] (1909) 26 TLR 139 (King's Bench Division).
[73] *Leigh* v. *Gladstone* (1909) 26 TLR 139 (Kings Bench Division) per Lord Alverstone CJ.

concerned is mentally competent,[74] the principle applies even if that person is in the custody of the Crown.[75] Conversely, a number of criminal cases have been tried on the basis of a failure to act where a duty of care exists, even though the alleged victim has declined to consent.[76]

In *R v. Stone and Dobinson*,[77] a case of manslaughter, the defendants were held to have voluntarily assumed a duty to care for the victim, by providing sustenance and assisting her with personal hygiene while she lived with them. The deceased was ill but declined medical aid and refused food and drink. She was ultimately found dead in her bed. Despite Stone's below average mental capacity, it was held that he and Dobinson, his common law wife, were aware of the victim's deteriorating condition and carried out ineffectual attempts to secure medical treatment for her. They had thereby neglected their duty to care for her and so were responsible for her death.

Like *Leigh* v. *Gladstone, Stone* assumes that the presence of a duty negates the need for individual consent. It offers no recognition of the fact that, even if the ineffectual carers had found a doctor to attend, the victim was at liberty to refuse treatment, and that she had already insisted that she was hostile to medical intervention. The couple may have been in dereliction of their duty because they failed to summon a doctor, but it should also be noted that a competent adult has an absolute right to refuse to be treated or diagnosed by a doctor. Should their failure have generated liability for homicide in the absence of evidence that the sister would have then consented to any treatment offered, or that it would have been legally permissible for treatment to be imposed without consent? Perhaps the court was implying here a principle enunciated in *R v. Smith*,[78] namely that, "if she appeared desperately ill then whatever she may say it may be right to override" her wishes.[79] However, this statement is clearly contrary to the obligation to respect individual autonomy and not to breach another's physical integrity without their consent. At issue in these cases is whether the individuals concerned were competent to decide for themselves? If they were, medical intervention cannot be justified in the absence of consent, and if they were not on what basis could treatment be legitimately administered? The

---

[74] In R v. *Ashworth Hospital Authority ex parte Brady*, [2000] Lloyd's Med Rep 355, [2000] 8 Med LR 251, Mr Justice Kay held that Moors murderer Ian Brady should not be allowed to starve himself to death and under s. 63 of the Mental Health Act force feeding constituted treatment of his mental disorder.

[75] A-G of *British Columbia* v. *Astaforoff* [1983] 6 WWR 322, and, in the British Columbia Court of Appeal, [1984] 4 WWR 385, expressly rejected the notion that the state had a duty to force feed an individual on hunger strike to prevent her suicide. Similarly, in *Airedale NHS Trust* v. *Bland* [1993] 1 All ER 821, at 861, Lord Keith, while discussing the principle of the sanctity of life, confirmed that "it does not authorise the forcible feeding of prisoners on hunger strike." See also *Home Secretary* v. *Robb* [1995] FLR 412, which upholds this position.

[76] R v. *Stone* [1977] QB 354, R v. *Wilkinson, The Times*, 19 April 1978, 5, and R v. *Smith* [1979] Crim LR 251, are the most notable.

[77] [1977] QB 354, [1977] 2 All ER 341, (CA).

[78] [1979] Crim LR 251.

[79] *Ibid*, at 252–3.

answers are highly significant for anybody considering avoiding medical intervention in a quest for death with dignity.

While the law supports doctors who treat incapacitated patients without consent in emergencies, in practice consent is often sought from relatives or next-of-kin. This custom has no legal authority. Its only significance is as a method of determining the supposed wishes of the patient regarding the unfolding medical situation in the same way that chapter two described instances where the views of relatives about proposed treatment options might be sought but could not be considered decisive. Medical treatment performed without consent may be more easily legitimated in any subsequent legal dispute if relatives have been consulted, but only because the opinions of relatives can provide evidence as to the presumed wishes of the patient, not because proxy consent has been obtained from the relatives.[80]

Despite this, some judges have erroneously assumed that valid consent to treat an incompetent adult may be acquired through the agency of relatives.[81] The American case of *Canterbury* v. *Spence*[82] has authoritatively been cited in favour of the proposition that relatives consent should be sought as a substitute where the patient is unable to comply. And close scrutiny reveals that the judgment referred to the earlier case of *Bonner* v. *Moran*,[83] apparently supporting the contention that a patient's relatives are eligible to give consent in circumstances where the patient is prevented from so doing. But *Bonner* v. *Moran* concerned the eligibility of an adult relative to give consent on behalf of a child patient and is therefore clearly distinguishable on its facts from *Canterbury* v. *Spence*. Consequently, *Canterbury* v. *Spence* cannot provide the authority claimed for it.

In general the courts are concerned that medical professionals, acting from laudable motives, should not be subjected to legal sanction if they treat incompetent patients without consent. This has sometimes been expressed in terms of protecting the public interest, in that it should be permissible as a matter of public policy, for doctors to legitimately give emergency treatment to patients, even in the absence of consent,

"... I would prefer to explain the emergency cases on the basis that it is in the public interest that an unconscious patient who requires treatment should be able to receive it and that those who give this treatment in an emergency should be free from any threat of an action for trespass to the person".[84]

However, there are some adult patients who are permanently incapacitated and therefore require medical treatment in routine situations that cannot be defined as emergencies. Incapacitated patients inevitably suffer from the same range of

---

[80] P D G Skegg, *Law, Ethics, and Medicine* (Oxford, Clarendon, 1984) at 72–3.

[81] See for example Johnson LJ in *Wilson* v. *Pringle* [1987] QB 237, who makes this assumption but offers no legal authority to support it.

[82] (1972) 464 F 2d 772 per Judge Robinson at 789.

[83] (1941) 126 F 2d 121.

[84] *Re F (A Mental Patient: Sterilisation)* [1990] 2 AC 1, [1989] 2 All ER 545 (HL), per Lord Goff.

minor and major ailments as the rest of the population but are unable to give legally valid consent for the treatment of these conditions. In the absence of special mechanisms to authorise treatment even the pain and distress associated with something as trivial as a toothache or an in-growing toe nail could not be remedied. Best interests criteria has been established as a method of legitimately providing treatment without consent in these circumstances.

Best Interests

The concept of best interests has purchase in respect of clinical decision-making for all patients, competent and incompetent, adults and children. The doctor's duty of care to every patient lies in providing treatment according to that patient's best interests. So whether or not a particular treatment is regarded as clinically indicated for a specific patient will depend on an analysis of the best interests of that patient.

A patient with the capacity to consent can choose whether or not to accept the treatment offered according to her own understanding of what constitutes her own best interests. She is at liberty to assess and articulate her own desires with respect to what kinds of terminal care intervention she finds acceptable. But an incompetent patient who needs treatment will be treated according to somebody else's interpretation of her best interests. Clearly this is likely to be beneficial in terms of general health and well-being, but it may be problematic for people who have previously been competent and have expressed a wish not to be treated in pre-determined circumstances. These issues will be specifically addressed in the context of advance directives in chapter five, but much of that analysis is underpinned by the concept of best interests, discussed here.

For patients who lack the mental capacity to consent to treatment the overriding legal principle governing their care is that at all times the treatment given must be in their best interests:

> "not only must (1) there be a necessity to act when it is not practicable to communicate with the assisted person, but also (2) the action taken must be such as a reasonable person would in all the circumstances take, acting in the best interests of the assisted person".[85]

The best interests approach is a founding principle in family law and has provided a framework within which the courts have adjudicated cases, whether they turned on welfare principles concerning children or on treatment decisions for incompetent adults, according to the merits of their individual facts. A range of criteria can and have been used to determine what constitutes the best interests of a particular person in particular circumstances. As a result the best interests test has often been rendered imprecise in its application and its definition

---

[85] *Re F (A Mental Patient: Sterilisation)* [1990] 2 AC 1, [1989] 2 All ER 545 (HL), per Lord Goff.

reducing it, in Kennedy's terms, to ". . . a somewhat crude conclusion of social policy".[86]

Re F,[87] has been highly influential in defining the circumstances under which it is lawful to treat an adult patient who is incapable of giving consent. It was determined according to the application of best interests criteria. The judgment sought to clarify the circumstances under which the test's application is germane. The House of Lords held that the best interests test is apposite where a person is unable to consent to medical treatment. It affirmed that referral to the judiciary for a declaration that a particular therapy was in the best interests of a patient, and therefore lawful, was appropriate and necessary, because

> "no court now has jurisdiction either by statute, or derived from the Crown as *parens patriae*, to give or withhold consent to . . . an operation in the case of an adult as it would in Wardship proceeding in the case of a minor".[88]

It also described the type of criteria that should be used to define the patient's best interests.

The *Bolam* test of professional competence provided the initial framework for the House of Lords' analysis of this patient's best interests. Accordingly, it was held that once it had been ascertained that a doctor had acted "in accordance with the practice accepted by a responsible body of medical men skilled in that particular art",[89] she would not be in breach of the duty owed to her patient. Thereafter, careful consideration should be given to the reasonableness of the proposed treatment, in the light of the circumstances of the case, and with regard to certain procedural guidelines. To be reasonable the procedure involved must be necessary in the medical circumstances, and ideally the carers and relatives of the patient should have been consulted. Where appropriate, the opinions of other specialists should also be obtained, so that decisions are not taken in isolation. Factors specific to each case should also be considered which, in *Re F*, included the woman's right to control her own reproduction, and the fact that even though she was physically healthy she would be subjected to a serious, invasive and irreversible operation. The reasonableness of the proposed treatment should be assessed by the clinicians considering whether and what treatment to administer, with the consequence that proceeding with any treatment subsequently shown to be unreasonable will attract liability for battery.

Procedural guidelines dictate that the person responsible for the care and proposed treatment of the patient, the Claimant, should make an application to the court for a declaration that the treatment decision concerned can be lawfully implemented in the absence of consent. Similar rules apply where treatment

---

[86] Ian Kennedy, *Treat Me Right: Essays in Law and Ethics* (Oxford, University Press, 1994) at 395.
[87] *Re F (A Mental Patient: Sterilisation)* [1990] 2 AC 1, [1989] 2 All ER 545 (HL), per Lord Goff.
[88] *Ibid*, per Lord Bridge.
[89] [1957] 1 WLR 582, [1957] 2 All ER 118.

withdrawal from an incompetent patient is being considered. The patient should normally be the Respondent in the case with representation by a litigation friend who will ordinarily be the Official Solicitor. Hearings are usually conducted in private, subject to the court's discretion, with the decision being given publicly.[90]

After *Re F* Ian Kennedy argued that medical and judicial decisions determined according to the consideration of best interests alone, often disregard fundamental issues of human rights and may therefore result in unsatisfactory outcomes.[91] Although *Re F* did not explicitly refer to human rights, F's rights were afforded some, albeit limited, protection since some of the rights issues pertinent to the sterilisation of an incompetent adult woman were considered. The fact that the controversial nature of sterilisation raises emotional and moral issues, that it is permanent and should never be performed involuntarily without the clearest justification was carefully assessed. Furthermore the inclusion of the requirement that patients have a right to representation and privacy indicates a recognition of the importance of these human rights. It remains debatable whether the outcome of *Re F* adequately protected her human rights or those of potential future patients and Kennedy's point may assume greater importance in the light of the introduction of the Human Rights Act 1998 incorporating ECHR into domestic law. Subsequent cases have further illuminated the application of best interests criteria, expanding the assessment to include more than best medical interests and incorporating "medical emotional and all other welfare issues".[92] Further the application of the *Bolam* test has recently been limited in the assessment of best interests, such that once it is established that the range of possible treatment options meet the *Bolam* criteria and would be acceptable to a responsible body of medical practitioners, then it is for the court to determine a patient's best interests, according to welfare considerations.[93]

These principles are clearly relevant to cases involving incompetent adults and children, where courts have been charged with identifying whether a patient's best interests lay in continuing futile medical treatment when the alternative is withdrawing treatment so that the patient dies.[94] Most notable amongst these cases is *Airedale NHS Trust* v. *Bland*,[95] the first British case concerning the discontinuation of treatment for a patient in permanent vegetative state. Here it was decided that the best interests test was appropriate where it is necessary to determine the extent of a doctor's duty of care to a particular

---

[90] *Re F (A Mental Patient: Sterilisation)* [1990] 2 AC 1, [1989] 2 All ER 545 (HL), per Lord Goff.

[91] Ian Kennedy, *Treat Me Right: Essays in Law and Ethics* (Oxford, University Press, 1994) at 395.

[92] *Re MB (An Adult: Medical Treatment)* [1997] 2 FCR 541, per Butler-Sloss at 555.

[93] *Re SL (Adult Patient) (Medical Treatment)* [2000] 2 FCR 452.

[94] There have to date been a number of such cases in the UK, see *Airedale NHS Trust* v. *Bland* [1993] 2 WLR 316, *Frenchay NHS Trust* v. *S* [1994] 2 All ER 403, *A National Health Service Trust* v. *D* [2000] Fam Law 803.

[95] *Airedale NHS Trust* v. *Bland* [1993] 2 WLR 316, per Lord Goff.

patient. The limitations of merging the *Bolam* standard for assessing medical negligence with criteria legitimating non-consensual treatment of incompetent adults as in *Re F*, become apparent on close inspection of this and subsequent judgements like *Bland*. Reference is made to the kinds of issues that ought to be considered when determining the best interests of a patient who is unable to consent, but consistency and cohesion are lacking due to the dearth of any explicit guidance clarifying how to assess what actually constitutes a patient's best interests. Lord Mustill expressed his anxiety about the problem in evidence presented to the House of Lords Select Committee on Medical Ethics when he explained that:

> "one of the things that is not very good is that the phrase *best interest* has been put into play without any description of what it means. This . . . actually increases the difficulties for the doctors rather than helps to solve them".[96]

Some of the vagaries associated with the definition of best interests were specifically addressed by the Law Commission in its Report on *Mental Incapacity* within it's remit to consider "the ways in which decisions may lawfully be made for those who are unable to make decisions for themselves".[97] The purpose of the Report was to provide certainty for medical and legal decision-makers, while offering protection to patients. Clause 3(1) of the Draft Bill proposed in the Report, contains the general recommendation that, "any thing done for, and any decision made on behalf of, a person without capacity should be done or made in the best interest of that person". So the best interests standard remains pivotal in the decision-making process.

During it's consultation process the Law Commission was made aware of the inadequacies of the legal position following *Re F*, and of the expressed desire of it's consultees for "clear and principled guidance" about the assessment of best interests.[98] Consequently the Report outlines a "checklist of factors" to be considered in determining the best interests of any particular individual, in order that the standard be judiciously applied to all health-care decisions made on behalf of those who lack the mental capacity to consent for themselves. These factors are contained in Clause 3(2) of the Draft Bill proposed in the Report, which recommends that, "in deciding what is in a person's best interests regard should be had to":

> "(1) the ascertainable past and present wishes and feelings of the person concerned, and the factors that person would consider if able to do so;
> (2) the need to permit and encourage the person to participate, or to improve his or her ability to participate, as fully as possible in anything done for and any decision affecting him or her;

---

[96] Select Committee on Medical Ethics (1993–4) HL 21-II, Oral Evidence at page 21 para 41 per Lord Mustill.

[97] The Law Commission Report No. 231 *Mental Incapacity. Item 9 of the Fourth Programme of Law Reform, Mentally Incapacitated Adults* (1995) London, HMSO at para 1.1.

[98] These comments are made in Consultation Paper No.119, paras 2.22–2.24.

(3) the views of other people whom it is appropriate and practicable to consult about the person's wishes and feelings and what would be in his or her best interests;

(4) whether the purpose for which any action or decision is required can be as effectively achieved in a manner less restrictive of the person's freedom of action".

The Report stresses the importance of any known views of the individual patient in respect of the decisions to be made in reference to the "ascertainable past and present wishes". It recognises the fact that some people have never had the capacity to consent while others may have been able to anticipate their present incapacity and recorded their opinions in advance of it. This would of course be crucial in a case where a person had expressed a wish not to be maintained in a state of permanent incapacity. Consideration should therefore be given to the factors that the individual herself "would consider" and any known convictions and preferences of the previously competent individual. If however a person has never attained the capacity to decide or express an opinion the court will imply the standard of "a normal decent person, acting in accordance with contemporary standards of morality".[99]

Where "other people" are to be involved in the decision-making process the Report is careful to point out that no one class of person is designated as any more appropriate than any other. It may be practicable and appropriate to consult relatives, or carers, or anyone nominated in advance by the patient to be involved in decision making.[100] Clearly any or all of these types of people should be consulted in an effort to determine the wishes of the incapacitated person and his or her best interests. The inclusion of the requirement to investigate less restrictive treatment options in point (4) is in line with established medical and legal practice and is particularly interesting in the context of medical decisions that will lead to death. Clearly death is the most restrictive option available, and where an action is brought with a view to obtaining a court declaration that it will not be unlawful to pursue a treatment option that will result in death the courts will effectively be making a life or death choice. The less restrictive option will never be able to achieve that purpose.

The Law Commission developed these recommendations in response to the inadequacies of the common law position in Britain, which offers minimal guidance to clinicians as to how they should proceed in practice. They have not yet been implemented by Government but remain authoritative. Other jurisdictions have attempted to address the problem of legitimating medical treatment without consent by adopting the principle of substituted judgement as an alternative method of decision-making.

---

[99] *Re C (A Patient)* [1991] 3 All ER 866, at 870.

[100] The Law Commission Report No. 231 *Mental Incapacity. Item 9 of the Fourth Programme of Law Reform, Mentally Incapacitated Adults* (London, HMSO, 1995) at para 1.1.

Alternative Decision-Making

Substituted judgement is founded on the principle of autonomy, as opposed to the best interests standard which is based upon beneficence and non-maleficence. It involves a designated proxy, or a court acting as proxy, making decisions on behalf of the patient that are intended to reflect what the wishes of the patient would have been, had she been able to respond. Arguably therefore substituted judgement is an expression of the patient's best interests "as that patient would have defined them",[101] and provides a means by which the best interests standard can be executed. However, as an autonomy based standard and as a measure of an individual's own assessment of her best interests, substituted judgement can, in practice, be an imperfect device.

Firstly, proxy decision-makers bring with them their own idiosyncrasies and prejudices, which will necessarily influence the decisions they make. Autonomy is worthless if a proxy consents to a procedure believing it to be in the patient's best interests but knowing that the incompetent individual would not have consented in the circumstances. The objectivity of the proxy decision-maker is crucial to the efficacy of the process of substituted judgement but is not easily guaranteed or verified. Hence, when the applicability of the substituted judgement test in English law was discussed in *Bland*[102] it was rejected by Lord Goff, "I do not consider that any such test forms part of English law", and by Lord Mustill, "the idea is simply a fiction, which I would not be willing to adopt". Yet both here, and in the earlier case *Re T*,[103] it was held to be appropriate to consider the opinions of relatives while compiling evidence about the patient's best interests.

Secondly, the substituted judgement test is not appropriate in all circumstances. Specifically, it is inappropriate to apply such a test to patients who have never been competent to make decisions for themselves, such as permanently mentally disabled adults and minors. Much of the discussion of the principle of substituted judgement in English cases has centred on cases where the test was inappropriately applied. For example, *Belchertown State School Superintendent v. Saikewicz*,[104] *Re Moe*,[105] and *Re Jane Doe*,[106] all of which purported to apply the principle of substituted judgement to patients who had never been competent and whose wishes therefore could never have been known or expressed. These examples have been responsible for much confusion about the application and appropriateness of the substituted judgement test. As a consequence English courts continue to be reluctant to adopt it despite the fact that in other

---

[101] P S Appelbaum, C W Lidz, A Meisel, *Informed Consent: Legal Theory and Clinical Practice* (New York, Oxford University Press, 1987).
[102] *Airedale NHS Trust v. Bland* [1993] 2 WLR 316, per Lord Goff.
[103] *Re T (Adult: Refusal of Treatment)* [1992] 4 All ER 649.
[104] 373 Mass 728 (1977).
[105] 432 NE 2d 712 (1982).
[106] 583 NE 2d 1263 (1992).

jurisdictions substituted judgement has clearly played a valuable role in deter-mining the preferences of patients who become incompetent.[107]

The proposals for legal reform within Law Commission Report 231[108] do go some way towards better defining the mechanisms of legitimately providing treatment to permanently incompetent adults, as do subsequent proposals for legislative reform.[109] New forms of decision-making are considered and recom-mendations are made concerning the introduction of a continuing power of attorney to deal with matters such as admission to hospital,[110] the appointment by the court of managers to manage property and financial matters,[111] and the expansion of the use of advance statements about health care.[112] Essentially however, the recommendations centre around defining what constitutes the best interests of any individual while leaving the existing legal framework largely in tact. They fail to strengthen principles of individual autonomy or to offer alter-native mechanisms for making decisions on behalf of people who cannot con-sent. Valuable support is advanced for greater use of living wills, and the potential impact of these on end-of-life decision-making will be assessed in detail in chapter five. The introduction of many of these recommendations would be helpful in terms of providing guidance for the medical profession but may also lead to a degree of inflexibility which the present common law approach of considering individual cases according to their particular facts tends to avoid.

CONCLUSIONS—A CONSENT TOO FAR?

Obvious tensions exist in the law of consent as far as decision-making at the end of life is concerned. Competent people who are able to articulate their own views may wish to have their lives ended to avoid the perceived indignities asso-ciated with protracted suffering, but their consent will not legitimate medical intervention leading to this conclusion. People who are not able to decide for themselves due to mental incapacity will have decisions made for them by oth-ers, according to an assessment of their best interests. Paradoxically they may be permitted to die and ironically, these people are usually not suffering or even aware of their potential to suffer. It is clear therefore that an inherent inconsist-ency exists in the legal approach to life limiting decisions. Those who can make

---

[107] Re Quinlan 70 NJ 10 (1976) is illustrative of the successful operation of substituted judge-ment.

[108] The Law Commission Report No. 231 Mental Incapacity. Item 9 of the Fourth Programme of Law Reform, Mentally Incapacitated Adults (London, HMSO, 1995) at para 1.1.

[109] Lord Chancellor's Department, Who Decides? Making Decisions on Behalf of Mentally Incapacitated Adults (London: HMSO, 1997) Cm 3808, Lord Chancellor's Department, Making Decisions (London: HMSO, 1999) Cm 4465.

[110] The Law Commission Report No. 231 Mental Incapacity. Item 9 of the Fourth Programme of Law Reform, Mentally Incapacitated Adults (London, HMSO, 1995) at para 7.1.

[111] Ibid at para 8.41.

[112] Ibid at paras 5.1–5.39.

valid and considered decisions on their own behalf are not permitted medical assistance, seemingly for fear of abuse, while those who cannot participate in the decision-making process are allowed to die. The deaths of each of these groups may in actuality appear similar. Withdrawing nutrition and hydration from a patient will result in a slow death as will the failure to intervene for the competent but incurable or terminally ill patient, but one is regarded as more dignified and the other less.

At present patients can only influence the manner of their dying through their ability to refuse medical treatment. Few concerns arise for those who are able to make autonomous medical decisions so long as their decisions are respected by the attending medical professionals. However, problems develop when the efficacy of a decision is questioned and where the patient's competence to make a decision is debatable, especially if consent is denied and death is the expected consequence. In this case autonomy may be compromised by an assessment that the patient is not competent, resulting in their treatment refusal being overridden.

Many people consider the possibility of becoming permanently incompetent before it happens to them. They may determine what action they would like to have taken on their behalf through a living will, hoping to ensure that they are not kept alive inappropriately against their known wishes. In reality the aspirations of this group need less protection of than others who retain competence but are powerless to act on their wish to die, because legal precedents and the application of best interests criteria favour allowing the permanently incompetent to die, while the criminal law prohibits deliberate actions causing death, even at the considered request of a competent patient.

The practical limits of individual autonomy are readily exposed when consent is considered in relation to best interests analysis and competency at the end of life. For example, are patients always able to exercise autonomy and in what circumstances will autonomous decisions be subjected to medical scrutiny? In theory the same legal mechanisms and rules apply to withholding or refusing consent and to giving consent but practical and ethical distinctions are often drawn which can be destructive of autonomy. The legal response to these issues is, at best in need of clarification, and at worst riddled with inconsistency

4

Autonomy, Self-Determination, and Self-Destruction

"Perhaps the most fundamental precept of the common law is respect for the liberty of the individual. In a medical context this means that a person's right to self-determination, to deal with his body as he sees fit, is protected by the law".[1]

INTRODUCTION—AUTONOMOUS CHOICES

In medical law the fundamental right of self-determination, described here by Ian Kennedy, represents the right of each person to exercise personal autonomy, to act as a sovereign individual, and to exercise independent choices. As such, autonomy provides the foundation to the law of consent, and has come to be regarded as the linchpin of health care decision-making.[2] Legal recognition of the right to self determination and autonomy in medicine dictates that individuals are not subjected to the arbitrary imposition of the wishes or ideals of others. It is no surprise then that autonomy is heralded as being pivotal to the right to make end-of-life decisions, but how far respect for decision-making autonomy extends and whether it can countenance life limiting decisions is questionable.

Personal autonomy can be seen as being composed of three separate categories; autonomy of thought, of will and of action.[3] Together these encompass the notion that individuals are able to think for themselves, make decisions and act accordingly. The physical integrity of the body is defended from unauthorised invasion, whether hostile or not, because any physical touching of one person by another without the authorisation of the person concerned is proscribed by the criminal and the civil law. Furthermore the prohibition against non-consensual contact exists even if the touching takes the form of life saving

---

[1] I Kennedy, *Treat Me Right: Essays in Medical Law and Ethics* (Oxford, Oxford University Press, 1991) at 320.

[2] See for example, *Schloendorff* v. *Society of New York Hospital* (1914) 105 NE 92, 93, per Cardozo J, *Sidaway* v. *Bethlem Royal Hospital Governors* [1985] 1 All ER 643 at 666. *Re T (Adult: Refusal of Treatment)* [1992] 4 All ER 649, at 652–3, and *Airedale NHS Trust* v. *Bland* [1993] 1 All ER 821, at 860. This right is also endorsed in the Government policy document *"A Guide to Consent for Examination and Treatment"* issued by Dept. of Health and the Welsh Office, and *The Patient's Charter*.

[3] R Gillon, *Philosophical Medical Ethics* (Chichester, Wiley, 1985).

medical treatment.[4] Intellectual self-determination, which is concerned with choices and decisions, is largely protected by the right of the individual to determine, by whatever means, whether or not to consent to medical intervention.[5] The renowned words of J S Mill that "the only purpose for which power can be exercised over any member of a civilised community, against his will, is to prevent harm to others"[6] provide the basis upon which this right is founded. Furthermore, it is a right that even prevents others interfering in decisions to harm oneself since such power should not be exercised for "his own good, either physical or moral, is not sufficient warrant".[7] This being the case individuals should be free to autonomously decide for themselves whether or not they choose to end their own lives, provided that no one else is harmed by the decision.

Choice is frequently associated with the preservation of human dignity in dying, so that to have ones choices respected, and thereby to maintain control, is regarded as inherently more dignified than being subjected to futile and unwelcome medical interventions at the end of life.[8] Autonomy is central to the ability to make valid end of life decisions, and the legal protection of autonomy ensures that individual choices are respected. Hence autonomy should play a pivotal role in end of life decision-making, permitting people the opportunity to decide the timing and circumstances of their own demise if that is what they wish. In practice however, individual autonomy is rarely absolute. The inherent limitations of our own capacity to understand and take action often restricts the exercise of autonomy. Autonomy fluctuates over time and is dependent upon factors like, how much information we have about the environment within which the decision is to be made. Similarly, where decisions are contingent upon knowledge of their potential impact on others. For example, one person might avoid choosing to die to protect loved ones from imminent trauma. Another might select a life-limiting option by acting altruistically to try to prevent family and friends experiencing distress and suffering at witnessing her gradual demise, or wishing to avoid becoming burdensome to those she cares for.[9] No person is an island and decisions are often influenced by considerations relating to our social surroundings and relationships with others.

---

[4] For example, in *Airedale NHS Trust* v. *Bland* [1993] 1 All ER 821, Lord Keith held that, ". . . it is unlawful, so as to constitute both a tort and the crime of battery, to administer medical treatment to an adult, who is conscious and of sound mind, without his consent . . . such a person is completely at liberty to decline to undergo treatment, even if the result of his doing so will be that he will die", at 860.

[5] *Re T (Adult: Refusal of Medical Treatment)* [1992] 4 All ER 649, at 652–3.

[6] J S Mill, *Utilitarianism, On Liberty and Considerations on Representative Government*, (London, Dent, 1972) at 73.

[7] *Ibid.*

[8] See for examples, T E Quill, *Death and Dignity. Making Choices and Taking Charge* (New York, Norton, 1993), C Seale, J Addington-Hall, "Euthanasia: Why People Want to Die Earlier" (1994) 39 *Social Science and Medicine*, 647–54.

[9] These concerns are explored more fully in H Biggs, "I Don't Want to be a Burden! A Feminist Reflects on Women's Experiences of Death and Dying" in S Sheldon and M Thomson (eds.), *Feminist Perspectives on Health Care Law* (London, Cavendish, 1998) at 279.

Janet Adkins, Dr Kevorkian's first "victim", seems to typify this sentiment. Diagnosed as suffering from Alzheimer's Disease she is reported to have planned her death at a time which would be least disruptive to her family, particularly by avoiding spoiling Christmas. She also selected a time that enabled her to organise her own memorial service and is said to have "arranged for a therapist to mediate final 'closure' sessions with her family".[10] Where choosing suicide amounts to one person wanting to sacrifice herself for the good of others because she feels socially pressured, serious misgivings arise about whether that person is making an autonomous decision. Whether the pressure is real or imagined, covert or overt,[11] doubts persist about the quality and efficacy of choices made in these circumstances. They may appear to be autonomous but are clearly defective if influenced by the needs of others.[12]

Temporary or permanent incapacity is also destructive of autonomy,[13] and conflicts are likely to arise concerning medical decisions with dangerous or life threatening consequences, where the patient appears to lack the competence to decide for herself. Kennedy illustrates one approach to the problem of how to enable those with diminished capacity to act autonomously with the example of a child who resists medical treatment fearing pain, discomfort or embarrassment. Somewhat paradoxically he asserts that where such a child lacks the capacity to act autonomously, failing to act on her wishes is actually autonomy enhancing. He defends his position with the logic that if an individual is unable to make decisions in her own best interests then allowing somebody else to do so in order to preserve her long term well-being is a way of affording respect and protecting that person from harm.[14] In many respects what Kennedy proposes here is perhaps an acceptable face of paternalism in the sense of a caring parent attempting to augment the autonomy of one whose decision is invalid for want of full information, and because she lacks sufficient maturity or experience to fully appreciate the gravity of her decision. Perhaps therefore, after reasoning has been tried and failed it may be an acceptable approach to protect the long term interests of young children. It is not an approach that can be readily applied to adult patients. Nevertheless, in the context of death and dying Kay Wheat applies similar reasoning and agrees with Kennedy that, "we can justify intervention in the short term, whilst respecting a long term wish to die as being taken in an autonomous, impartial way".[15] Her view is that time is needed to

---

[10] S Gutmann, "Dr Kevorkian's Woman Problem: Death and the Maiden" 24 June 1996, *New Republic*, 3.

[11] See R M Cole, "Communicating with People who Request Euthanasia" (1993) 7 (2) *Palliative Medicine* 139–43.

[12] John Harris considers the shortcomings of idealised notions of autonomy in decision making in J Harris, *The Value of Life: An Introduction to Medical Ethics,* (London, Routledge, 1985) at 195.

[13] A full discussion of the assessment of capacity and its implications for decision-making is included in ch. 5.

[14] I Kennedy, *Treat Me Right: Essays in Medical Law and Ethics* (Oxford, Oxford University Press, 1991) at 320.

[15] K Wheat, "The Law's Treatment of the Suicidal" [2000] 8 *Medical Law Review* 182–209, at 208.

permit considered and reflective decision-making in case a different conclusion might be reached. But a general acceptance of this attitude would surely be destructive of autonomy, particularly if it entails ignoring the final wishes of dying patients.

Despite well publicised misgivings,[16] many clinicians do regard paternalism of this type as acceptable, or even beneficial. Raanan Gillon comments that

> "sometimes one has as a doctor to be paternalistic to one's patients—that is, to do things against their immediate wishes or without consulting them, indeed perhaps with a measure of deception, to do what is in their best interests".[17]

This model does not dictate riding roughshod over patients' autonomous decisions, but implies that wherever possible every effort should be made to promote understanding and autonomy. Other commentators take a more rigorous stance however, suggesting that "a certain amount of authoritarianism, paternalism and domination are the essence of the physician's effectiveness".[18] Even if adopted in the name of the patients best interests this approach is questionable, especially if the pursuit of a clinical perception of best interests might restrict the effective choices of a patient seeking dignity in dying. Surely a physician's effectiveness should never be secured by failing to respect the patients right to self-determination through deceit and lies?

Respect for patient autonomy dictates that a doctor "has a duty to respect the integrity and individuality of the person before him"[19] and John Harris has persuasively described medical rejection of a competent patients wishes as "the most profound of insults".[20] In line with his reasoning, dicta from *Re T (Adult: Refusal of Medical Treatment)* insist that

> "an adult patient who . . . suffers from no mental incapacity has an absolute right to choose whether to consent to medical treatment, to refuse it or to choose one rather than another of the treatments being offered".[21]

So in theory the autonomous choices of a competent adult ought to be respected in all circumstances, regardless of the substance, perceived morality, or certain outcome of the decision made.

Deliberate subversions of patients' autonomous medical decisions are thankfully becoming less commonplace, but there are still those who are potentially able to act autonomously yet find their autonomy and freedom to choose compromised, either by the level of information they receive, or because they have difficulty understanding and applying that information. Similarly, the circumstances

---

[16] See generally, R E Sartorius, (ed.) *Paternalism* (Minneapolis, University of Minnesota Press, 1983), M M Shultz, "From Informed Consent to Patient Choice: a New Protected Interest" (1985) 95 *Yale Law Journal* 219, M Brazier, *Medicine Patients and the Law* (London, Penguin, 1987) chapters 1–4, and S A M McLean, *A Patient's Right to Know* (Aldershot, Dartmouth, 1989).

[17] R Gillon, *Philosophical Medical Ethics* (Chichester, Wiley, 1985).

[18] F J Ingelfinger, "Arrogance" (1980) 303, *New England Journal of Medicine* 1507–11.

[19] I Kennedy, *The Unmasking of Medicine* (London, Paladin, 1983).

[20] J Harris, *The Value of Life* (London, Routledge, 1985) at 80.

[21] [1992] 4 All ER 649 at 652–3.

within which medical care is administered may effectively undermine the patient's right to self-determination, especially if the patient is contemplating making choices that will be instrumental in her own death.

In any institutional setting individuals may be unusually insecure, and unfamiliar surroundings with unknown personnel and routines will almost inevitably impinge upon a person's ability to act as an autonomous agent. In situations involving medical care, illness, lack of understanding and fear may compound and intensify these insecurities. O'Neill recognised many years ago that when stripped of clothing, familiarity of surroundings and emotional support, patients can find it difficult to express doubts and fears about the efficacy of proposed forms of treatment:

> "One patient can indeed be expected to come to an informed and autonomous (if idiosyncratic) decision; another may be too confused to take in what his options are. A third may be able to understand the issues but be too dependent or too distraught to make decisions".[22]

Clearly some people are more assertive than others. Self-assured people will probably be able to grasp and control the situations where their awareness and consent is required and ensure that their own wishes prevail. Others however do not posses the ability or comprehension to challenge the received wisdom of those who can determine their immediate medical future. Furthermore, because of the complexity of the situation when a patient wants to make a life-limiting decision, the personnel responsible for providing medical care may be poorly equipped to recognise those who give consent, or perhaps refuse to, despite their taciturn scepticism or ignorance. Here again the patient's ability to act as an autonomous agent is compromised.

In the context of clinical decision-making Len Doyal defines respect for autonomy as an indeterminate morality. His model describes respect for autonomy as often imperfect, and the exercise of autonomy as ill-defined and made up of weak and strong elements. All who have the ability to make ordinary everyday decisions in their lives possess weak autonomy, while strong autonomy attaches only to those who are able to scrutinise the information they receive in terms of impact and outcome, and thereby make fully informed choices.[23] Accordingly some patients might never be able to make autonomous medical decisions while others achieve autonomy in some situations but not others. Close inspection of autonomy in medical decision-making reveals therefore, that the ability to effectively exercise individual autonomy and self-determination can be easily invalidated. It is not surprising then that questions about the nature of autonomy are considered fundamental when people seek to have decisions that will lead directly to the end of their lives upheld by the law. Perhaps the most visible end-of-life decisions are taken by people who opt to kill themselves by suicide, and it

---

[22] O O'Niell, "Paternalism and Partial Autonomy" (1984) 10 *Journal of Medical Ethics* 177.

[23] L Doyal, "Medical Ethics and Moral Indeterminacy" (1990) 17 (1) *Journal of Law and Society* 1.

is here that many of the tensions inherent in the debate about autonomy and self-determination at the end of life are poignantly identified.

CHOOSING TO DIE—SUICIDE AND AUTONOMY

The relationship between death with dignity and respect for individual autonomy is always complex and intriguing, and nowhere less so than with respect to suicide and assisted suicide. Suicide can appear to be the ultimate act of self-determination since it implies that a person has deliberately opted to bring about the end of life but reality may not confirm this view.

Suicide, or self-murder, was decriminalised in England in 1961.[24] It remains, however, for a coroners court to return a verdict of suicide having determined that death was intentionally caused by the victim's own hand. The inclusion of *actus reus* and *mens rea* as criteria for determining that a death was caused by suicide satisfies requirements usually associated with criminal law and demonstrates the tensions that still exist between the social perception of suicide and its legal status. Metaphorically, suicide might be described as the vampire in the mirror of murder; it is invisible as a crime since it is not proscribed by law but must be defined by a court of law within the same parameters as murder.

Suicide has existed in all social settings throughout history, but in different cultures and across time it has been differently regarded. Social, legal, and philosophical approaches to suicide across the ages inform modern day perceptions of the phenomenon through theological and philosophical theory, references in literature and more latterly depictions in the media. Biblical references to suicide are apparently devoid of condemnatory remarks[25] and throughout the Roman Empire suicide was considered honourable where it reflected a commitment to high political or moral ideals.[26] Similarly, in medieval society, suicide was sometimes accepted as a noble conclusion in the aftermath of sexual assault or rape. More often though it was considered to be an offence against God and the State, and categorised as criminal.

> "... the law of England wisely and religiously considers, that no man hath a power to destroy life ... and as the suicide is guilty of a double offence; one spiritual, in evading the prerogative of the Almighty ... and the other temporal, against the King ... the law has ranked this among the highest crimes, making it a peculiar species of felony, a felony committed on oneself".[27]

Modern day Judaeo-Christian taboos on suicide reportedly stem from Saint Augustine's description of it as a "mortal sin" in his fourth century work, *City of God*.[28] His pronouncement seems to have been based on anxieties within the

---

[24] Attempted suicide was a criminal offence until the enactment of the Suicide Act 1961.
[25] B Barraclough, "The Bible Suicides" (1990) 86 *Acta Psychiatrica Scandinavia* 64–69.
[26] M G Velasquez, "Defining Suicide" (1987) 37 (3) *Issues in Law and Medicine* 40.
[27] Blackstone, *Commentaries on the Laws of England* (1769) 4 at 189.
[28] C Pritchard, *Suicide—The Ultimate Rejection* (Buckingham, Open University Press, 1995) at 10.

Church at the time about false martyrdom, and led to practices such as the prohibition on burying the bodies of those who had committed suicide in hallowed ground.

Even after these concerns had faded the religious and social sanctions against suicide persisted so that it carried enormous social stigma. In England attempted suicide was considered a felony from the fourteenth century onwards. As a result, anyone who survived a suicide attempt would face the death penalty and have their assets seized by the state.[29] The primary purpose behind the criminalisation and punishment of suicide appears to have been to raise income for the Government, since there can be little point in censuring someone who has tried, and failed, to kill themselves by executing them. The property and possessions of successful suicides would also be forfeited and their bodies would have stakes driven through them before being placed at a cross-roads. Perversely, in France, the body of a suicide might even have been put on trial before being publicly crucified.[30]

Despite the stigma often attached to it, suicide has tended to be romanticised in popular culture. Shakespeare's Romeo and Juliet typifies a rather sentimental portrayal of suicide as an ultimate act of love, and Cleopatra's suicide has also been idealised as a noble and honourable death. Even where a character contemplates suicide in tragic circumstances the contemporary audience frequently admires the courage and logic if not the motivation. The reverence with which the Hamlet soliloquy is regarded exemplifies this response:

> "To be or not to be, that is the question:- Whether 'tis nobler in the mind to suffer the slings and arrows of outrageous fortune; Or take up arms against a sea of troubles, And, by opposing, end them? . . . To die,—to sleep;—To sleep!—Perchance to dream; ay, there's the rub; for in that sleep of death what dreams may come, when we have shuffled off this mortal coil . . ." (Hamlet III. i).

The lines were written at a time when suicide was generally regarded as a mortal sin and stigmatised even more profoundly than today. Yet then, as now, these words evoke the misery of the dilemma and provoke sympathy and perhaps admiration for the person faced with the ultimate awful choice.

Today, suicide represents the highest cause of death in young people in all developed western countries and is more often regarded as a tragic waste of life rather than a noble death. The actual statistical incidence of suicide is hard to determine, since it remains socially stigmatised and is consequently thought to be underreported. Many deaths are recorded as accidental when they may have been the result of misadventure or suicide, because coroners tend only to attribute the most obvious cases to death by suicide. As a result statistics relating to suicide are generally regarded as underestimating the magnitude of the

---

[29] G Williams, *The Sanctity of Life and the Criminal Law* (London, Faber and Faber, 1957) at 274–5.
[30] C Pritchard, *Suicide—The Ultimate Rejection* (Buckingham, Open University Press, 1995) at 10.

incidence, and reputed to represent a minimum figure.[31] Difficulties in recording and reporting may be due in part to the methods selected by those who attempt to kill themselves. Men tend to be impulsive and choose drastic methods, which are more likely to succeed but may be recorded as accidental death, especially if the impulse allowed no time for the traditional suicide note. [32] Women, on the other hand, tend to favour less dramatic methods, like self-poisoning, which are less likely to be misconstrued.[33] World Health Organisation figures point to a suicide rate of one hundred and twenty-one per million head of population in the United Kingdom for the year 1992. That year 4,628 were suicides recorded, and official figures for 1997 attribute 5,993 deaths to suicide,[34] demonstrating a year on year increase. Pritchard explains that this amounts to more than ten times the homicide rate, even taking into account terrorism in Ireland, and that this has enormous resource implications. The figures are similar in other western countries.[35]

Within these statistics most suicides are characterised by mental illness, with the suicide rate amongst people with mental illness being equivalent to more than 80 times that of the general population.[36] Legitimate concerns arise here as to whether the individuals involved have exercised an autonomous choice to take their lives. People diagnosed as suffering from mental illness may not be competent to make free and independent moral decisions, hence respecting their decisions as autonomous is problematic. Decisions taken in these circumstances may therefore be overridden, for example if such a patient is admitted to hospital requiring emergency life saving treatment,[37] despite an apparently deliberate choice having been made. The unmistakable assumption here is that a wish to commit suicide can be distinguished from other decisions affecting health and welfare. Protectionism born of paternalism, as described earlier by Kennedy and Wheat, is the probable justification but conflicts are unavoidable where clinical discretion conflicts with a patient's apparently autonomous decision.

Celia Wells has eloquently described the dilemma experienced by all who are involved in this kind of decision-making process:

> "On the one hand the image of the surgical team bearing down on an unwilling patient with its spectre of naked self-defence in the face of coercion is offensive. On the other,

---

[31] S Ridley, "Sudden Death from Suicide" in D Dickenson et al (eds.), *Death Dying and Bereavement* (London, Sage, 2000) at 54.

[32] S Mayor, "Suicide in Young Men Needs Multiagency Solutions", (2000) 320 *BMJ* 1096.

[33] C Pritchard, *Suicide—The Ultimate Rejection* (Buckingham, Open University Press, 1995) at 55–6.

[34] Office for National Statistics, *DVS3.H Mortality Statistics* (1997) London.

[35] C Pritchard, *Suicide—The Ultimate Rejection* (Buckingham, Open University Press, 1995) at 56.

[36] Department of Health, *The Health of the Nation: A Strategy for England and Wales* (London, HMSO, 1992).

[37] See M Brazier, M Lobjoit, *Protecting the Vulnerable* (New York, Routledge, 1991).

there is the competing thought of the sense of despair that must affect those seeking to help, to do that which is both a natural and in this instance a professional reflex, to preserve the life of another".[38]

Thus, in a clinical emergency where medical attendants confront a patient who has apparently irrationally refused to consent to the available treatment, legal clarification may be sought, especially if the failure to treat has life threatening consequences. Such disputes are particularly likely to arise in relation to emergency treatment that has been refused by a patient, or by a parent on behalf of a minor. The legal resolutions of tensions generated by conflicts between clinical judgement and patient's treatment preferences are frequently illustrative of paternalistic legal attitudes,[39] where the expressed wishes of a patient were overridden by the court in an unfolding clinical emergency. At issue are respect for patient autonomy (the right to give or withhold consent to treatment), the rationality of the decision to refuse consent and treatment and the efficacy of proceeding with treatment in the absence of consent.

In favour of the courts approach, it must be remembered that in medical decision-making generally the choices made by patients sometimes seem less than rational or autonomous. Many patients encounter illness without the knowledge or expertise to understand and address the issues raised by treatments proposed by their doctors. Moreover, clinical practice often precludes any more than the most superficial notification process, and the shortcomings of the rudimentary knowledge of the workings of the human body which many patients exhibit, may be exacerbated by the specialised language used by medical professionals. Understanding disease and therapy requires an awareness of anatomy, physiology and pharmacology, not normally possessed by people without medical qualifications. It is probable therefore that, even in the presence of understandable and detailed explanations from medical professionals, many patients give or refuse consent while unaware of all the potential implications and complications of the therapy or investigation that is proposed. In emergency situations greater confusion and consternation is understandable.

Consent forms designed to guard against unauthorised treatment interventions require that medical professionals should provide patients with the information necessary to anticipate the implications and complications of proposed treatments. Within this framework opportunities are provided for patients to gather complete information prior to giving consent by inviting them to question information they do not understand, or would like explained more fully, as a means of protecting their autonomy. But, in order to avail themselves of this safeguard patients need a level of understanding about their own medical conditions and the procedures and techniques likely to be adopted in treating or

---

[38] C Wells, "Patients, Consent and Criminal Law" (1994) 1 *Journal of Social Welfare and Family Law* 65 at 69.

[39] Examples include, *Re S (Adult: Refusal of Medical Treatment)* [1992] 4 All ER 671, *Re T (Adult: Refusal of Treatment)* [1992] 4 All ER 649, *St George's Healthcare NHS Trust v. S* [1998] 3 All ER 673.

diagnosing them, which is beyond many people's experience. It is simply not possible to know whether you have received sufficient information to make an informed decision if you are ignorant of the details involved and are reliant on somebody else furnishing good advice. Thus, in doctor's surgeries and hospital wards anecdotal comments like, ". . . I don't understand what is happening so I just let them get on with it", are perhaps not surprising. Consequently, an apparently autonomous consent or refusal could later prove to be invalid because the patient failed to fully comprehend the information upon which it was based. Urgent decision-making will undoubtedly compound the difficulties.

Against this, some patients are well aware of their own limitations in processing and responding to medical information and might prefer to deliberately distance themselves from the decision-making process. Even when fully fit some patients may be afraid or reluctant to discover the full ramifications of their condition and its management, or may just prefer to remain ignorant. On finding themselves in hospital and redefined as patients, others can experience profound insecurity when they are weakened by illness and in an alien environment. As a result, many patients choose to "positively and deliberately delegate doctors to manage their case".[40] They distance themselves from clinical decision-making and defer unconditionally to the judgements of health care professionals, purposefully placing themselves in the hands of their doctors because that is where they feel most comfortable. It is debatable whether or not autonomy is upheld in these circumstances but, a consent is likely to be entirely legally valid in these circumstances, given that:

> "when questioned specifically by a patient of apparently sound mind about risks involved in a particular treatment proposed, the doctor's duty must . . . be to answer both truthfully and as fully as the questioner requires".[41]

While, ideally, full information should always be provided, especially in very grave situations concerning end-of-life decisions, patients who are resistant to receiving that information may exercise their autonomy by choosing to defer to medical expertise. Even in this context, it can however be "wrong to conceive of respect for autonomy as being just a matter of honouring an individual's right to choose without coercion".[42]

Just as it can be difficult to understand how deliberately depriving oneself of information upon which to base decisions can be autonomy enhancing, the notion of a person exercising self-determination by deciding to end her own life could be regarded as bizarre and irrational. Yet to some, suicide may appear to be a rational choice in response to an intolerable situation. Closer scrutiny might reveal that the level of autonomy in the decision-making process is sometimes questionable, and with it the oft unchallenged relationship between autonomy and choice.

[40] R Gillon, *Philosophical Medical Ethics* (Chichester, Wiley, 1985).
[41] *Sidaway* v. *Board of Governors of the Bethlem Royal Hospital and the Maudsley Hospital* [1985] 1 All ER 643, per Lord Bridge at 662.
[42] L Doyal, "Medical Ethics and Moral Indeterminacy" (1990) 17 (1) *Journal of Law and Society* 1.

People who contemplate suicide frequently do so because they believe they have no choice. To them the options are so limited that the decision is really out of their hands,[43] so that they feel they have no alternative but to follow their instincts and end their lives. Furthermore, once the decision has been made and steps have been taken towards suicide, it seems that this dearth of alternatives is simply magnified. Accordingly, one suicide survivor reported that, "it was as if I'd already gone over, somehow—the problem was not how to die but would have been how to stay alive".[44] If a person is constrained, perhaps by lack of information or understanding, and feels compelled to act, autonomy plays a very limited role in the suicide decision. Suicide in these circumstances may be considered misguided, on the basis that it probably does not represent a rational choice. Medical intervention can be easily legitimated where a person's motivation is this uncertain. The law is clear though: even choices that will result in death need not be rational in order to be valid.[45] It is mental capacity that governs the validity of decisions. Strong arguments can be made for autonomy to be respected where it is certain that a competent person is acting intentionally.

Where it is not possible for a person to terminate their own life without assistance however, clear legal prohibitions exist. Active euthanasia, involving deliberate steps being taken by one person to bring about the death of another, amounts to murder, and assisting suicide is prohibited by statute.[46] Advocates of legal reform to permit euthanasia and assisted death contend that people should be empowered to maintain independence and control of their lives up to and including the moment of death, and that within this the ability to decide the time, place and manner of dying is fundamental. Conversely, it is arguable that neither euthanasia nor assisted suicide should be construed as true expressions of absolute individual autonomy however, since both require the active participation of other people. Where they do occur, interesting tensions exist between the autonomy of the recipient of euthanasia and that of the actor, which may ultimately be destructive of the dignity of each.[47]

Medically assisted suicide is not usually sought because of despair due to "community or circumstance, which shatters [one's] hold on the value of life"[48] and questions one's competence. It is generally contemplated because life and medicine have nothing left to offer except a prolongation of the dying process, where dependence and loss of control will inevitably follow. Hence, where a patient declines further treatment because of its perceived futility, concerns about compulsion and rationality should be avoided. Those who bring about

---

[43] A Alverez *The Savage God* (London, Weidenfield and Nicholson, 1971).

[44] Recounted in S Ridley, "Sudden Death from suicide" in D Dickenson et al (eds.), *Death Dying and Bereavement* (London, Sage, 2000) at 54.

[45] *Re T (Adult: Refusal of Treatment)* [1992] 4 All ER 649.

[46] s.2 (1) Suicide Act 1961 imposes a maximum penalty of 14 years imprisonment for those who aid, abet, council or procure the suicide of another.

[47] This point is discussed in greater detail in ch. 6.

[48] C Pritchard, *Suicide—The Ultimate Rejection* (Buckingham, Open University Press, 1995) at 2.

their own demise in these circumstances do so in order to preserve their auto-nomy and dignity until the end of their lives. These are the actions of people who can apply the independence of thought, will and action described by Gillon as fundamental to autonomy and human dignity. In seeking release from a life they perceive as intolerable and choosing to bring about their own death they are shaping their own destiny.

The law permits people to follow this course of action, provided they possess mental capacity. Interestingly decisions of this nature are not characterised as sui-cide,[49] neither are those of hunger-striking prisoners, as the courts and clinicians prefer to regard them as refusals of treatment and nutrition.[50] Distinguishing these actions as other than suicidal is problematic however, especially in the case of prisoners who apparently intend that their decisions should be upheld even if death is the inevitable consequence. They refuse food and hydration for a variety of reasons, often involving political pressure and a desire to manipulate prison authorities, motivations which are not readily applied to cases involving patients who seek to terminate their lives. The desire to terminate a life deemed as intolerable by declining further medical treatment is an entirely different matter.

Brian Clark's play *Whose Life is it Anyway?*[51] epitomises the plight of many who feel condemned to a life of dependence and indignity by the intervention of modern medical technology. The play's main character, Ken Harrison, was paralysed in a road accident and is fighting a legal battle to have his decision to be discharged from hospital upheld. Leaving hospital will inevitably result in his death because he is physically incapacitated and needs assistance with food and fluids and to keep his lungs functioning. Harrison bases his claim on arguments about autonomous choice and human dignity, pleading dramatically:

> "I know that our hospitals are wonderful. I know that many people have succeeded in making good lives with appalling handicaps. I'm happy for them and respect and admire them. But each man must make his own decision. And mine is to die quietly and with as much dignity as I can muster".[52]

Ken Harrison's plight is profoundly disturbing and raises real dilemmas con-cerning the ability of any person to act as a truly autonomous agent within con-temporary society. It recognises the significance of social interaction and the fact that people's choices and hence their autonomy are necessarily constrained by the needs, preferences and reactions of others.[53] The play also makes important comments about the nature of suicide, especially calculated suicide, within the context of terminal or incurable illness.

---

[49] See for example, *Airdale NHS Trust v. Bland* [1993] 1 All ER 821, per Lord Goff at 866.

[50] *Secretary of State for the Home Department v. Robb* [1995] 1 All ER 677, and *R v. Ashworth Hospital Authority ex patre Brady* [2000] Lloyd's Re Med 355, [2000] Med LR 251, provide exam-ples.

[51] B Clark, *Whose Life is it Anyway?* (New York, Dodd Mead, 1979).

[52] *Ibid*, at 76–7.

[53] See S Jinnet-Sack, "Autonomy in the Company of Others" in A Grubb (ed.) *Choices and Decisions in Health Care* (Chichester, Wiley, 1993).

"Perhaps we ought to make suicide respectable again. Whenever anyone kills himself there's a whole legal rigmarole to go through . . . and it all seems designed to find something to blame. Can you ever recall a coroner saying something like: 'We've heard all the evidence of how John Smith was facing literally insuperable odds and how he made a courageous decision. I record a verdict of noble death?' "[54]

While Ken Harrison and his plight are fictional, a series of legal cases demonstrate that his quest to autonomously determine the timing and circumstances of his death are grounded in medical and social reality. There really are people who are able to make autonomous decisions and would fervently desire to take their own lives but are physically prevented from so doing by the nature of their disease. Others desire a clinical and certain suicide, so that they are assured that there will be no mistakes and no return from the brink of death, but they cannot achieve their goal without assistance. Carole Smith has discussed the ways in which physical disability is often destructive of autonomy.[55] By contrasting the range of legal mechanisms formulated to protect the autonomy of those with mental disability, with the poorly addressed issue of the impact of physical disability on people's autonomy, she argues that a positive notion of autonomy is required to enable people to act autonomously.

SUICIDAL INTENTIONS

Positively endorsing autonomy in this way might have a significant impact on the law as it relates to assisted suicide. For example, Smith's argument is highly relevant to the 1993 case of Canadian born Sue Rodriguez,[56] whose potential physical disability would ultimately prevent her from taking her own life. In essence Rodriguez argued that her autonomy and dignity were compromised, not only by the Canadian Criminal Code, which prohibited assisted suicide, but also by the physically disabling nature of her disease, which would prevent her from independently taking her own life. She was competent to make an autonomous choice that she wished to take her own life when she decided that the time was right. But, in much the same way that the fictional Ken Harrison could not accomplish his objective independently, she would by then be unable to act upon it. Sue Rodriguez failed in the Supreme Court, where it was held that the Criminal Code was not discriminatory, and that such fundamental decisions should only be taken by the legislature.

---

[54] B Clark, *Whose Life is it Anyway?* (New York, Dodd Mead, 1979) at 102.

[55] C Smith, "Disabling Autonomy: The Role of Government, the Law, and the Family" (1997) 24 (3) *Journal of Law and Society* 421–39.

[56] *Rodriquez* v. *A-G British Columbia* (1993) 107 DLR (4th) 342, [1993] 7 WWR 641. A detailed analysis of the case is given in ch. 6 which emphasises Rodriguez' contention that barring her from receiving assisted suicide was destructive of her dignity.

In England, Annie Lindsell, brought a similar case before the courts in October 1997.[57] She too suffered from motor neurone disease and sought a legal right to die by assisted suicide. It was her belief that she would want the opportunity to end her own life when she reached the terminal stages of her disease, but that the nature of the disease would prevent her from acting. She therefore wished her autonomy to be respected and her decision to be acted upon by somebody else, preferably by her doctor. The case received a great deal of media attention but was eventually dropped after Annie Lindsell received assurances that she could legally be given any medication required to keep her comfortable in the terminal stages of her disease, even if that meant her life would incidentally be shortened. She died in December 1997.

Legislative intervention of the type mentioned in the Rodiguez case would be welcomed by advocates of permissive reform favouring death with dignity in many jurisdictions, but to date only those in Oregon and Holland have demonstrated an enduring commitment to this end. Australia's Rights of the Terminally Ill Act 1996, permitted medically assisted suicide in the Northern Territory, but was overruled by the federal Parliament, after being successfully employed by only four patients. Generally, assisted suicide remains prohibited either by criminal law specifically, as demonstrated in the English and Canadian cases, or constitutionally, as in the cases of *State of Washington et al v. Glucksberg et al* and *Vacco et al v. Quill et al*,[58] which were discussed in chapter one.

Both common law and constitutional law are open to judicial interpretation and the reluctance of the judiciary to intervene permissively in this area is readily observed. For example, New York State's ban on assisted suicide was challenged on the basis that it violated the Fourteenth Amendment's Equal Protection Clause, but was upheld based on the argument that anybody is permitted to refuse treatment while nobody is entitled to assist suicide. Therefore everybody is treated equally by the prohibition of assisted suicide. When comparisons are drawn with other rights, either constitutional or common law, judicial interpretations of this nature can appear to result in an inconsistent application of legal principles.

In America, the right to abortion is regarded as eligible for constitutional protection because it, "falls within the constitutionally protected sphere of liberty requiring medical assistance".[59] The 1967 Abortion Act in Britain permits the termination of pregnancy in a range of specified circumstances that can be roughly equated to the protection of the health and well being of the pregnant woman and thereby protect her life and liberty. Neither physician assisted

---

[57] The case is unreported, but see E Wilkins, "Dying Woman Granted Wish for Dignified End" (1997) *The Times*, 29 October, 3.

[58] *Washington* v. *Glucksberg*, Supreme Court 2258 (1997), *Vacco* v. *Quill*, Supreme Court 2293 (1997).

[59] B Geobel, "Who Decides if There is 'Triumph in the Ultimate Agony?' Constitutional Theory and the Emerging Right to Die with Dignity" (1995) 37 (2) *William and Mary Law Review* 827, at 879.

suicide, nor the termination of pregnancy can be achieved without the help of medical professionals, and a perceived right to assisted suicide can be made out on the understanding that unnecessary suffering may be avoided and self-determination could be protected.

If, as has been claimed, the right to abortion represents a unique thread of individual liberty and is justified by concerns for the woman's suffering,[60] how can it be distinguished from claims for a right to assisted suicide founded on the need to relieve individual suffering? What more unique expression of liberty and self-determination could there be than the considered wish to die in order to escape terminal suffering? One way to explain this apparent inequity might be to consider the interests that are being protected.

Like the illusive right to die with dignity, the right to a pre-viability abortion is often viewed as a right to terminate life, albeit a potential life rather than a life in being. Here the interests of the living woman are protected by the law and her liberty to make an autonomous decision to abort her pregnancy takes priority over the unprotected "rights" of the unborn child.[61] The entity that "dies"[62] has no legal rights and therefore no interests that the State can protect. The individual who dies as a result of assisted suicide possesses a right to life, which the State considers worthy of a degree of protection. Although in recent years suicide has been recognised more as, either an expression of self-determination and individual autonomy, or the result of mental illness, the criminal prohibition of assisted suicide is regarded as necessary to guard against the potential for subversion of the right to self-determination. Suicide itself does not ordinarily attract the attention of the criminal justice system because of the absence of culpable *mens rea*, but even if the potential victim seeks death, it is considered necessary to guard against the potential for unlawful killing that allowing assisted suicide might open up. Therefore, when a person wants to kill herself and cannot do so without help, her adjutant is regarded as a criminal accomplice and can be sentenced to a maximum penalty of fourteen years imprisonment.[63] Classifying assisted suicide as a criminal act akin to unlawful killing is anomalous because it amounts to aiding and abetting the commission of an action that is not in itself a crime, while aiding and abetting, counselling and procuring are more usually regarded as the actions of an accomplice who participates, to a greater or lesser degree, in the commission of a crime.

Of course there is a role for the criminal law in preventing people becoming victims of malevolent intentions, for example where "vulnerable people who do not desire death, despite their suffering, might be killed by others for reasons of

[60] *Planned Parenthood v. Casey*, 112 S Ct 2791 (1992) at 2810–11.

[61] The term "unprotected rights" is used here to express the lack of legal protection for the moral rights of the unborn child which are recognised by some.

[62] The word "dies" is used figuratively here to denote a comparison between the two concepts, abortion and euthanasia. Legally of course an aborted foetus does not "die" in the literal sense of the word, because it has never been born alive and hence has not lived.

[63] Suicide Act 1961, s.2.

their own".[64] Such actions are of course harmful and should be prevented. But where is the harm when assistance is provided at the voluntary request of a person wishing to exercise an autonomous choice to die? Perhaps perversely, while it may be difficult to identify harm to the person who dies, the present law might indirectly offer a protection not generally envisaged.

People who are asked to assist in the suicide or euthanasia of a patient or loved one, might feel compelled to comply out of loyalty or compassion, regardless of their own misgivings. Just as a patient might find her autonomy constrained by concerns about the impact of her actions upon others, so those who care for her, either professionally or emotionally, may find their autonomy compromised by being asked to participate in, or condone, conduct that will result in loss of life. Furthermore, any ensuing criminal investigation might give rise to criminal culpability, the outcome of which may vary depending on the status of the assistant. Andrew Ashworth has examined this area and theorises that there may be some inequity in the legal response to those who assist suicide. He suggests that, despite the legal prohibition, doctors who participate in assisted suicide are more likely to receive a sympathetic response than friends and relatives, who "must run the gauntlet of a legal process which affords no formal recognition to the circumstances under which they killed".[65] The consequences of the legal prohibition on assisted suicide for clinicians may in fact be rather less obvious. Clinicians are used to exercising discretion in the conduct of their everyday practice, but where end of life decisions are concerned, the ways in which judgements are made and decisions implemented may be influenced by patients' attitudes and the law.

AUTONOMOUS CLINICAL DISCRETION

It is to be expected that doctors introduce their own value judgements into treatment decisions so that clinical or technical decisions can become inherently moral in nature.[66] Frequently, therapeutic decision-making cannot be accomplished without considering the wider social and moral environment within which the decision is taken. Often such bias is introduced unwittingly and with the kindest of intentions, and the implications for the exercise of patient autonomy can be profound. Decisions to terminate a pregnancy, or not; to provide contraception to an underage girl, or not; to confine a person suffering from mental illness involuntarily, or not, are just a few examples of clinical situations which cannot be considered in isolation from their social consequences. The ramifications of treatment decisions like these dictate that they cannot, and perhaps should not, be determined in a vacuum. But neither should they be unduly influenced by the experience and morality of the clinician responsible for patient

---

[64] A Ashworth, *Principles of Criminal Law* (Oxford, Oxford University Press, 1995) at 286.
[65] *Ibid.*
[66] I Kennedy, *The Unmasking of Medicine* (London, Paladin, 1983) especially ch. 4.

care at the expense of the need of the patient concerned to make an autonomous decision. Yet if a deliberate decision to terminate life were under consideration, how could a clinician trained to preserve life advise a patient dispassionately? The patient's need to make an autonomous decision and the clinicians' professional judgement would almost certainly conflict.

Medical staff generally possess well-intentioned desires to provide the best possible treatment regime and achieve the best possible outcome for their patients. As a result, there are bound to be occasions when doctors feel "justified in going to great lengths to persuade a patient",[67] especially if the patient is apparently too overwrought, afraid, and confused, to be competent to make an autonomous choice. Determining what is best is always a subjective judgement and patients are entitled to reach their own decisions, even if the choices they make do not seem rational to medical staff or the disinterested onlooker.[68] But the biggest impact of any treatment decision is on the life of the patient receiving the treatment, so it should be for that individual to decide on the basis of her own ethics, not those of her doctor, though the professional experience and expertise of the doctor will provide valuable information upon which to base a decision. Where tensions exist between the patient's wishes and what clinical judgement declares to be the best treatment option, the law of consent is designed to provide the patient with a safeguard against medical paternalism. It bears repeating that a competent patient has an absolute right to consent to or refuse medical treatment, even if a refusal will lead to death, and where the patient lacks the capacity to select an option the application of best interests criteria is crucial to the decision-making process. It is in the evaluation of capacity and the exercise of clinical discretion that the value judgements of medical practitioners may conflict with those of the patient.

Clinical judgement is based upon the assessment and understanding of available medical data and the exercise of each physician's expertise and experience.[69] Doctors are in a unique position to evaluate the available information and to make judgements about prognosis and potential therapies. They also have responsibility for providing the patient with the information she requires before she can give valid consent to any proposed treatment. The determination of what information is relevant in order to make a rational decision about treatment in any given clinical situation is therefore the prerogative of the medical personnel concerned. Hence, the patient's decisions about whether and which treatment options to accept are inevitably governed by the amount of information provided and the way it is presented. Whether or not any clinician is able

---

[67] P D G Skegg, *Law, Ethics, and Medicine* (Oxford, Clarendon Press, 1988) at 98.

[68] See *Re T (Adult: Refusal of Treatment)* [1992] 4 All ER 649, where Lord Donaldson explained that patients choices are not limited to those which others may regard as sensible or rational, at 652–3.

[69] The practical problems associated with paternalism, beneficence and autonomy are discussed at length by T Beauchamp and J Childress, *Principles of Medical Ethics* 4th edn. (Oxford, Oxford University Press, 1989) at 271–290.

to offer independent neutral information knowing that the patient is choosing to live or die is questionable.

DECIDING TO LIVE OR DIE—WHOSE DECISION?

"[P]erfect autonomy, decisions taken without any defect at all either of information or reasoning or of control, is, like any ideal, unattainable. But the fact that autonomy, like many important and desirable things, is a matter of degree does not make it any the less worth striving for, nor does it make it any the less important to have as much of it as possible".[70]

John Harris's words succinctly identify the value of autonomy and the associated concerns that have been the focus of this chapter.

The right of every individual to make autonomous choices about the medical care they receive, especially when life is ending, has been repeatedly endorsed as an absolute right, but the examples shown here demonstrate that it is often a highly contingent right. As a counter measure patients presented with treatment choices at the end of life must be provided with sufficient information upon which to base their decisions so that they are able to act autonomously, according to their own will and ensure that their selections are meaningful.

"To make an optimally informed choice, patients require active help . . . when, for whatever reason, they are confused or think they know more than they do, the duty not to coerce in the long term tells doctors little about how to help them to be more critically autonomous in the short term".[71]

Clearly the ability to enhance patient autonomy requires more than simply the provision of information in a way that says, here are the options, now make your choice.[72] "There is no such thing as informed consent unless there is equal knowledge",[73] choices must be presented and autonomy encouraged without sacrificing the decision-maker to her autonomy.

Many have rightly argued that "the law relating to consent pays little more than lip service to patient autonomy"[74] so autonomy presently extends only as far as legal and medical paternalism allows it to. Given the complexities of the medical decision-making environment this appears unavoidable, although, in the context of consent to treatment, some western jurisdictions are committed to upholding autonomy and extending patient choice.[75] Two reasons explain

---

[70] J Harris, *The Value of Life* (London, Routledge, 1985) at 200.

[71] L Doyal, "Medical Ethics and Moral Indeterminacy" (1990) 17 (1) *Journal of Law and Society* 1, at 12.

[72] F J Inglefinger, "Arrogance", (1980) 303 *New England Journal of Medicine*, 1507–11.

[73] The words of Professor Max Hamilton cited in, C Pritchard, *Suicide—The Ultimate Rejection* (Buckingham, Open University Press, 1995) at 166.

[74] M Brazier, *Medicine, Patients and the Law* (London, Penguin, 1992) at 92.

[75] K Tickner, "*Rogers v. Whitaker*—Giving Patients a Meaningful Choice" (1995) 15 (1) *Oxford Journal of Legal Studies* 110 at 118, suggests that this is the case in Australia, Canada, New Zealand and more than half of the jurisdictions of North America.

why stressing patient autonomy alone fails to provide a solution. Firstly, patient autonomy will always be contingent upon clinical and judicial discretion and interpretation, at least for some. And secondly, were legislative support for assisted dying to be introduced in order to enhance patient autonomy, it would certainly be to the detriment of significant numbers of clinicians who would regard it as a challenge to their professional and moral integrity. The central tenet of medical ethics is first do no harm, but providing a patient with the means to kill herself clearly contravenes this ethic. Anecdotal evidence suggests that many of the Dutch doctors who have assisted with suicide do so only once because of the trauma involved, and it has been postulated that doctors sometimes feel like "a victim of the social and cultural circumstances in which the medical treatment of the patient takes place".[76] Hence, if assisted suicide were to be permitted as a means of enforcing patient autonomy doctors would need to be enabled to exercise their own autonomous choice not to participate if they so desired, particularly where participation is regarded as undignified.

The task of protecting the autonomy of all parties is not an easy one. It is evident that:

> "attempts to provide uniform guidelines for treating patients as persons, respecting their autonomy and avoiding unacceptable medical paternalism are bound to be insensitive to the radical differences of capacity of different patients".[77]

Combine this with the inevitable emotional and clinical tensions that will arise when a patient embarks on a course that will result in death and, in an imperfect world, autonomy may be aspired to but never achieved.

Multiple reforms are required if autonomy at the end of life is to be effectively promoted, but this may need to be achieved incrementally. Clinical and judicial respect for autonomous decisions must be strengthened, initially by permissive reform allowing for greater recognition and promotion of living wills. Were assisted death to become legally permissible, the formulation of adequate safeguards to ensure that it was performed only after careful consideration and at the repeated voluntary request of the recipient would protect against abuse. But, while assisted suicide continues to be outlawed, many people's measured, autonomous decisions to kill themselves will be nullified by the absence of the physical autonomy to act for themselves. It is not enough however for law and medicine to simply insist that we'll save you, or prevent you from acting now so that you can go away and reflect. Like countless women who seek abortions only to have their decisions questioned once they enter the medical arena, most of those who contemplate euthanasia or assisted suicide will already have reflected and considered their options before settling on their final choice. Their autonomy will be seriously compromised by doubt and delay, as will their

[76] W Grey, "Right to die or duty to Live? The Problem of Euthanasia" in D Dickenson et al (eds.), *Death, Dying and Bereavement* 2nd edn. (London, Sage, 2000) 270–283 at 280.
[77] O O'Niell, "Paternalism and Partial Autonomy" (1984) 10 *Journal of Medical Ethics* 177.

dignity. Perhaps an immediate way forward is to promote greater recognition of and respect for living wills, so that people's considered choices could be upheld without being distracted by the imminence of death. Dignity in dying through the exercise of autonomous choice might then be a real possibility.

5

Living Wills and the Will to Die

INTRODUCTION

The concept of the living will or advance directive, originated in America[1] and is now gaining currency in most Western countries as a device that can enable people to retain control of their lives until they die. Where a person anticipates that she will become incapable of any form of medical decision-making, a living will can provide an opportunity to make known her aspirations regarding the type and extent of medical treatment she finds acceptable. Through a living will, decisions about future treatment can be taken in consultation with medical professionals before the treatment is required and while the person concerned still has the mental capacity to decide for herself. Family and friends can be included in the decision-making process so that the patient's wishes are clearly understood, and decisions can be anticipated by all concerned. Thus, even if the hypothetical patient depicted earlier remains unconscious and unable to communicate, her concerns and opinions can be made known to her clinicians and acted upon.

Usually a living will is thought of as a statement indicating a person's preferred treatment options at the end of life, but the term "living will"[2] is also "sometimes used for advance directives which are concerned with other situations or which can be used to express a willingness to receive particular treatments".[3] Some stipulate that specific treatments are acceptable while others are not,[4] while others insist that all available appropriate medical resources should be utilised to maintain life.[5] Living wills are not therefore exclusively associated with end-of-life decisions, although generally the purpose of a living will is to promote individual autonomy and choice for the patient; characteristics which have long been associated with euthanasia as a means of achieving death with dignity.

---

[1] Living wills have been recognised by statute in America since the introduction of the Natural Death Act in California in 1976, and in South Australia since the Natural Death Act 1983. In the USA the Patient Self-Determination Act 1990 now requires that all federally funded hospitals in America advise their patients of their right to make a living will.

[2] Note that living wills are also variously described and defined as advance directives, advance declarations and anticipatory decisions about medical treatment.

[3] The Law Commission Consultation Paper No 129, *Mentally Incapacitated Adults and Decision Making: Medical Treatment and Research* (London, HMSO, 1993) at 29, n18.

[4] For example, *The Watch Tower: Bible and Tract Society of Pennsylvania* issues a directive for use by its members that states that the transfusion of blood and blood products is refused in all circumstances, but the administration of non-blood volume expanders such as saline and Ringer's solution is acceptable.

Some people make living wills because they would prefer a quick dignified end to protracted dying and therefore wish not to be kept alive once any hope of cure or improved quality of life is lost. Some simply want to spare their loved ones the potential trauma of having to make life-limiting medical decisions on their behalf, or having to sanction such decisions made by clinicians. Similarly, a person may prepare a living will in order to avoid adding to the distress of loved ones who might otherwise have to care for her during a lengthy period of physical deterioration.[6] Alternatively she may object to the prolongation of futile treatment, perhaps because of a sense that the resources needed to delay her inevitable death could be better used for people with more optimistic prognoses. Regardless of the motivation for formulating a living will those who do so expect that their decisions will be respected in the appropriate circumstances. Whether this is a legitimate expectation is the subject of this chapter.

Preceding chapters described how every competent adult has a legal right to give or withhold consent to treatment. Founded upon respect for individual autonomy this is a right that operates through the law of consent to protect patients from unfettered medical paternalism.[7] Common law holds that patients with the capacity to give consent are also competent to refuse or withhold consent, "even if a refusal may risk personal injury to health or even lead to premature death".[8] Furthermore, a "refusal of treatment can take the form of a declaration of intent never to consent to that treatment in the future, or never to consent in some future circumstances".[9] Accordingly, any consent or refusal of consent made by a competent adult patient can also be valid in respect of the same treatment at any time in the future. However, in so far as these protections exist, they are available only to those who have the capacity to express their desires by giving, or withholding, their consent.[10]

Ordinarily the mental capacity necessary for full participation in an interactive decision-making process develops with maturity, but mental handicap, mental illness, or trauma may prevent its acquisition. A person who gains capacity on achieving the age of majority may subsequently lose it through, trauma,

---

[5] See the Terrence Higgins Trust and King's College London, Living Will (2nd edn.) in M Molloy, V Mepham, *Let Me Decide* (London, Penguin, 1993).

[6] R Pearlman, K Cain, D Patrick, M Appelbaum-Maizel, H Starks, N Jecker, R Uhlmann, "Insights Pertaining to Patient Assessments of States Worse than Death", in L Emanuel (ed.) *Advance Directives: Expectations, Experience and Future Practice* (1993) 4 (1) *Journal of Clinical Ethics* 33.

[7] But see, Sally Sheldon, "Subject Only to the Attitude of the Surgeon Concerned: The Judicial Protection of Medical Discretion" (1996) 5 (1) *Social and Legal Studies* 95, which suggests that in many clinical situations, perhaps most notably those concerning women's reproductive rights, medical paternalism appears to remain unfettered and is frequently upheld by the courts.

[8] *Re T (Adult: Refusal of Treatment)* [1992] 4 All ER 649, per Lord Donaldson at 653.

[9] Law Commission Report 231, Mental Incapacity, *Item 9 of the Fourth Programme of Law Reform: Mentally Incapacitated Adults* (London, HMSO, 1995) para 5.2, at 65–66. *Re C (Adult: Refusal of Treatment)* [1994] 1 WLR 290.

[10] Chs. 3 and 4 provide background and insights into the legal status of the right to give and withhold consent. See also J Montgomery, "Power Over Death: The Final Sting" in R Lee, D Morgan (eds.) *Death Rites: Law and Ethics at the End of Life* (London, Routledge, 1996) 37–53, at 37.

degenerative disease, or mental illness resulting in temporary or permanent incapacity. Here a person who was once competent to make decisions will no longer have the capacity so to do. In these circumstances a properly executed living will can serve to express the views of the person concerned despite her inability to communicate them herself. Hence, capacity is crucial to assessing the validity of a persons consent or refusal to consent both at the time the decision is made and when the treatment becomes necessary.

The special mechanisms designed to legitimate the provision of medical treatment in the absence of consent from the patient were described in chapter three, and, in summary, these allow treatment to be administered if it is medically necessary and in the patient's best interests.[11] Consequently incapacitated patients are not ordinarily afforded the luxury of participation in the decision-making process. So, even though no person has authority to consent on behalf of another, these patients effectively become the object of decisions made about them by others, rather than interested contributors. In these circumstances living wills become relevant because they can help those who once were competent to maintain some control over treatment decisions.

Living wills can take a variety of different forms. They may encompass generalised expressions of the patient's desires, or include anticipatory decisions about specific prospective therapies but their authority does not extend to requests or demands for treatments that are not clinically indicated.[12]

> "[W]here a doctor has formed a reasonable and responsible clinical judgement that treatment is not called for, the law will not second-guess him by ordering him to provide the treatment".[13]

So a reasonable medical judgement that a certain treatment regime is inappropriate, cannot be overridden by interjection from the patient or anyone else, even if it is stipulated in a living will. Nonetheless patients and their representatives may form the impression that any requests for treatment made within a formally executed living will must be complied with. Doctors, on the other hand, have expressed concerns that they may be required to perform treatments specified in a patient's advance directive which are contrary to their clinical judgement, or even against the law.[14] Both viewpoints are clearly misinformed and have been described by the Law Commission as "another example of excessive influence being attributed to the fact that 'advance directives' are often written down and signed".[15]

---

[11] *Re F (Mental Patient : Sterilisation)* [1990] 2 AC 1, [1989] 2 All ER 545 (HL).

[12] See *Re J (A Minor) (Wardship: Medical Treatment)* [1992] 4 All ER 614 (CA), where the court refused to insist that a doctor should treat a child in a way that was contrary to clinical judgement. See also, *R v. Secretary of State for Social Services ex p Hincks* [1992] 1 BMLR 93.

[13] I Kennedy, A Grubb, *Medical Law: Text with Materials* 2nd edn. (London, Butterworths, 1994) at 1278.

[14] The Law Commission Consultation Paper No 129, *Mentally Incapacitated Adults and Decision Making: Medical Treatment and Research* (London, HMSO, 1993) para 3.12.

[15] Law Commission Report 231, Mental Incapacity, *Item 9 of the Fourth Programme of Law Reform: Mentally Incapacitated Adults* (London, HMSO, 1995) para 5.6, at 66–67.

Regardless of misconceptions like these a living will whose provisions will lead to the death of a patient who is terminally ill, or incurable and inevitably dying, is likely to generate relatively few ethical and medical dilemmas. However, sometimes patients use advance directives to refuse treatments, not because of a wish to die, but because their beliefs about the therapy and its religious, philosophical or practical consequences make that treatment undesirable to them, even if refusal means death. Examples include advance refusals of blood transfusion or particular types of surgical intervention necessary to preserve life, where the treatment could, if given, restore health and prolong life. Here tension is created between respect for the individual's autonomy and the medical imperative to do no harm and restore health wherever possible. As a consequence the law concerning the applicability and validity of living wills is largely informed by cases defining the scope of advance directives and anticipatory decisions that do not directly refer to terminal care, and these will provide a focus for much of this discussion.

Living wills are often promoted as a mechanism through which autonomy can be safeguarded in order to provide dignity in dying. Whether or not such claims are legitimate depends largely on the forms living wills take, how widely they are recognised and used and the legal response to them. In individual cases it may also depend on whether they have been drafted clearly enough to uphold the patient's particular wishes hence their practical significance and legal standing will be examined through a discussion of when they become operative and the factors that determine their scope and validity. Finally the responsibilities of health care professionals to patients who have composed living wills will be considered so that some conclusions may be drawn about their effectiveness in protecting autonomy and choice, and providing death with dignity.

I KNOW MY WILL

The form and content of living wills varies enormously depending on the intentions of the person designing them and their desired outcome. Distinctions can be drawn between those decisions that favour particular types of treatment, and others, which effectively withhold consent in opposition to specific therapies. The Terrence Higgins Trust has formulated an interesting example of a living will that incorporates both elements. Included are the statements,

> "I wish to be kept alive for as long as reasonably possible using whatever forms of medical treatment are available."

> and "If I become permanently unconscious with no likelihood of regaining consciousness, I wish medical treatment to be limited to keeping me comfortable and free from pain, and I *REFUSE* all other medical treatments".[16]

---

[16] The Terrence Higgins Trust and King's College London, Living Will (2nd edn.) in M Molloy, V Mepham, *Let Me Decide* (London, Penguin, 1993).

Clearly this advance directive is designed to meet the needs of a particular group of users, specifically those suffering from the terminal stages of AIDS, who seek to prolong life for as long as there is hope but not once treatment becomes futile. Being constituted as a formal document evidenced in writing, it is not typical of all advance directives, since many take the form of informal oral statements outlining the intentions of the person concerned. As such they may represent anticipatory decisions about specific forms of treatment, or perhaps constitute an expression of personal preferences and opinions regarding future therapy.

The variability of content and form of advanced health care declarations has proven problematic in America, where living will legislation was originally designed only to enable people to forgo life-sustaining medical care in their final days and die unencumbered by intrusive medical technology. In practice many statutes were too limited in their application allowing only those who were diagnosed as terminally ill to gain the protection of living wills. Additionally the phrase "terminally ill" was often defined so narrowly that many people died before completing the required waiting period between being diagnosed as terminally ill and signing their living will. Seemingly however, the greatest difficulty was that many people wanted to give power of attorney to others who could then make health related decisions for them; a solution not easily achieved within existing legal frameworks. Recent legislation has therefore combined the provisions in the living will and the enduring power of attorney statutes and twenty states have now enacted measures enabling family members to make health care decisions even if the patient has no advance directive. Here the expectation is that a living will designed to delegate decision-making power to others means the proxy will use personal knowledge about the patient's convictions and beliefs to inform their decisions, and that the outcome will be in keeping with the patient's own principles.[17] Although this sounds like an ideal solution for a patient who wants to be certain that the provisions contained in her living will are upheld, the practice and theory may diverge.

Will You Decide? Proxy Decision-Making

Unlike other jurisdictions English law does not recognise substituted judgement or facilitate the giving or withholding of consent by anyone other than the patient herself.[18] Treatment decisions concerning incompetent adults will ordinarily be made according to the application of best interests criteria, as they would for minors or those of adult years who never attained competence, and the views of significant others, including anybody who had been appointed as a proxy decision-maker, can be considered in the assessment of the patient's best

---

[17] This pattern is being reflected in Canada and Australia and a British example can be seen in the advance directive drawn up by the Voluntary Euthanasia Society 13, Prince of Wales Terrace, London W8 5PG (1995).

[18] Ch. 3 discusses the concept of substituted judgement and its application.

interests.[19] Indeed, the Law Commission recommended that others should be consulted where it is "appropriate and practicable",[20] but case law demonstrates that their views will not be decisive.[21]

Strengthening the role of proxy decision-makers would require significant legal reform, which Andrew Grubb considers to be "beyond the role of the courts and could only be done by Parliament".[22] At present the Enduring Powers of Attorney Act 1985, allows those with power of attorney to continue to administer the affairs of a person after she has lost mental capacity. Medical treatment decisions are however excluded from the scope of the Act so that advance directives appointing proxy decision-makers are presently limited in their application.

The Law Commission considered the issues surrounding the appointment of continuing power of attorney in conjunction with advance directives and recommended it as an alternative strategy for medical decision-making.[23] Subsequently the Government set up a public consultation entitled *Who Decides?*[24] to consider a range of options for reform, including legislation on living wills and the use of a medical power of attorney. That was followed by a White Paper, *Making Decisions*[25] proposing to enable adults to draw up continuing powers of attorney, to appoint friends or relatives to make health care decisions and to introduce a modern Court of Protection to take health care decisions in appropriate circumstances.

Apparently then proxy decision-making is soon to be possible in this jurisdiction, but will it enhance individual patient autonomy and promote dignity at the end of life? People may feel more secure in the knowledge that somebody they trust will be deciding for them but the substance of the decisions taken is surely of greater import than who ultimately takes them. How can anybody be sure that their proxy will decide as she would herself, and could those responsible for patient care verify that the decisions made by the proxy were in keeping with the views of the incompetent patient? Carers, whether professional or voluntary, usually favour treatment that corresponds to their own understanding of the best interests of the patient. This ethos may strongly conflict with decisions made by a proxy, particularly if the proxy is inclined towards a course of treatment, or non-treatment, which will culminate in the death of the patient. In a sense this is the best possible solution if it means that the views of the patient

---

[19] See *Airedale NHS Trust* v. *Bland* [1993] 1 All ER 821, [1993] 2 WLR 316, and *Re T (Adult: Refusal of Treatment)* [1992] 4 All ER 649, and ch. 4.

[20] Law Commission Report 231, Mental Incapacity, *Item 9 of the Fourth Programme of Law Reform: Mentally Incapacitated Adults* (London, HMSO, 1995) para 3.33–3.36, and Clause 3(1) of the draft Bill.

[21] *Re G (Persistent Vegetative State)* [1995] 2 FCR 46, at 51.

[22] A Grubb, "Commentary on *Re T (Adult: Refusal of Treatment)* (1993) 1 Med LR 83, at 87.

[23] Law Commission Report 231, Mental Incapacity, *Item 9 of the Fourth Programme of Law Reform: Mentally Incapacitated Adults* (London, HMSO, 1995) para 7.1.

[24] Lord Chancellor's Department, *Who Decides? Making Decisions on Behalf of Mentally Incapacitated Adults* (London, HMSO, 1997) Cm 3808.

[25] Lord Chancellor's Department, *Making Decisions* (London, HMSO, 1999) Cm 4465.

will be strongly represented in opposition to those of the professional carers, because, assuming that accords with the patient's desires, autonomy will be maximised in this. But what if the proxy fails to fight the patient's corner, or superimposes her own, different, opinions on to those of the patient? Where is the patient's autonomy then?

Furthermore, what happens if the patient, though now technically incompetent, denies the authority of the proxy to decide for her, or challenges the efficacy of the proxy's decisions? How can valid treatment decisions be made in such circumstances? The appointment of a proxy decision-maker in a living will might appear to be the perfect way to ensure that life ends in a way that reflects the dignity of the way it was lived but less complex provisions, like clearly articulated anticipatory decisions, may be more successful. It is therefore vital to ensure that the form of a living will reflects the needs of its author and is sufficiently authoritative that its provisions will be upheld.

THIS IS MY WILL

The simplest form of advance directive is a statement made by a competent person in respect of medical treatment that will occur in the future rather than contemporaneously. Kennedy and Grubb therefore correctly assert that the commonest form of advance directive is the surgical consent form, which takes the form of an anticipatory decision about future surgical intervention.[26] This kind of anticipatory decision is designed largely as a means of protecting medical professionals from legal action by authorising in advance the physical contact involved in medical treatment. Advance directives taking the form of properly executed and exercised anticipatory decisions or declarations tend to be uncontroversial and unremarkable, but this is not always the case.

Early examples of living wills tended to focus on avoiding being subjected to heroic medical interventions or cardiopulmonary resuscitation, designed to save and prolong life at all costs. Observance of the provisions included in these directives usually culminated in immediate death. More contemporary approaches to end-of-life decision-making have seen the development of less precisely worded advance directives, a good example of which is the living will formulated by the Voluntary Euthanasia Society (VES).[27]

Here a detailed schedule is provided of the kinds of medical conditions that should trigger the operation of the directive when the signatory is unable to speak for herself. These include, advanced disseminated malignant disease, severe immune deficiency, advanced degenerative disease of the nervous system,

---

[26] I Kennedy, A Grubb, *Medical Law: Text with Materials* 2nd edn. (London, Butterworths, 1994) at 1325.

[27] Published by The Voluntary Euthanasia Society, 13 Prince of Wales Terrace, London W8 5 PG (1995).

severe and lasting brain damage due to injury, stroke, disease or other cause, senile or pre-senile dementia and any other condition of comparable gravity.

Although detailed, the list exhibits a degree of uncertainty about exactly when the provisions of the living will come into force, and each element allows for clinical discretion in determining when the advance directive should be implemented. There is, for example, no precise clinical definition of when disseminated malignant disease, or degenerative disease of the nervous system becomes *advanced*, or how extensive brain damage or immune deficiency must be before it is classified as *severe*. "Any other condition of comparable gravity" is similarly imprecise. In practice these apparently minor interpretative discrepancies could result in a failure to safeguard the patient's wishes and may become a source of discord between the patient's clinicians and representatives. To help avoid undignified disputes developing and resulting in failure to respect the patient's choices, the VES living will also includes a declaration designed to assist in the interpretation of the schedule. It explains that, if the author becomes unable to participate in medical decision-making while suffering from any condition described in the schedule, and is, in the opinion of two medical practitioners, unlikely to recover, then she should not be subjected to any medical intervention or treatment aimed at prolonging or sustaining life. Further clarification is provided by the insistence that:

"any distressing symptoms (including any caused by lack of food or fluid) are to be fully controlled by appropriate treatment, even though that treatment may shorten [my] life".

Perhaps most importantly the VES living will also contains a compelling statement of opinions and intentions, which states,

"I wish it to be understood that I fear degeneration and indignity far more than I fear death. I ask my medical attendants to bear this in mind when considering what my intentions would be in an uncertain situation".

The emphasis on the fear of "indignity" and "degeneration" as being inherently less desirable than death demonstrates that the bearer of the document would choose death over a life considered undignified or one where the ability to function has been reduced by "degeneration". Whether "indignity" has been sufficiently explained or is in fact a concept that can be widely applied without extensive clarification is questionable, since dignity itself is generally poorly defined. But the statement can be regarded as indicative of the author's general preferences and is therefore in line with arguments put forward by many commentators about the importance of "value histories"[28] in medical decision-making.

The VES also supplies a medical emergency card that functions in a similar way to the organ donors card, and is designed to operate in conjunction with the

    [28] J Gibson, "Values History Focuses on Life and Death Decisions" (1990) 5 *Medical Ethics* 1, P Lambert et al, "The Values History: an Innovation in Surrogate Medical Decision-Making" (1990) 18 *Law Medicine & Health Care*, 202, C Docker, "Living Wills/Advance Directives" in S A M McLean (ed.) *Contemporary Issues in Law, Medicine and Ethics* (Aldershot, Dartmouth, 1996) 179, C Docker, "Decisions to Withdraw Treatment" (2000) 320 *British Medical Journal* 54.

living will. The card incorporates the patient's signature, some medical information, the name of the next of kin, and details of where the advance directive is lodged. Individuals carry the card with them in case they require emergency treatment and are unable to express their wishes at the time. The reader of the card is advised that the individual named does not wish resuscitation or artificial prolongation of life, if there is no "reasonable prospect of recovery". However, these apparently self-explanatory provisions may in practice be of limited value in a genuine medical emergency.

Physicians are trained to react to emergencies with speed and skill. Their strategy is usually confined to overcoming the initial crisis and observing the therapeutic duty of care owed to the patient. For these reasons scant attention may be paid to whether in the long term the patient has a "reasonable prospect of recovery". Managing an emergency situation requires different skills from those necessary for accurately assessing prognosis and recovery. Such assessments are neither practically feasible nor appropriate in the emergency room where the clinical emphasis is on immediate resuscitation and stabilisation.

The phrase "reasonable prospect of recovery" itself allows for a variety of interpretations, since recovery is a value-laden assessment. Some people consider the prospect of recovery with full mental capacity but physical disability unreasonable and undesirable, while others would tolerate, even relish, physical survival, despite the impairment of cognitive function. Similarly, does the prospect of recovery need to be reasonable or the recovery itself? Without a subjective understanding of what constitutes a reasonable prospect of recovery for the person concerned those responsible for the provision of medical care are bound to exercise a wide discretion, the result of which may not accord with the patients intentions in the circumstances.

Despite these shortcomings, the living will of the Voluntary Euthanasia Society is likely to be as effective in practice as any advance directive can be. The document takes a legalistic form, incorporating a formal declaration to be signed by two witnesses. It makes provision for updating, confirmation of its applicability and for its revocation. Signatories are also urged to discuss the stipulations within the directive with their general practitioner and to lodge a copy of it at their doctor's surgery. These provisions offer the maximum possible security that the desires espoused within the advance directive will be acted upon at the appropriate time.

However, not all living wills are made in writing or as formally as the VES example, nor need they be. A verbal declaration of a patient's opinions and wishes can be equally influential in determining future medical care. In its Report No 231, *Mental Incapacity*, the Law Commission of England and Wales was anxious to stress the importance of both written and oral advance health care statements, as expressions of individual preferences and value systems.[29]

---

[29] Law Commission Report 231, Mental Incapacity, *Item 9 of the Fourth Programme of Law Reform: Mentally Incapacitated Adults* (London, HMSO, 1995) para 5.3.

Despite this, unless oral statements are recorded in such a way that all those responsible for the provision of medical care to the patient are aware of their existence and validity, their practical value is bound to be limited. They are necessarily less easily evidenced and therefore less readily confirmed as valid and applicable.

If, for example, a patient explains her wishes and preferences regarding future medical care in a particular set of circumstances, she is reliant on those wishes being accurately recorded and made available to others who might subsequently become responsible for her care. Such a statement made to a general practitioner would probably have greater impact than if it were made to a friend or family member but only if it were recorded and readily accessible to other medical personnel. The American case of *Cruzan v. Missouri Department of Health*,[30] clearly illustrates this point. The judgment held that, while a patient's wishes should be respected in order to uphold self-determination, "clear and convincing" evidence was required, before such views could be acted upon. Here only a formally executed living will was considered sufficiently authoritative for this purpose. Hence a person who wants her living will to be decisive should perhaps take all practicable steps to formalise it, especially where it anticipates specific medical circumstances and expresses what action should be taken. Couching a living will in such terms effectively anticipates future clinical events, what decisions might be taken and dictates whether or not the author consents. Anticipatory decisions relating to the acceptance of treatment where consent is *given* in advance have generally not been regarded as problematic. Advance decisions refusing consent to specific kinds of treatment which, in the unfolding medical situation would lead to the patient's death, have however prompted intense legal and ethical debate.

The legal status of anticipatory decisions in Britain has been informed by several leading cases, but these cases have tended to be confined to the discussion of the status of anticipatory decisions in general, rather than with the operation of living wills specifically related to end of life decisions.[31] For example, in *Re T* Lord Donaldson MR explained that:

"an adult patient . . . has an absolute right to choose whether to consent to medical treatment, to refuse it or to choose one rather than another of the treatments being offered".[32]

And these sentiments were reiterated in *Bland* where Lord Keith said:

". . . a person is completely at liberty to decline to undergo treatment, even if the result of his doing so will be that he will die".[33]

---

[30] 110 S Ct 2841 (1990) (US Supreme Court).

[31] *Re T* [1992] 4 All ER 649, *Re S* [1992] 4 All ER 671, and *Re MB (Medical Treatment)* [1997] 2 FLR 426, all concerned pregnant women who declined particular types of treatment. *Airedale NHS Trust* v. *Bland* [1993] 1 All ER 821, and *Re C* [1994] 1 WLR 290, specifically discussed advance directives with potentially life-limiting consequences.

[32] *Re T (Adult: Refusal of Treatment)* [1992] 4 All ER 649, per Lord Donaldson at 653.

[33] *Airedale NHS Trust* v. *Bland* [1993] 1 All ER 821, at 860.

Whilst these judgments apparently confirm the validity of anticipatory decisions where the individual concerned was competent to consent to treatment at the time of their formulation, the outcomes of the cases often belie the effectiveness of substantively valid anticipatory decisions. For example, in *Re T* the general efficacy and importance of valid advance decisions was revered, but T's own advance decision was overruled.

In line with this it is clear that only anticipatory decisions appertaining to the particular circumstances of the patient's condition will be valid. If specific treatments are refused in advance, but there is no evidence that the patient was aware when she made her decision that death would result from the circumstances that have subsequently arisen, then the refusal will be invalid.[34] For example, a patient may refuse a blood transfusion when she is agreeing to undergo a minor operation, knowing that blood transfusions are not normally necessary for this procedure. She may not anticipate that blood could become essential to save her life due to unforeseen complications of the surgery. In this case the advance refusal will not be valid because it does not apply to the situation that has developed.

Similarly the effectiveness of a living will, as a mechanism for enhancing patient autonomy, might be significantly impaired if the provisions within it are couched too generally. Andrew Grubb addresses the issue in his discussion of *Re T*,

> "the requirement in *Re T* that the patient be as specific as possible may well mean that a 'living will' is less comprehensive than would be a general statement of the patient's wishes. Provided that the specific situation contemplated arises, there is no legal problem . . . If a different situation arises, however, the 'living will' may miss the mark and the patient's more general intention to, for example, forego life-sustaining treatment will be frustrated".[35]

It seems that a living will containing anticipatory decisions that are either too general or too specific could be considered inapplicable. Acknowledging this as a point for concern Jonathan Montgomery has protested that:

> "the law represents that they [patients] may choose to die, but allows this power over their dying to be withheld from them at the very point at which its exercise is sought".[36]

Various methods of overcoming this problem were considered by the Law Commission, which concluded that primary legislation would be unlikely to succeed, while:

> "the technique (adopted by the THT/King's College model form) of referring to treatments with particular purposes rather than any particular treatments may be one way of avoiding some of the difficulties".[37]

[34] *Re T* [1992] 4 All ER 649.

[35] A Grubb, "Commentary on *Re T (Adult: Refusal of Treatment)*, (1993) 1 Med LR 83, at 87.

[36] J Montgomery, "Power Over Death: The Final Sting" in R Lee, D Morgan (eds.) *Death Rites: Law and Ethics at the End of Life* (London, Routledge, 1996) 37–53, at 39.

[37] Law Commission Report 231, Mental Incapacity, *Item 9 of the Fourth Programme of Law Reform: Mentally Incapacitated Adults* (London, HMSO, 1995) para 5.22.

One further important issue, relating specifically to women, and created by the tension between the dicta of *Re C*,[38] endorsing the validity of anticipatory decisions, and *Re S*,[39] and subsequent obstetric cases,[40] concerning a contemporaneous decision to refuse consent for a Caesarean section, cannot be so easily resolved.

In a ruling that has been widely discredited,[41] *S*'s decision to refuse treatment was overruled because of the imminent danger to the life of her unborn child. Protection of the interests of unborn children was thereby afforded greater importance than respect for the autonomy of pregnant women. Following *Re S*, it seemed likely that any anticipatory decision with life-limiting implications could be legitimately invalidated, simply because the author was a pregnant woman. Advocates of patient autonomy, like the Law Commission greeted the judgment with considerable unease,

"we do not, however, accept that a woman's right to determine the sorts of bodily interference which she will tolerate somehow evaporates as soon as she becomes pregnant".[42]

Re S and similar judgments, encourage the interpretation that any advance directive relating to a pregnant woman, would be invalid, unless it specifically addressed the circumstances in question, notably her pregnancy.[43] Therefore, the Law Commission recommended that

"Women of child bearing age should . . . be aware that they should address their minds to this possibility if they wish to make advance refusals of treatment".[44]

Women of child bearing age and pregnant women are thereby distinguished as a separate class to whom special rules relating to the formation, application and validity, of advance directives will apply.[45] The effect on advance directives of

---

[38] [1994] 1 All ER 819.

[39] [1992] 4 All ER 671.

[40] See for example, *Re L (An Adult: Non-consensual Treatment)* [1997] 1 FCR 60, and *Re MB (Medical Treatment)* [1997] 2 FLR 426.

[41] D Morgan, "Whatever Happened to Consent?" (1992) 142 *New Law Journal* 1448, J Bridgeman, "Medical Treatment: The Mother's Rights", [1993] Fam Law, 534, I Kennedy and A Grubb, *Medical Law: Text with Materials* 2nd edn. (London, Butterworths, 1994) at 359, M Thomson, "After *Re S*" (1994) 2 Med LR 127.

[42] Law Commission Report 231, Mental Incapacity, *Item 9 of the Fourth Programme of Law Reform: Mentally Incapacitated Adults* (London, HMSO, 1995) para 5.25, at 75–6.

[43] The American case of *Werth v. Taylor* (1991) 474 NW2d 426 (Mitchigan CA) where a pregnant patient, Cindy Werth, brought an action in battery against Dr Taylor when he failed to respect her advance directive not to transfuse blood, similarly illustrates the controversy. Here under dicta taken from *In Re Estate of Dorone* 517 pa3, 543 A 2d 452 (1987) it was held that, ". . . in a situation . . . where there is an emergency calling for an immediate decision, nothing less than a fully conscious contemporaneous decision *by the patient* will be sufficient to override evidence of medical necessity". And ". . . without contemporaneous refusal of treatment by a fully informed, competent adult patient, no action for battery lies".

[44] Law Commission Report 231, Mental Incapacity, *Item 9 of the Fourth Programme of Law Reform: Mentally Incapacitated Adults* (London, HMSO, 1995) para 5.25, at 75–6.

[45] Similar distinctions have been included in other models for living wills, for example, the first legislative provision for living wills, the Natural Death in California Act 1976 and Age Concern Institute of Gerontology and Centre of Medical Law and Ethics King's College London, *The Living Will: Consent to Treatment at the End of Life* (London, Edward Arnold, 1988) at 60.

subsequent dicta in *Re MB*,[46] confirming that there is no jurisdiction to balance the interests of a foetus against those of a competent pregnant woman, remains uncertain since it hinges on the assessment and demonstration of maternal competence.[47]

Furthermore, the Law Commission's Draft Bill includes the general recommendation that, unless there are contrary indications, a presumption will operate that an anticipatory refusal of treatment does not apply if it threatens the life of the author or, if the author is a pregnant woman, if it threatens the life of her unborn child.[48] Effectively this recommendation amounts to a "presumption in favour of the preservation of life",[49] so that unless a living will makes specific reference to the potential for an advance refusal of treatment to result in death its provisions may be invalidated. Any anticipatory decision about health care must relate to the specific circumstances that arise and women of child bearing age must acknowledge the possible threat to the life of an unborn child alongside the general content of their living wills in order to safeguard validity. Autonomy is always compromised "in the company of others" but in this context it may be non-existent.

Protecting individual autonomy is obviously the primary purpose of a living will, but how successfully this is achieved depends not only on the wills format and content, its scope and the clinician's responsibility relative to it, but also on the establishment of a clear understanding about when its operation is invoked. It is imperative for patient autonomy that a living will becomes operative once its author's mental capacity becomes so diminished that she is no longer able to decide for herself. Therefore, the definitive answer as to when a particular living will becomes operative usually depends upon an assessment of when its author is no longer competent to participate in medical decision-making. Alternatively, a directive might include the provision that some other "trigger" mechanism stimulates its implementation. The triggering factor may be a specific deterioration in the patient's medical condition, or a particular medical occurrence that the author considers significant for her prospects of survival. Examples might include, loss of the ability to communicate, urinary or faecal incontinence, or perhaps a confirmed diagnosis of a terminal or degenerative disease. Living wills of this type are gaining in popularity in jurisdictions where advance statements about health care are supported by legislation. They are not commonplace in Britain where loss of mental capacity is the event that would usually be expected to trigger the initial introduction of the provisions of a living will.

---

[46] *Re MB (Medical Treatment)* [1997] 2 FLR 426.

[47] Established authority exists in *Paton* v. *BPAS* [1979] QB 276 and *C* v. *S* [1988] QB 135 supporting the proposition that an unborn child has no right to have its interests balanced against those of its potential mother. Yet numerous cases, including *Re T (An Adult) (Consent to Medical Treatment)* [1992] 4 All ER 649, *Re S* [1992] 4 All ER 671 and *Re L (An Adult: Non-consensual Treatment)* [1997] 1 FCR 60, have overruled refusals of consent in order to safeguard foetal interests.

[48] Law Commission Report 231, Mental Incapacity, *Item 9 of the Fourth Programme of Law Reform: Mentally Incapacitated Adults* (London, HMSO, 1995) Draft Bill, clause 9(3), 76.

[49] *Ibid*, para 5.26, at 76.

In cases of prolonged illness the desire and ability to fully engage with medical decision-making may be gradually reduced or destroyed, generating vulnerabilities that render an assessment of mental capacity problematic. There is often only limited awareness, both clinically and socially of the significance of declining autonomy in these circumstances.[50] Crucially the impact of fading autonomy may be compounded if a patient only decides to devise a living will as her illness begins to progress and her capacity decreases, since both autonomy and competence may be questionable at precisely the time that protection from arbitrary decisions and indignity are sought.

I WILL DECIDE

It has been stated that, "the right to decide one's own fate presupposes a capacity to do so",[51] suggesting that the ability to exercise individual personal autonomy is only available to people who are intellectually competent. In actuality a recognition of fluctuating or declining competence may prompt a person to construct an advance directive to protect her ability to control her own fate and thereby preserve her dignity. But, because the validity of the content of a living will is dependent upon the competence of its author to make anticipatory health care decisions at the time it is composed, a will constructed in these circumstances may be ineffective. Accurately gauging competency is therefore vitally important in establishing the applicability of a living will both at its inception and at the point of its activation, and the reliable evaluation of capacity is central to this analysis.

A Test for Competence

In most instances there is no doubt about a person's competence to give or decline consent to treatment in real time or for the future. For example, an adult patient who is fully conscious and suffering no mental impairment will usually be competent to decide. Similarly, an unconscious patient is clearly devoid of the mental capacity and physical ability required to make a competent medical decision. Another person may be mentally ill, or suffering from impaired mental capability, yet still be considered competent for some purposes. Competence is assessed in relation to the type of decision being made and it is widely recognised that competence can be "both partial and fluctuating".[52] Indeed it is possible for

---

[50] Interestingly, as financial awareness deteriorates a representative may be appointed to oversee a patient's monetary affairs but the law does not presently recognise a similar mechanism concerning medical care.

[51] *Re T (Adult: Refusal of Treatment)* [1992] 4 All ER 649, per Lord Donaldson at 653.

[52] Law Commission Report 231, Mental Incapacity, *Item 9 of the Fourth Programme of Law Reform: Mentally Incapacitated Adults* (London, HMSO, 1995) para 3.5.

a person to have the capacity to marry, but, on the same day, to be incompetent to make a detailed will.[53]

Where consent to medical treatment is concerned a patient with capacity should understand the nature of the treatment and any potential complications, as well as the implications of not being treated.[54] Competence to consent should be assessed for each decision and does not confer an overall status of competence or incompetence on a patient.[55] Basing the determination of an individual's competence to consent to treatment on clinical and legal criteria, in relation to each particular clinical situation creates inherent uncertainties and inconsistencies in the evaluative process, as *Re C,*[56] clearly illustrates.

C was a sixty-eight year old man who had been diagnosed as suffering from chronic paranoid schizophrenia and had been an inpatient of Broadmoor secure mental hospital for thirty years. He was delusional, believing that he had been a world renowned vascular surgeon who had pioneered techniques to avoid amputating limbs. Ironically, C's leg became gangrenous after he sustained a minor injury, and surgeons recommended amputation as clinical indications suggested that his life would otherwise be endangered. C refused to consent to surgical intervention and sought the legal right to have his refusal respected even though the treatment was seen as potentially life saving. The questions for the court to decide were firstly, was C competent to refuse consent, and secondly, if his refusal was valid would it also be valid in respect of the same treatment at any time in the future, even if C later became incompetent?[57]

Varying opinions and assessments of C's mental capacity were offered by three separate consultant psychiatrists, a surgeon, and the court, before it was eventually decided that C was competent. The difficulties encountered in *Re C* in evaluating a patient's competence to decide are reflected in the tests and standards proffered as mechanisms for determining competence in the case law and legislation in this area. Three types of assessment have commonly been used.

The first is a cognition-based test, involving an assessment of the patient's ability to understand information. Sections 57 and 58 of the Mental Health Act 1983 include such a test and require that a patient who is competent to consent to treatment should be, "capable of understanding the nature, purpose and

<hr>

[53] *In the Estate of Park, Park v. Park* [1954] P 112, the particular facts of this case are explained in M Brazier, *Medicine, Patients and the Law* (London, Penguin, 1992) at 100–101.

[54] The Mental Health Act 1983 Code of Practice discusses the issue of capacity to make medical treatment decisions in great detail.

[55] This principle is enshrined in the Mental Health Act 1983 which permits some patients to be treated against their will but only for conditions which relate to their mental illness. The assessment of capacity is also relevant in Part VII of the Act, which deals specifically with the issue of competence to manage "property and affairs" and again illustrates that while a person may be considered incompetent for the purposes of this provision she may retain capacity in respect of other decisions.

[56] *Re C* (Adult: Refusal of Treatment) [1994] 1 WLR 290.

[57] For further commentary see, R Gordon, C Barlow, "Competence and the Right to Die" (1993) 143 *New Law Journal* 1719–20, E Roberts, "*Re C* and the Boundaries of Autonomy" (1994) 10 (3) *Professional Negligence* 98–101.

likely effects" of the treatment in question. In *Re C* Thorpe J applied a modified form of this type of test to determine C's competence. He held that the patient would *not* be competent if he failed to "sufficiently understand the nature, purpose and effects of the proffered amputation".[58] His test assessed the patient's subjective understanding rather than with his *ability* to understand, which distinguishes it from the cognition test in the Mental Health Act 1983.

The second type of test recognises that cognition alone is often an insufficient assessment of a person's competence to make health care decisions, and reflects the reasoning applied in *Gillick v. Norfolk and Wisbech Area Health Authority*.[59] It was held here that children under the age of sixteen possess competence if they demonstrate maturity together with intelligence and understanding.[60] There is no presumption of competence for minors in this situation; they must effectively prove they are competent to make health-care decisions on their own behalf. Being institutionalised and isolated from everyday decision-making, due to mental illness or instability can similarly lead to the presumption that patients are not competent to make their own choices. Consequently these patients will need to demonstrate their competence and ability to function autonomously in circumstances where it is likely to be seriously impaired.[61]

In *Re C* doctors presented evidence disputing C's understanding of the information given to him regarding the proposed amputation because he expressed his disbelief in their assertions that he might die without the treatment. The clinicians contended that if he understood but nevertheless failed to believe that he could die, he was not competent to decide. Fennell argues that this test poses particular practical difficulties.[62] If a patient believes the assessment of her situation and the suggested treatment must she accept the treatment offered in order to demonstrate her belief in it, or can she still decide for herself in the face of the information provided, thereby implying an element of disbelief?

Thorpe J based his assessment of C's competence largely on the patient's reactions and responses at the court hearing, and found that C was cognisant of his situation and was therefore competent to decide. He made his evaluation regardless of the psychiatrist's diagnosis of paranoid and delusional schizophrenia, and the thirty years C had spent as an inpatient of Broadmoor, demonstrating that the fact that a person is mentally disordered is not in itself sufficient to destroy her decision-making capacity. The operation of the test was subsequently clarified in *B v. Croydon District Health Authority*[63] where Thorpe J explained that absolute disbelief amounts to being "impervious to reason,

---

[58] *Re C* (Adult: Refusal of Treatment) [1994] 1 WLR 290 at 295.
[59] [1985] 3 All ER 402.
[60] In *Re E* [1993] 1 Fam Law Reports 386, Ward J endorses the notion that a minor may be both intelligent and well-informed but may, nevertheless lack the maturity to attain *Gillick* competence.
[61] *Kaimowitz v. Michigan Dept. of Mental Health* 42 USLW 2063 (1973), Law Commission Consultation Paper No 128, "Mentally Incapacitated Adults and Decision-Making" (1993) at 31.
[62] P Fennell, *Treatment Without Consent* (London, Routledge, 1996) at 257.
[63] [1995] 2 WLR 294.

divorced from reality, or incapable of judgement after reflection" and that this can be distinguished from, "the tendency which most people have when undergoing medical treatment to self assess and then to puzzle over the divergence between medical and self assessment".[64]

The third test of competence is perhaps the most contentious and the most difficult to demonstrate as a test. It focuses on the rationality of the decision made, and is contentious because respect for individual autonomy dictates that the rationality of any one person's decision should not be challenged on the basis that it fails to conform with accepted norms or the opinions of those required to assess competence. As long as the patient is legally competent to decide she has an absolute right to choose whether to give or refuse consent to medical treatment. Legal precedent suggests that the choice made is not limited to, "decisions which others might regard as sensible. It exists notwithstanding that the reasons for making the choice are rational, irrational, unknown or even non-existent".[65] Any decision made by a competent patient should therefore be binding, irrespective of whether or not that decision appears rational or sensible to others. Yet, the principle is far from absolute. Examples of cases where women have undergone court authorised caesarean sections despite their refusal to consent have already been referred to, and a series of cases concerning young adults also reveals that individual autonomy can indeed be devalued by other people's perceptions of what would constitute a rational or sensible choice in a given situation.

Re R[66] and *Re W*[67] clearly demonstrate the contingent nature of autonomy with their confirmation that, "no minor of whatever age has power by refusing consent to override a consent to treatment by someone who has parental responsibility for the minor and a fortiori a consent by the court".[68] Similarly in *Re E*[69] where a fifteen year old boy declined consent to a blood transfusion on the basis of his religious beliefs. Although this was a contemporaneous decision rather an advance directive, upholding *E*'s choice would inevitably have led to his death. The judge expressed admiration for *E*'s intelligence and composure but none the less felt that he had failed to comprehend the full significance of the process of dying he would confront if his decision were upheld. However, the level of understanding and insight described in this judgment as necessary to demonstrate competence:

> "effectively set the test of competence so high that it was not only beyond the range of a 15 year-old boy but arguably beyond the range of most adults".[70]

---

[64] *Ibid.*

[65] *Re T (Adult: Refusal of Treatment)* [1992] 4 All ER 649, per Lord Donaldson at 653.

[66] *Re R (A Minor) (Wardship: Medical Treatment)* [1991] 4 All ER 177.

[67] *Re W (A Minor) (Medical Treatment)* [1992] 4 All ER 627.

[68] *Ibid*, at 639.

[69] *Re E* [1993] 1 Fam Law Rep 386.

[70] E Roberts, "*Re C* and the Boundaries of Autonomy" (1994) 10 (3) *Professional Negligence* 98–101.

Implicit in the judgment is the suggestion that although the boy was competent the apparent irrationality inherent in his decision, because of its inevitable consequence, negated its validity.

Apparently then, a person's competence may be otherwise firmly established, but the substance of a particular medical decision can raise doubts about her mental capacity, particularly in the case of minors. Jo Bridgeman's assessment of the inconsistencies in these cases focuses on the tension between, on the one hand, seeking to uphold the autonomy of the minors involved and, on the other, wanting to protect them from their potential to make ill informed and immature decisions with dangerous consequences. She argues that "because we care" it is often too difficult to accept an irrational but otherwise autonomous decision by a young adult where its consequences will cause irrevocable harm.[71]

Refusals of consent are especially vulnerable to this kind of reasoning because the implications of refusing consent are often far greater than when giving consent. Refusing a potentially life-saving therapy can be sufficient reason to question the integrity of a patient's decisions and her competence to make them. Indeed some commentators have argued that a higher degree of comprehension is required to make an informed refusal than is necessary for a competent consent.[72] In the absence of an established doctrine of informed consent, accepting treatment may amount to little more than following the advice of an experienced medical professional. Declining consent in similar circumstances takes on the appearance of a rejection of the same expertly formed opinion, ostensibly from a position of relative ignorance. Thus a decision to refuse life-sustaining treatment may appear irrational and be challenged on the basis of the questionable competence of the individual concerned.

With regard to advance directives, Kristina Stern has raised concerns that such decisions may be taken as evidence of a patient's incompetence simply because they fail to comply with expert opinion and are idiosyncratic.[73] Where a treatment refusal is made in advance and remote from the clinical situation to which it becomes relevant, the appearance of irrationality may be compounded. Stern suggests that in cases where a diagnosis of incapacity is disputed, perhaps by the patient, the family, or carers, an independent assessment of competency could be required to clarify the situation. Any mechanism to assist in ascertaining capacity and the validity of anticipatory decisions would be useful to clarify when an advance directive becomes operative due to incapacity but its application in respect of anticipatory decisions would clearly be limited. The Law Commission did not consider this possible solution, though it has been

---

[71] J Bridgeman, "Because We Care? The Medical Treatment of Children" in S Sheldon and M Thomson (eds.), *Feminist Perspectives on Health Care Law* (London, Cavendish Publishing, 1998) at 97.

[72] J A Deverereux, D P H Jones, D I Dickenson, "Can Children Withhold Consent to Treatment?" (1993) 306 *British Medical Journal* 1459.

[73] K Stern, "Advance Directives" (1994) *Medical Law Review* 57–76 at 62.

addressed in other jurisdictions.[74] Some of the more general problems associated with the assessment of mental capacity in the face of apparently irrational decision-making were discussed at length by the Law Commission.

Describing what it defined as the "outcome" approach to the assessment of capacity, Law Commission Report 231 states:

> "An assessor of capacity using the 'outcome' method focuses on the final content of an individual's decision. Any decision which is inconsistent with conventional values, or with which the assessor disagrees, may be classified as incompetent . . . A number of our respondents argued that an 'outcome' approach is applied by many doctors; if the outcome of the patient's deliberations is to agree with the doctor's recommendations then he or she is taken to have capacity, while if the outcome is to reject a course which the doctor has advised then capacity is found to be absent".[75]

Subsequently the Law Commission recommended that a legislative definition of incapacity is needed which would become operative

> "when a person is unable by reason of mental disability to make a decision on the matter in question, or unable to communicate a decision on that matter because he or she is unconscious or for any other reason".[76]

Mental disability is here defined as meaning, "any disability or disorder of the mind or brain, whether permanent or temporary, which results in an impairment or disturbance of mental functioning".[77] Further provision was included in the Draft Bill concerning the link between a person's competence to decide and her understanding of the likely consequences of that decision:

> "*We recommend* that a person should be regarded as unable to make a decision by reason of mental disability if the disability is such that, at the time the decision needs to be made, he or she is unable to understand or retain the information relevant to the decision, including information about the reasonably foreseeable consequences of deciding one way or another or failing to make that decision".[78]

To date the Law Commission's proposals have not been incorporated into statute but many have been included in the 1999 White Paper *Making Decisions.*[79] In the mean time, *Re MB,*[80] where stress, fatigue and medication were considered by the clinicians, and the court of first instance, to have temporarily impaired the patient's capacity to refuse consent to a caesarean section, has further clarified the test of capacity. The Court of Appeal held that,

---

[74] The Manitoba Law Reform Commission refers to independent assessment of competence in its Report No. 74, June 1991, *Self-determination in Health Care (Living Wills and Health Care Proxies)*.

[75] Law Commission Report 231, Mental Incapacity, *Item 9 of the Fourth Programme of Law Reform: Mentally Incapacitated Adults* (London, HMSO, 1995) para 3.4.

[76] *Ibid*, Draft Bill Clause 2 (1).

[77] *Ibid*, Draft Bill Clause 2 (2).

[78] *Ibid*, Draft Bill Clause 2 (2)(a).

[79] Lord Chancellor's Department, *Making Decisions* (London, HMSO, 1999) Cm 4465.

[80] *Re MB (Medical Treatment)* [1997] 2 FLR 426.

"A person lacks capacity if some impairment or disturbance of mental functioning renders the person unable to make a decision whether to consent to or refuse treatment. That inability to make a decision will occur when:
a) the patient is *unable to comprehend and retain the information* which is material to the decision, especially as to the likely consequences of having or not having the treatment in question;
b) the patient is *unable to use the information* and weigh it in the balance as part of the process of arriving at a decision". (emphasis added)[81]

Useful guidance on assessing capacity has thus been formulated which will be valuable in the clinical setting. But, even where it is easily established that a patient either does or does not possess decision-making capacity, a living will may still be ineffective if it is not clearly expressed or if its substance conflicts with a clinical understanding of the patients best interests.

WILL MY WILL BE DONE?

It is settled law that if a patient is devoid of the capacity to give or refuse consent, the clinicians, or the courts, will decide for her on the basis of a determination of her best interests. If, in similar circumstances the patient has executed a living will, her own wishes about the kind of care she desires will be known and can be given effect. However, in some situations the provisions contained within a person's living will may be considered, by those responsible for her medical care, as contrary to her best interests. The living will may include anticipatory decisions with which the carers disagree, or decision-making health care proxies may have been appointed whose opinions differ from those of the professionals involved. In order to dispel conflict in these circumstances it will become necessary to determine the scope and validity of the particular living will and this will normally be achieved by examining the provisions contained in it, and their legal status. Although living wills are usually promoted on the assumption that they enhance patient autonomy and individual choice, there may be situations where rigid adherence to the provisions contained in an advance directive can limit choice and apparently become less than beneficial to the patient concerned.[82] Earlier discussion focussed on the validity of general provisions contained within living wills but more specific issues, relating to the alteration and revocation of an advance directive, and the refusal of basic care are also likely to be contentious and might limit the effectiveness of an otherwise valid advance directive.

---

[81] *Re MB (Medical Treatment)* [1997] 2 FLR 426, at 437.
[82] See for example, J Lynn, "Why I Don't Have a Living Will" in A Capron (ed.) "Medical Decision Making and the 'Right to Die' After Cruzan" (1991) 19 *Law Medicine & Health Care* 101, and, Law Commission Report 231, Mental Incapacity, *Item 9 of the Fourth Programme of Law Reform: Mentally Incapacitated Adults* (London, HMSO, 1995) para 5.4, at 67.

Basic Care

Proposals to prohibit the validity of advance directives declining either the provision of pain relief or basic care,[83] were included in Law Commission Report 231. Revisions were introduced following the British Medical Association's expression of concerns that effectively outlawing all anticipatory decisions refusing pain relief would mean that those individuals who sought to remain alert, through abstention from certain types of medication, might be denied that opportunity. Vetoing the refusal of treatment aimed at alleviating *severe* pain was thought more pertinent than denying the opportunity to refuse strong pain relief, particularly where patients suffered inappropriate side effects. Spoon-feeding was also originally referred to as an element of basic care that should not be refused. The words "direct oral hydration and nutrition" were later substituted however, since this terminology better reflects the practicalities of nursing care, which often dictates that nutrition and hydration are administered via spouted cup or syringe.

Denying the right to refuse basic care in an advance directive is clearly destructive of individual rights of self-determination and autonomy, yet it may be necessary to protect the interests of others who need to have contact with the patient concerned. Endorsing the provisions of a living will which stipulated the complete withdrawal of basic care, including elementary hygiene and symptomatic pain control, may be traumatic for medical staff and other patients who would have to observe its effects and could therefore be regarded as contrary to public policy and destructive of dignity. It would certainly be considered unethical and against public policy to withhold basic care from an incapacitated patient. But the public policy argument takes no account of the fact that a patient with full mental capacity may legitimately decline the provision of basic care, including efforts to wash and nourish her, in an effort to impress her personality on the situation.[84]

Alteration and Revocation

Criticisms offered by some commentators relate to the perceived inability of a living will to adequately cater for a person's complex care requirements[85] and

---

[83] *Basic care* has been defined by the Law Commission as the alleviation of severe pain, the maintenance of bodily hygiene, and the provision of direct oral hydration and nutrition. See also Law Commission Report 231, Mental Incapacity, *Item 9 of the Fourth Programme of Law Reform: Mentally Incapacitated Adults* (London, HMSO, 1995) at para 5.34, and Draft Bill, clause 9(7)(a) and (8).

[84] I am indebted to the doctors at Northgate Medical Practice, Canterbury, for their practical insights into this situation.

[85] See J Lynn, "Why I Don't Have a Living Will" in A Capron (ed.) "Medical Decision Making and the 'Right to Die' After Cruzan" (1991) 19 *Law Medicine & Health Care* 101.

the possibility patients might inadvertently deprive themselves of "professional medical expertise or of beneficial advances in treatment".[86] Consequently many authorities, including the Law Commission, recommend the formulation of special mechanisms to facilitate the alteration and revocation of advance directives. Since new therapies are continually being developed, and people often revise their opinions about the kinds of treatment they find acceptable when they actually confront the practicalities of illness, such concerns are inevitable. It would be a travesty if the provisions of an advance directive operated to prevent the director receiving a valuable, even curative therapy, which was unknown when the advance directive was formulated.

Existing case law stipulates however that the validity of a living will is dependent on its author being sufficiently informed to have intended her anticipatory decisions to apply in the circumstances that have subsequently arisen.[87] Under these criteria, the availability of clinical or pharmaceutical developments not envisioned when the advance directive was formulated would almost certainly imply that the directive would be invalid in the specific situation that had arisen. Furthermore, while she retains mental capacity the author of a living will can alter, or revoke, its provision as she chooses, and her contemporaneous decisions cannot be overridden.

In respect of the formulation, alteration and revocation of advance directives the Law Commission favours a policy of "maximum flexibility",[88] designed to enable patients to review the provisions contained within their living wills in the light of developing medical circumstances and changes in their own values and opinions. Specifically, concerns have been expressed that people should not be constrained by the need to formally repudiate their advance directive, "it would seem entirely wrong to stipulate that an advance refusal must stand until, for example, paper and pencil and an independent witness can be found".[89] At first glance then, given the need for precision in drafting and clarity regarding the circumstances where an advance directive becomes operative, there would seem to be little need for specific guidelines relating to their revocation and alteration. Perhaps of greater significance is the need to ensure that health care professionals encountering living wills are aware of their significance and their professional obligations in relation to them. Regardless of its content an advance directive will be ineffective unless the medical professionals caring for the patient are aware of its existence and their responsibility towards it.

---

[86] Law Commission Report 231, Mental Incapacity, *Item 9 of the Fourth Programme of Law Reform: Mentally Incapacitated Adults* (London, HMSO, 1995) at para 5.4.

[87] *Re T* [1992] 4 All ER 649, *Airedale NHS Trust* v. *Bland* [1992] 1 All ER 821.

[88] Law Commission Report 231, Mental Incapacity, *Item 9 of the Fourth Programme of Law Reform: Mentally Incapacitated Adults* (London, HMSO, 1995) at para 5.32.

[89] *Ibid*, para 5.31.

WHERE THERE'S A WILL

Advance statements about medical care hold significance for both patient autonomy and clinical responsibility. They can simultaneously offer a reassurance for the patient and pose a threat to clinical freedom, particularly where treatment decisions designed to culminate in death are endorsed and encouraged. In this situation an advance directive might represent a stark choice between "prior personal choice and immediate well-being".[90] Clinicians may experience this choice as a tension between the obligation to respect individual autonomy and the duty to treat a patient according to her best interests. Hence a living will can present real professional and ethical dilemmas.

Members of all medical professions, and the professions supplementary to medicine, may have responsibilities relating to the operation of living wills. The patient's general practitioner, and any doctor by whom the patient is treated in hospital, will have particular obligations since it is they who must ensure that valid consent for medical treatment is given. Other health-care professionals also have a role to play depending upon when they come into contact with the patient. For example, nursing staff, particularly those involved in long-term or terminal care, tend to develop close relationships with patients, and may be aware of anticipatory decisions that are unknown to other carers. Conversely medical workers, such as ambulance drivers and para-medics, may encounter a patient for the first time in an emergency situation and be completely unaware of that individual's concerns or preferences, even though this is precisely the situation the living will anticipates. How far the directions in a living will are observed depends therefore not only on how clearly it is drafted and the capacity of its author, but also on the practical environment within which it operates and the clinical relationship between the patient concerned and the medical staff in attendance.

In Britain the care and treatment of the population is divided between primary and secondary care under the umbrella of the National Health Service. General practitioners (GPs) operate as family doctors with responsibility for primary care. They conduct most initial consultations, and refer patients to hospitals or clinics for specialist secondary care. Superimposed on this system is the facility for people to self-refer to hospital accident and emergency departments without seeing a GP. Hospital consultants and GPs take overall responsibility for the patients under their care, even where they are not directly involved in service provision. Other members of the clinical team, such as junior doctors, nurses, and members of the professions allied to medicine,[91] generally answer to the clinician in charge of the patient's care under the terms of their contracts of employment, and according to their professional Codes of Practice. Paramedics

---

[90] D Lamb, "Refusal of Life-prolonging Therapy" (1995) 1 (2) *Res Publica* 147 at 156.
[91] For example physiotherapists and radiographers.

occupy an almost unique position with respect to living wills here because they work in environments where doctors are not usually available to make decisions, and where they often have to react to unforeseen situations.

Most paramedics are ambulance staff or nurses who have been specially trained to provide emergency care and life-sustaining treatment until such time as medical assistance is available. If confronted with an unconscious patient who is not competent to give consent the paramedic will administer treatment as the clinical situation dictates. Frequently this involves first aid, resuscitation and maintenance while a patient is transported to hospital. If the patient is competent and can give or refuse consent the paramedic must act accordingly; like doctors they are not authorised to treat a patient in the absence of consent unless it is an emergency and the patient is not competent but needs urgent treatment.

Faced with a situation where the patient is not conscious but the relatives or friends insist they have made a valid living will refusing treatment in the situation that has occurred, the paramedic must judge whether or not treatment is appropriate.[92] However, just as for doctors, if there is any doubt about the validity or applicability of a living will paramedics are authorised by their Code of Practice to administer treatment in accordance with the patient's best interests. Paramedics are likely to take this course rather than risk neglecting the duty of care they owe to their patients by failing to treat in an emergency.[93]

General practitioners are the clinical group most likely to be involved with the formulation of living wills and will often be responsible for holding a copy of a patient's living will in her medical records. Historically patients have tended to have long-standing professional relationships with their family doctors. In these circumstances the GP would usually have been aware not only of the patient's medical history but also of their social circumstances and background,[94] so the GP may be regarded as an appropriate source of guidance about future medical treatment and anticipatory decision-making. By contrast, clinical staff in the hospital setting are less likely to be involved in the composition of patient's living wills, other than in the context of long term care, where anticipatory decisions taken in consultation with hospital staff, may constitute an advance directive. These personnel are the ones with ultimate responsibility for complying with the terms of a previously executed living will. They may only become aware of its existence at the point where it becomes clinically significant because the exact medical circumstances anticipated by the patient have arisen, perhaps raising tensions between the wishes of the patient and the professional discretion

[92] K V Irerson, "Forgoing Hospital Care: Should Ambulance Staff Always Resuscitate?" (1991) 17 *Journal of Medical Ethics* 19–24.

[93] This conclusion was reached following informal consultation with ambulance crews and paramedics in the Canterbury area, in August 1996.

[94] In the present health care and social environment this may represent a rather idealised view, since the population is increasingly geographically mobile and many patients attend large health centres where they might encounter several different doctors. The move towards casual "drop-in" medical centres and co-operative out of hours services can also contribute to a loss of continuity in patient services.

of the clinical team. Disputes here would do little to enhance patient autonomy and dignity.

Clearly health-care professionals must be aware of the legal status of advance directives and how they relate to clinical responsibility if they are to adequately protect the autonomy of the patients who are their authors. Hence the British Medical Association, in conjunction with the Royal College of Nurses, has published guidelines for its members which are intended to operate as a Code of Practice for practitioners dealing with advance directives.[95]

In summary these guidelines state that "advance directives refusing some or all medical procedures must be followed where valid and applicable". To ensure their validity, checks should be made that directives refusing life-prolonging treatments were made by the patient, of her own free will, and without undue influence. Furthermore, oral objections or opinions about particular treatments may constitute an advance directive, as long as the patient was informed and competent at the time. Where a patient's wishes are not known or unclear, appropriate treatment should be given in accordance with the clinical assessment and health professionals may contact GPs to confirm the existence and validity of advance directives.

Following the guidelines, and case law,[96] a doctor who is aware that a patient has made an advance directive that is relevant to the unfolding clinical situation, should consider its contents before taking treatment decisions on behalf of a patient who has become incompetent. A living will that is applicable in the clinical circumstances should be regarded as "the settled wishes of the patient" and doctors are advised to "act upon it if the clinical situation requires".[97] Yet its effectiveness will be compromised unless it is sufficiently detailed to apply to the specific situation that has arisen because its validity will be vulnerable to challenge. Jurisdictions on both sides of the Atlantic have adopted a similar approach and analysis of the British cases concerned with treatment refusal[98] clearly indicates the level to which they are informed by judgments from America and Canada.[99] Much academic debate has been generated as a result of these court decisions because they appear to subjugate the autonomous decisions of the patients in favour of a paternalistic clinical response. Exceptionally

---

[95] The BMA, *Advance Statements about Medical Treatment* (1995) London, BMA publications was published following recommendations made in the Law Commission Report 231, Mental Incapacity, *Item 9 of the Fourth Programme of Law Reform: Mentally Incapacitated Adults* (London, HMSO, 1995) at paras. 5.39,and 5.4, and by the House of Lords Select Committee on Medical Ethics para. 265.

[96] *Re C* (Adult: Refusal of Treatment) [1994] 1 WLR 290.

[97] The MDU, *Problems in General Practice: Consent to Treatment,* July 1996, London: The Medical Defence Union, 10.

[98] *Re R* [1991] 4 All ER 177, *Re W* [1992] 4 All ER 627, *Re T* [1992] 4 All ER 649, *Re S* [1992] 4 All ER 671, *Re L (An Adult: Non-consensual Treatment)* [1997] 1 FCR 60, and *Re MB (Medical Treatment)* [1997] 2 FLR 426 are recent examples.

[99] The judgements in *Re T* [1992] 4 All ER 649 and *Re S* [1992] 4 All ER 671 in particular, are certainly directly informed by the judgements in *In Re Estate of Dorone* 517 pa 3, 543 A 2d 452 (1987) and (1991) 474 NW 2d 426 (Michigan CA).

however, the Canadian case *Malette* v. *Shulman*[100] offers a judgment that is rather more sympathetic to the desires of patients formulating advance directives.

After Mrs Georgette Malette and her husband were involved in a road accident in which Mr Malette had been killed. Mrs Malette was rushed unconscious to hospital where, under the care of Dr Shulman, she was found to be suffering from head and facial injuries and was "bleeding profusely". The bleeding had induced severe clinical shock for which Ringer's Lactate and glucose were immediately administered, which is a typical treatment for shock resulting from blood loss. Whole blood would later be transfused if the patient's condition failed to improve after this initial treatment.

Mrs Malette's condition did not improve but before any further treatment decisions were made a card identifying her as a Jehovah's Witness was discovered in her belongings. As Mrs Malette was a French speaking Canadian the card was written in French; on translation it read:

"NO BLOOD TRANSFUSION!

As one of Jehovah's Witnesses with firm religious convictions, I request that no blood or blood products be administered to me under any circumstances. I fully realise the implications of this position, but I have resolutely decided to obey the Bible command: 'Keep abstaining . . . from blood'. (Acts 15:28, 29). However, I have no religious objection to the use of nonblood alternatives, such as Dextran, Haemaccel, PVP, Ringer's Lactate or saline solution".

Dr Shulman was informed of the contents of the card. A surgeon had also examined Mrs Shulman and both doctors had formed the opinion that her blood volume must be maintained to avoid irreversible shock. While undergoing further diagnostic tests the patient's condition deteriorated and Dr Shulman personally administered the transfusions of blood he regarded as necessary to preserve her life. He was fully aware of the card and its contents, but was not entirely satisfied that the opinions expressed represented Mrs Malette's steadfast opinion in this life threatening situation. The doctor took responsibility for disregarding the instructions on the card and later raised questions concerning its validity, in defence of his actions. Robins JA articulated these queries in the Ontario Court of Appeal:

"he did not know whether she might have changed her religious beliefs before the accident; whether the card may have been signed because of family or peer pressure; whether at the time she signed the card she was fully informed of the risks of refusal of blood transfusions; or whether, if conscious, she might have changed her mind in the face of medical advice as to her perhaps imminent but avoidable death".[101]

The concerns expressed by Dr Shulman are not dissimilar to those voiced in *Dorone, Werth* v. *Taylor* or indeed in *Re T* and *Re S*. However, Robins JA responded to them quite differently, arguing that,

---

[100] (1990) 67 DLR (4th) 321, [1991] 2 Med LR 162 (Ont CA).
[101] *Ibid*, per Robins JA.

"there was no reason not to regard this card as a valid advance directive. Its instructions were clear, precise and unequivocal, and manifested a calculated decision to reject a procedure offensive to the patient's religious convictions".[102]

Furthermore, he expressed the view that, because the opposition of Jehovah's Witnesses to blood transfusions is well known and the card carried by Mrs Malette explicitly referred to her understanding of the implications of such a refusal in all circumstances, the doctor could not defend his actions with the argument that he held a "reasonable belief that the patient would have consented had she been in a condition to do so". The fact that the situation was one of emergency was similarly dismissed:

"A doctor is not free to disregard a patient's advance instructions any more than he would be free to disregard instructions given at the time of the emergency. The law does not prohibit a patient from withholding consent to emergency medical treatment, nor does it prohibit a doctor from following his patient's instructions. While the law may disregard the absence of consent in limited emergency circumstances, it otherwise supports the right of competent adults to make decisions concerning their own health".[103]

Robins JA stated categorically that Dr Shulman's conduct in transfusing Mrs Malette despite the objections raised in her card was not authorised, even though she was unconscious and could not verify that the views described on the card were an expression of her firmly held beliefs. He described the doctors actions as contrary to the principles of individual autonomy and self-determination, "violating" the patient's right to control her own body and disrespectful of her religious beliefs. According to him, the very fact that Mrs Malette carried a card in anticipation of an emergency situation where she would be unable to communicate her wishes was evidence of her continuing commitment to the opinions stated on the card. The unconscious patient's stated opinions should have been respected by the clinical staff. In disregarding them Dr Shulman's action constituted a battery.

The facts of *Malette* v. *Shulman*, clearly demonstrate the tension that often exists between established, and well intentioned, medical practice, and the kind of provisions contained within advance directives. With the exception of those whose advance directives are designed to ensure that they obtain every possible medical advantage, people usually construct their advance directives because they wish to decline certain forms of treatment in certain situations. Often this will amount to a declaration that the individual concerned does not wish to be kept alive beyond what they consider to be dignified bounds. This of course, conflicts with the ethos that exists within the medical profession of using all available resources to save life.

Malette v. *Shulman* also illustrates the difficulties that exist within the BMA guidelines for the administration of advance directives. The level of scrutiny

---

[102] *Ibid.*
[103] (1990) 67 DLR (4th) 321, [1991] 2 Med LR 162 (Ont CA).

necessary to ascertain the validity and applicability of advance directives is outside the ordinary experience of most medical practitioners. Doctors do not routinely need to interrogate statements made by patients concerning their present or future health care. The absence of a legal doctrine of informed consent in Britain means that even decisions made by patients concerning their consent to medical intervention rarely require detailed scrutiny. Hence, practitioners may not possess the skills required to determine the validity of an advance directive, particularly where the presence or absence of legally defined concepts like duress and undue influence are concerned. To expect doctors to ascertain that patients have executed their advance directives of their own volition and free from external pressure is to encumber them with a burden which can only compound the pressures they bear in everyday clinical practice. Dr Shulman raised this issue with his concerns about whether Mrs Malette had signed her refusal of blood transfusion card because of family or peer pressure, and his concerns were overruled by the court. Further uncertainty is introduced by the requirement in the BMA guidelines that doctors must ensure that the wishes expressed are those of the patient, made freely and without undue influence. It is unclear whether the assessment should be made, and presumably recorded, at the time when the advance directive is executed or at the time when its provisions are put into effect. Clearly it will be virtually impossible for a doctor to ascertain whether an advance directive was made freely and in the absence of duress if, as is probable in an emergency setting, her first contact with the patient and the directive, occur simultaneously. This is the situation where living wills could perhaps most benefit patients and where they will in practice probably be of the least benefit.[104]

The BMA guidelines include the provision that if there is doubt as to a patient's intentions, treatment should be given according to a determination of her best interests. Any patient who is incapacitated upon presentation and is not known to the doctor concerned is likely therefore to be treated according to best interests criteria, whether or not there is an existing advance directive, particularly in an emergency situation. This may provide a safeguard for those doctors who can demonstrate genuine doubts as to the validity of a living will, or it may offer a clinician the opportunity to disregard a directive that does not correspond with her assessment of clinical need. The result may be that a properly executed directive fails to operate in the way its author intended because a clinician is uncertain about it's validity. However, a doctor who wrongly assesses the validity of an advance directive and disregards it, as did Dr Shulman, may not be authorised to treat the patient and may incur tortious or criminal liability as a consequence.

Perhaps perversely the BMA guidelines do not significantly improve the chances of a patient's living will being upheld by a clinician who is unfamiliar

---

[104] See D Morgan, "Odysseus and the Binding Directive: Only a Cautionary Tale?" (1994) 14 *Legal Studies* 411, at 423.

with the patient's medical and social history, such as when family doctors use deputising or co-operative systems to provide emergency services outside of normal surgery hours. The stipulation in the guidelines that GPs may be contacted by other health workers to verify the existence of a living will or clarify its terms, dictates that family doctors must devise mechanisms for identifying which patients have composed living wills. Also, because verbal statements may constitute valid advance directives, any statements made by a patient that may be considered an advance directive should be documented and similarly identifiable. Anecdotally, some general practitioners do make provision for these circumstances by ensuring that their deputising or co-operative administrators are aware of all of their patients who have living wills and the contents of those wills, but this appears to be an uncommon practice, calling into question how effective advance directives are in practice.

A patient's expectation is that if she has gone to the lengths necessary to formulate and record an advance directive then the provisions contained within it will be acted upon. Yet, despite the Law Commission's recommendation that no liability should flow where a doctor withholds treatment according to the provisions of an advance directive believed to apply in the circumstances,[105] doctors will be reluctant to act upon an advance directive whose validity they cannot verify because they do not personally know the patient, particularly in circumstances which might lead to death. Imagine the hypothetical situation where a patient arrives in an emergency room unconscious but in a treatable condition. The accompanying family members insist that the living will they have with them, which decrees that no treatment should be administered, is observed, and that the patient be allowed to die. Is the attending clinician going to examine the document to ascertain its authenticity and validity while the patient's condition deteriorates, or is she, like the para-medics referred to earlier, going to treat the patient according to best interests criteria and ask questions later?

CONCLUSIONS

In Britain the Law Commission, the BMA and the common law, all now support the principle of patients being enabled to make advance declarations and decisions about the medical treatment they will receive if they become incapacitated. The Law Commission has recommended that advance refusals of care should be presumed to have been validly made, if they are "in writing, signed and witnessed" and there is "no indication to the contrary",[106] and these views are reiterated in the BMA Code of Practice relating to advance statements about

---

[105] Law Commission Report 231, Mental Incapacity, *Item 9 of the Fourth Programme of Law Reform: Mentally Incapacitated Adults* (London, HMSO, 1995) Draft bill, clause 9(4).

[106] Law Commission Report 231, Mental Incapacity, *Item 9 of the Fourth Programme of Law Reform: Mentally Incapacitated Adults* (London, HMSO, 1995) Draft Bill clause 9(5).

medical care. However, the BMA guidelines associated with the Code of Practice, and the common law interpretation of the issues involved in cases concerning refusal of treatment in life threatening circumstances, suggest that, to paraphrase Sally Sheldon, the effectiveness of a living will is subject to the discretion of the doctors and courts involved.[107]

In America and Canada, where there is a significant body of legislation protecting the right to make an advance directive, a number of cases have arisen concerning the application of the provisions contained within living wills, most revolving around the issue of the administration of treatment in the absence of consent.[108] However, the Voluntary Euthanasia Society reports that more recently, civil cases concerning "wrongful life" have been brought by patients who did not wish to be resuscitated or treated. Edward Winter brought such a case after he was resuscitated by a nurse following a heart attack. Prior to this he had witnessed the lingering death of his wife and expressed his wish that if ever he should need to be resuscitated no action should be taken because he wished to be allowed to die. He was left in a severely debilitated condition and later sued the hospital for actions he believed had deprived him of the ability to die with dignity.[109]

Experience, and the cases referred to in this chapter, demonstrate that anticipatory decisions made by patients about their future medical care have often been overruled or disregarded. Similarly, treatment decisions declining consent in circumstances where non-treatment is likely to result in death are less readily complied with than those consenting to intervention. As Derek Morgan suggests, considering the nature of the doctor/patient relationship and the responses of the courts to it, the assessment of advance directives by doctors and the courts cannot be regarded as "value-neutral".[110] Living wills should be valuable in enhancing individual autonomy in the context of medical care. They could also be useful as a means of protecting doctors from litigation in circumstances where treatment is withdrawn. But how effective they can be in promoting death with dignity by "protecting patients from the final sting, the broken promise which leaves them powerless to control their last days",[111] remains uncertain.

---

[107] S Sheldon, "Subject Only to the Attitude of the Surgeon Concerned: The Judicial Protection of Medical Discretion" (1996) 5 (1) *Social and Legal Studies* 95, which suggests that in many clinical situations, perhaps most notably those concerning women's reproductive rights, medical paternalism appears to remain unfettered and is frequently upheld by the courts.

[108] *In Re Estate of Dorone* 517 pa 3, 543 A 2d 452 (1987), *Werth* v. *Taylor* (1991) 474 NW 2d 426 (Michigan CA), *Malette* v. *Shulman* (1990) 67 DLR (4th) 321, [1991] 2 Med LR 162 (Ont CA).

[109] Voluntary Euthanasia Society, *Your Ultimate Choice: The Right to Die with Dignity*, (London, Souvenir Press, 1992) at 16. Of course it must be remembered that this incident occurred in a jurisdiction where costly health care must be privately funded.

[110] D Morgan, "Odysseus and the Binding Directive: Only a Cautionary Tale?" (1994) 14 *Legal Studies* 411, at 423.

[111] J Montgomery, "Power Over Death: The Final Sting" in R Lee, D Morgan (eds.) *Death Rites: Law and Ethics at the End of Life* (London, Routledge, 1996) 37–53, at 37.

6

Is Euthanasia a Dignified Death?

"I have had a good life and I would dearly like a good death . . . my last wish is to die with dignity".[1]

INTRODUCTION—WHY DIGNITY?

Previous chapters have considered medically assisted dying and the preservation of autonomy at the end of life through treatment refusal and living wills. In order to further scrutinise the close association between autonomy and dignity at the end of life this chapter will assess whether dignity in dying can indeed be achieved through these mechanisms. Can dignity ever be attained by curtailing treatment or by medical interventions that hasten death, or is the whole process of dying despite the best efforts of modern medicine so inherently undignified that no action can possibly succeed in providing dignity?

Respect for human dignity has been described as "the most important feature of Western political culture".[2] Respect for human dignity means respecting the intrinsic value of human life and as such it underpins the high regard for individual autonomy that is pivotal to the perceived quality of a person's life. At the end of life this dictates that dying should be attended by a degree of dignity that reflects the quality of the life lived until that time. Hence the ability to govern one's own conduct according to self-formulated rules and values should be upheld and personal choices endorsed, enabling people to control their own destinies.

Modern medicine has developed the ability to maintain life in the face of intractable illness, often at the cost of prolonging the dying process and

"sophisticated new medical and psychotherapeutic technology can constitute a threat to the physical and intellectual integrity of the individual, minimising the degree of control and choice he has over his own life".[3]

Science and nature then become rivals in a contest where death represents the ultimate medical failure and:

---

[1] C Taylor-Watson in Margarette Driscoll "After a Good Life, Why Can't we Choose a Good Death?" *The Sunday Times* Jan 15 1995.
[2] R Dworkin, *Life's Dominion: An Argument about Abortion and Euthanasia* (London, Harper-Collins, 1993) at 166.
[3] L Sampaio, "To Die with Dignity", (1992) 35 (4) *Social Science and Medicine* 433–42, at 433.

"the quality of life remaining to many terminally ill people has been tragically compromised by an ideology driven by the medical technical imperative to treat, . . . where
curative medicine is prioritised at the expense of individuals".[4]

For a person seeking death with dignity, overriding autonomy by insisting on
utilising every available therapy is inherently destructive of human dignity and
can compromise her quality of life.

When medical technology intervenes to prolong dying like this it does not do
so unobtrusively. It does so with needles, tubes, pain and discomfort, accompanied by the bright lights, noise, odours and loss of privacy associated with
institutional caring. In this environment death represents, "the ultimate form of
consumer resistance, (where) natural death is that point at which the human
organism refuses any further input of treatment".[5] By contrast, the opportunity
to die unencumbered by the intrusion of medical technology and before experiencing loss of independence and control, appears to many to extend the promise
of a dignified death. As a result, euthanasia and death with dignity have become
inextricably linked.

Concerns about excessive treatment have generated much of the debate about
and support for euthanasia. Fuelled by the increasing longevity of the population and the further development of medical expertise, the euthanasia debate is
therefore gaining momentum and proponents of voluntary euthanasia argue
that by taking control when death is inevitable and avoiding the futile excesses
offered by medicine, greater dignity can be achieved.

NEEDING DIGNITY

Death and dying are elements of life over which human beings can exert only
limited control. Death itself is not an experience that can be recounted or shared
with others, but dying is an observable phenomenon whose contemplation
shapes peoples' perceptions of their own lives and their expectations for their
own demise. "Fear of dying, fear of the possible mode of dying, fear of death
itself are part of the human condition"[6] and the combining of these fears with
new anxieties about the excesses of inappropriate medical care has fostered the
convergence of euthanasia and death with dignity that is now well established
in Western culture. Furthermore, it has been acknowledged that individual
choice and self-determination are central to this debate.[7] Surveys of patients'
attitudes to terminal care in various jurisdictions suggest that the possibility of

---

[4] B McNamara, et al, "The Institutionalisation of the good Death" (1994) 39 11 *Social Science
and Medicine* 1501–8, at 1505.

[5] I Illich, *Medical Nemesis: The Exploration of Health* (Delhi, Rupa, 1975) at 149.

[6] J Sanders, "Medical Futility: CPR", in R Lee & D Morgan, *Death Rites: Law and Ethics at the
End of Life* (London, Routledge, 1994) 72–90 at 77.

[7] M Kelner, I Bourgeault, "Patient Control Over Dying: Responses of Health Care Professionals"
(1993) 36 *Social Science and Medicine* 757–765.

choosing an alternative to becoming dependent upon medical carers and burdensome to family is fundamental to dignity in this context.[8] A similar view is expressed by Angell in her moving account of how, in the pursuit of a dignified death, her father shot himself the night before he was to be admitted to hospital for treatment for prostate cancer.[9]

Evidence of these attitudes has been clearly demonstrated in Holland where, prior to recent legislative changes, euthanasia was regarded as legally permissible subject to established procedural guidelines,[10] and was practised openly. In 1990, as part of its preparation for further discussions about the legalisation of euthanasia, the Dutch Government sought a national review of "Euthanasia and Other Decisions Concerning the End of Life" and commissioned the Remmelink study.[11] Three distinct areas of study were undertaken. Firstly, detailed interviews were conducted with 405 physicians; secondly, questionnaires were sent to the doctors of a sample 7,000 deceased persons, and thirdly, the 405 doctors interviewed provided information about the 2,250 deaths that had occurred in their collective practices in the six months following the interviews.

Three types of medical decision at the end of life (MDEL) were considered: non-treatment decisions, the administration of high doses of opioids to relieve pain and control symptoms and active euthanasia. The results showed that MDEL had been taken in 38 per cent of all deaths and in 54 per cent of non-acute deaths. Life was shortened by the use of high doses of opiates in 17.5 per cent of all deaths and by non-treatment in a further 17.5 per cent. Euthanasia by the administration of a lethal dose of medication at the request of the patient was estimated to occur in 1.8 per cent of all deaths annually.[12]

The participants in the study were questioned about the reasons patients gave for requesting euthanasia. Their responses showed that 57 per cent of patients, the largest proportion, mentioned loss of dignity, 46 per cent mentioned pain, 46 per cent were concerned about unworthy dying, 33 per cent wanted to avoid being dependent on others, and 23 per cent mentioned tiredness of life. In less than 5 per cent of the cases pain was given as the primary reason for requesting euthanasia. A similarly constructed study reported in the *British Medical*

---

[8] See for example, P J Van Der Mass, J J M Van Delden, L Pijnenborg, and C W N Looman, "Euthanasia and Other Medical Decisions Concerning the end of Life" (1991) 338 *The Lancet* 669, C Seale and J Addington-Hall, "Euthanasia: Why People Want to Die Earlier" (1994) 39 *Social Science and Medicine* 647–54, and, R Hunt, I Maddocks, D Roach, A McLeod, "The Incidence of Requests for a Quicker Terminal Course" (1995) 9 (2) *Palliative Medicine* 167–8.

[9] M Angell, "The Supreme Court and Physician-Assisted Suicide—the Ultimate Right, (1997) 336, *New England Journal Of Medicine* 50–3.

[10] J Griffiths, "The Regulation of Euthanasia and Related Medical Procedures that Shorten Life in the Netherlands" (1994) 1 *Medical Law International* 137–58, at 143.

[11] P J Van Der Mass, J J M Van Delden, L Pijnenborg, and C WN Looman, "Euthanasia and Other Medical Decisions Concerning the end of Life" (1991) 338 *The Lancet* 669.

[12] R Fenigsen, "The Case Against Dutch Euthanasia" (1989) *Hastings Centre Report*, Special Supplement 22–30, claims that the incidence of active euthanasia in Dutch AIDS patients is 11.2%, suggesting that the incidence of active euthanasia is variable according to the disease group.

Journal in October 2000,[13] demonstrated strikingly similar statistics, with 56 per cent of patients whose request for euthanasia was granted siting "avoiding loss of dignity" as a main reason for seeking death. In both studies retaining dignity and control was considered more important than relief from terminal pain as a reason for requesting euthanasia, illustrating the close link between euthanasia and dignity in the minds of patients.

Similar findings were also recorded in a survey of 3,696 people in 20 health authorities in England.[14] The participants were questioned about relatives and friends who had recently died, of whom 3.6 per cent were shown to have requested euthanasia at some time during their final year of life. As in the Dutch samples, a dread of dependency and the indignity associated with it was more prominent than fear of pain amongst this group. Preserving dignity through the avoidance of dependency and the maintenance of autonomy, was of greater significance to those surveyed than was relief from pain. Indeed there was an expectation that pain could be controlled, but that some of the methods of pain relief could themselves lead to indignity. For these people euthanasia represented an attractive alternative to conventional medical therapy, suggesting that perhaps the issue of dependence and indignity needs to be more fully appreciated and catered for than at present. Wider issues than the purely medical, including the social and economic, also need to be addressed. To this end, Seale and Addington-Hall comment:

> "if good care is to obviate the desire to die sooner, it needs to address the problem of dependency as well as to provide the symptom control in which hospice practitioners have developed such impressive expertise".[15]

In the post war period patients have become consumers of health care services who demand to be recognised by medical professionals as people first and patients second.[16] Today many patients insist on more than just a right to health care in general, they seek a right to choose specific types of treatment. They want to be able to retain control throughout the entire span of their lives and to exercise autonomy in all medical decisions concerning their welfare and treatment. A survey of members of the Voluntary Euthanasia Society substantiates evidence of the trend in that the reason most often given for joining was "to be

[13] I Haverkate, B D Onwuteaka-Philipsen, A Van Der Heide, P J Kostensa, G Van Der Wal, P J Van Der Mass, "Refused and Granted Requests for Euthanasia and Assisted Suicide in the Netherlands", (2000) 321 *British Medical Journal* 865–6.

[14] C Seale & J Addington-Hall, "Euthanasia: Why People Want to Die Earlier" (1994) 39 *Social Science and Medicine* 647–54.

[15] *Ibid.*

[16] Arguments about emerging consumerism in health care have been rehearsed over many years. Some examples include, W Arney, B Bergen, ""The Anomaly, the Chronic Patient and the Play of Medical Power" (1983) 5 *Sociology of Health and Illness* 12. L Darvall, *Medicine, Law and Social Change* (Aldershot, Dartmouth, 1993), Lord Irvine of Lairg, "The Patient, the Doctor, Their Lawyers and the Judge: Rights and Duties" (1999) 7 *Medical Law Review* 255–268.

able to control myself in the circumstances of my own death".[17] The concepts of autonomy, self-determination and control at the end of life are therefore, key factors in conflating euthanasia and dignity, but the concept of dignity itself remains esoteric and difficult to define.

FINDING DIGNITY

The Oxford English Dictionary defines dignity as, "true worth, excellence, high estate or estimation, honourable office, rank or title; elevation of manner, proper stateliness", so that to dignify is to, "make worthy; confer dignity upon, ennoble". "Dignity commands emphatic respect".[18] In the context of dying, the word dignity engenders a sense of serenity and powerfulness, fortified by "qualities of composure, calmness, restraint, reserve, and emotions or passions subdued and securely controlled without being negated or dissolved".[19] This being so, a person possessed of dignity at the end of life, might induce in an observer a sense of tranquillity and admiration which inspires images of power and self-assertion through restraint and poised composure.

Though dignity is firmly identified in modern bio-ethics, it is not a concept that is presently recognised by the law. It has however been alluded to in cases concerning medical decisions at the end of life. For example, in *Airedale NHS Trust v. Bland*[20] Lord Goff stated that, ". . . account should be taken of the indignity to which . . . a person has to be subjected if his life is to be prolonged by artificial means", and in *Re A (A Minor)*[21] Johnson J held that, ". . . it would be wholly contrary to the interests of that child . . . for his body to be subjected to what would . . . be the continuing indignity to which it is subject".[22] Dignity is also gaining currency through the language of human rights in other jurisdictions, and not always in respect of decisions at the end of life.

Signatories to the Council of Europe's Convention on Human Rights and Biomedicine resolve to "take such measures as are necessary to safeguard human dignity and the fundamental rights and freedoms of the individual with regard to the application of biology and medicine",[23] as do those to numerous other national and international treaties and conventions. In France the principle of

---

[17] See R Lam, "Who is Concerned about the Right to Die with Dignity? A Postal Survey of Exit Members" occasional paper (London, Institute for Social Studies in Medical Care, 1981).

[18] A Kolnai, "Dignity", in R S Dillon (ed.) *Dignity, Character, and Self-Respect* (London, Routledge, 1995) 53–75, at 55.

[19] A Kolnai, "Dignity", in R S Dillon (ed.) *Dignity, Character, and Self-Respect* (London, Routledge, 1995) 53–75, at 56.

[20] *Airedale NHS Trust v. Bland* [1993] 1 All ER 821.

[21] *Re A (A minor)* [1992] 3 Med L R 303.

[22] *Ibid* at 305.

[23] Council of Europe, *Convention for the Protection of Human Rights and Dignity of the Human Being with Regard to the Application of Biology and Medicine: Convention on Human Rights and Biomedicine* (DIR/JUR (96) 14) (Strasbourg, Directorate of Legal Affairs, November 1996).

safeguarding human dignity was recently identified within the preamble to the 1946 constitution, coming to light when the French Constitutional Council was reviewing proposed new laws on bio-ethics to ensure their conformity with the constitution. Since then the principle has been referred to in a number of cases concerning, for example, the constitutionality of legislation on housing and the morality of the bizarre practice of dwarf throwing.[24] Here, two mayors objected to dwarf throwing competitions being conducted in their localities, on the basis that the spectacle violated human dignity. Exactly how human dignity should be interpreted in these circumstances, and from whose perspective, fell to be determined. The *Conseil d'Etat* decided that both the dignity of the individual dwarf, who was being thrown, and that of those assembled to view the event were to be considered, and that dignity was compromised both collectively and individually. Dwarfs, including the participant, who regarded his own dignity as unblemished, were at risk due to the degrading nature of the process, which would devalue the social worth of dwarfs generally. The spectators were also likely to be debased by their association with the indignities imposed during the show. Thus it was that this extraordinary case established human dignity as a valuable constitutional principle in French law, albeit without clearly defining its extent or application. The concept remains even less well defined in other jurisdictions.

In America numerous Acts and proposals for legislative reform permitting assisted dying have included "dignity" in their titles.[25] The 1991 Natural Death Act of California refers specifically to the, "recognition of the dignity and privacy that a person has a right to expect", in its endorsement of a person's right to "make a written declaration instructing his or her physician to withhold or withdraw life-sustaining treatment . . . in the event that the person is unable to make those decisions".[26] The Act does not condone mercy killing or assisted suicide, but it does acknowledge that a person's dignity may be preserved through the availability of the choice to decline treatment, even if the exercise of that choice results in death. It makes no attempt to define dignity in this context.

The concept of human dignity was also central to the case of *Rodriguez* v. *Attorney General of Canada and Others*,[27] mentioned in chapter four, where the plaintiff argued that her constitutional right to basic human dignity was nullified by section 241 (b) of the Canadian Criminal Code. Sue Rodriguez was forty-two years old and suffering from motor neurone disease.[28] She had requested the assistance of a doctor to commit suicide because her physical condition prevented her from acting alone, but was denied help because aiding and abetting suicide is contrary to section 241(b) of the Canadian Criminal Code.

---

[24] S Millns, "Dwarf-Throwing and Human Dignity: A French Perspective" (1996) 18 (3) *Journal of Social, Welfare and Family Law* 375–80.

[25] Examples include: in California, the Death with Dignity Act 1992 and the Humane and Dignified Death Act 1988, in New Hampshire, the Act Relative to Death with Dignity for Certain Persons Suffering Terminal Illness 1992, and in Oregon, the Death with Dignity Act 1994.

[26] Natural Death Act California, 1991, 7185.5, Legislative Findings and Declaration (d).

[27] *Rodriquez* v. *A-G British Columbia* (1993) 107 DLR (4th) 342, [1993] 7 WWR 641.

[28] Also known as amyotrophic lateral sclerosis or ALS.

She therefore applied for an order declaring section 241(b) invalid, on the grounds that it violated her rights under sections 7,12, and 15(1) of the Canadian Charter of Rights and Freedoms.

The Court of British Columbia dismissed her application, as did the Court of Appeal of British Columbia. She appealed to the Supreme Court of Canada. The thrust of her argument was that section 7 of the Canadian Charter of Rights and Freedoms, which refers to "security of the person" encompasses autonomy as well as "control over one's physical and psychological integrity", and that these principles are essential to dignity. This was said to be pivotal to her case since she was seeking a right to die with dignity. The dissenting judgments of L'Heureux-Dube and McLachin agreed as to the significance of dignity in dying, while Cory J declared that

> "it follows that the right to die with dignity should be as well protected as is any other aspect of the right to life. State prohibitions that would force a dreadful, painful death on a rational but incapacitated terminally ill patient are an affront to human dignity".[29]

However, the five to four majority opinion accepted that while section 241(b) did impinge on the security of her person as defined in section 7, and thereby encroached upon her dignity, this was not contrary to the principles of fundamental justice under section 7. It was argued that the state has an interest in the protection of life and the avoidance of any devaluation of human life which might result from permitting lives to be deliberately terminated. As a means of protecting vulnerable individuals from potential abuse the measures in section 241 (b) were not unfair or arbitrary. Hence the correlation between dignity and the ability to make choices concerning the time and manner of one's own death was recognised but ultimately not endorsed by the court. The decision rested on the need of the state to protect the interests of those who may suffer abuse if euthanasia were legally permitted. As in the French dwarf throwing case, individual rights were insufficient to overrule fundamental collective interests. A wider public interest existed and was prioritised.

The dichotomy between dignified and undignified dying was central to the argument in *Rodriguez*, but the ability of euthanasia to provide a dignified death, though endorsed in the dissenting judgments, was not scrutinised. The definition and application of dignity remains ambiguous in the context of death and dying as elsewhere. Paradoxically therefore, opponents of euthanasia also speak of the centrality of dignity in dying but contend that there are alternative, more dignified, methods of achieving the same goal.

ACHIEVING DIGNITY IN DYING

In much the same way that euthanasia is preferred by it supporters as an alternative to traditional western medicine at the end of life, so the *good death* ideal

---

[29] (1993) 107 DLR (4th) 342 at 413.

is revered by many ancient and eastern religions. Buddhism, Jainism, and Hinduism, in particular, embrace the concept of the *good death* as a means of achieving dignity and spiritual fulfilment at the end of life without resorting to artificially shortening its span. The modern hospice movement, founded in Britain, espouses a similar philosophy which emanates from a rather different environment. Our understanding of the concept of the good death, as it relates to euthanasia, may be usefully informed by considering these specific examples.

The Good Death in Ancient Eastern Religions

Buddhism, Jainism and Hinduism are indicative of some of the many ancient eastern cultural and religious philosophies that inform alternative approaches to death, dying and euthanasia. Contemporary Buddhists have extensively questioned whether euthanasia has a role to play within Buddhist philosophy.[30] As a result it is suggested that

"there is much more to Buddhist thinking on euthanasia than a purely pragmatic concern to keep the First Precept—not to take life—while practising the virtue of compassion".[31]

It has, for example, been argued that in Buddhism "volition constitutes a man's essential *beingness*" which implies that the intrinsic value of human life lies in the capacity for conscious choice. So, at least in principle, the Buddhist should be in favour of "*voluntary* euthanasia, provided it applied within narrowly defined limits".[32]

In opposition, the doctrine of *karma* asserts that positive acts and thoughts bring good *karma* while the opposite is true for evil or negative thinking and conduct. These goods and evils are carried over into subsequent lives. Taking this into account, Phillip Lecso argues that

"if the complete evolution of a karmic debt were to be disrupted by an active intervention on the part of a physician, it would then need to be faced again in another existence".[33]

Accordingly, he favours the hospice model for coping with the needs of the terminally ill because it appears to allow calm and controlled dying without active intervention.

---

[30] See for example, M Barnes, "Euthanasia: Buddhist Principles" (1996) 52 (2) *British Medical Bulletin* 369–75, P A Lecso, "Euthanasia: a Buddhist Perspective" (1986) 25 *Journal of Religion and Health* 51–7, Louis Van Loon, "A Buddhist Viewpoint", in G C Oosthuizen, H A Shapiro, S A Strauss (eds.) *Euthanasia* (1978) 65 Human Sciences Research Publication (Cape Town, Oxford University Press, 1978) at 73–79.

[31] M Barnes, "Euthanasia: Buddhist Principles" (1996) 52 (2) *British Medical Bulletin* 369–75, at 369.

[32] Louis Van Loon, "A Buddhist Viewpoint", in G C Oosthuizen, H A Shapiro, S A Strauss (eds.) *Euthanasia* (1978) 65 Human Sciences Research Publication (Cape Town, Oxford University Press, 1978) at 73–79.

[33] P A Lecso, "Euthanasia: a Buddhist Perspective" (1986) 25 *Journal of Religion and Health* 51–7.

Yet Barnes regards both of these conclusions as problematic for other Buddhists; the first because it, "is only doubtfully Buddhist in its account of the human person" while the second, Lecso's analysis, "begs the question by failing to acknowledge that *any* treatment will have karmic consequences".[34] The implication here is that, whether or not medical intervention results directly in death it will influence the manner and possibly the time of dying and will therefore disrupt the *karmic* cycle. The diversity of these opinions demonstrates the absence of an established Buddhist position on euthanasia, which some commentators regard as entirely appropriate.[35]

Jainism similarly emphasises the autonomy of the moral subject and reveres a practice called *ahimsa* which extends the notion of non-violence to include positively wishing well to all beings. Jainism also acclaims the custom known as *sallekhana*: the ultimate act of heroism. *Sallekhana* involves fasting to the death in a manner which is reminiscent of religious martyrdom or suicide. The process takes the form of personal penance which is believed to purge the body of all pernicious, detrimental and negative factors as the moment of death approaches. It is not, however, considered to be a form of euthanasia or suicide because it is constrained and legitimated by religion. Instead the practice of *sallekhana* is described as a kind of "self-willed death" that better resembles a religious sacrifice.[36]

While similar to Jainism in many respects, Buddhism forbids the taking of ones own life in any fashion. The distinction seems to be that the Jains believe people are shaped by their history so that the *karmic* process is ongoing and the causes of *karma* can be identified and eliminated. By comparison, for Buddhists *karma* can never be destroyed. A person's volition or intention determines the moral status of her act such that, "the moral quality of the act is to be determined by the interior state of the individual".[37] Actions motivated by greed or hatred for example will always be immoral and the opposite will apply for pure actions and deeds. Buddhists believe that human existence is rare and rebirth as a human is rarer still. Consequently it is best approached cautiously without attempting to exert control over the dying process. At the point of dying, a Buddhist should ideally be conscious, rational and alert, prompting the Dalai Lama to comment, that,

"from a Buddhist point of view, if a dying person has any chance of having positive virtuous thoughts, it is important—and there is a purpose—for them to live even just a few minutes longer".[38]

---

[34] M Barnes, "Euthanasia: Buddhist Principles" (1996) 52 (2) *British Medical Bulletin* 369–75, at 369.

[35] See A Sumedho, cited in M Barnes, "Euthanasia: Buddhist Principles" (1996) 52 (2) *British Medical Bulletin* 369–75, at 370, n.4.

[36] P Dundas, *The Jains* (London, Routledge, 1992) at 155.

[37] M Barnes, "Euthanasia: Buddhist Principles" (1996) 52 (2) *British Medical Bulletin* 369–75, at 372.

[38] In P Anderson, "Good Death: Mercy, Deliverance and the Nature of Suffering" (1992) *Tricycle, The Buddhist Review* 36–42.

It is crucial for Buddhists to prepare for the moment of death because the quality of that moment will dictate the prestige of the new birth. Thus,

> "whichever of the two kinds of karma dominates at the time of death determines one's next life . . . by forgetting or ignoring death one is unworthy of human existence, thinking only of the pleasures of this life. Lack of death awareness affects one's way of life and leads to regret at the time of death".[39]

Within this framework, Keown's statement, that "any affirmation of death or choice in favour of death is a rejection of the vision of human good"[40] clearly explains why the self-willed death revered by the Jains appears to Buddhists as a kind of escapism which cannot succeed because the *karma* will have to be relived.

Traditional Hindu religious culture is informed by both the Jain and the Buddhist religions and also emphasises the *good death* as a reflection of the quality of the life that preceded it. If a good, dignified death is attained, it is perceived as evidence of having lived a worthy life because "the manner of one's passing out-weighs all previous claims and intimations of one's moral worth".[41] In much the same way that exponents of voluntary euthanasia advocate that the manner of dying should reflect the inherent quality of the life lived, both ancient and contemporary Hindu religious philosophers acknowledge death as an ordinary occurrence which is of extraordinary significance in that "a good death certifies a good life".[42]

But a *good death* does not automatically happen. It is a goal to be accomplished, one which must be striven for and attained. The *good death* is achieved when death occurs in full consciousness, in a chosen place and at a chosen time. In ideal circumstances the chosen location will be the home, or alternatively a holy place. As with Buddhism great significance is attached to the element of choice and the maintenance of control,[43] so if at all possible, "one must be in command and should not be overtaken by death. To be so overtaken is the loss of dignity".[44] Thus the final moments of life should be calm, easy and peaceful if dignity is to be preserved. A sharp contrast to the kind of institutional death which many in the West would seek to avoid through euthanasia, and many more expect and fear.

Many of the insights of these traditional religions are echoed in the modern Western understanding of euthanasia, as a means of achieving death with dignity, which focuses on avoiding dependence and loss of control. Choosing to deliberately end one's life allows control over the time, place and method of

[39] Geshe Ngawang Dhargyey, *Tibetan Tradition of Mental Development* (Dharamsala, Library of Tibetan Works and Archives, 1974) at 54–5.

[40] D Keown, *Buddhism and Bioethics* (London, Macmillan, 1995) at 187.

[41] T N Madan, "Dying with Dignity" (1992) 35 (4) *Social Science and Medicine* 425–32.

[42] T N Madan, "Living and Dying" in *Non-Renunciation: Themes and Interpretations of the Hindu Culture* (New Delhi, Oxford University Press, 1987).

[43] J Parry, *Death and the Regeneration of Life* (Cambridge, Cambridge University Press, 1982).

[44] T N Madan, "Dying with Dignity" (1992) 35 (4) *Social Science and Medicine* 425–32.

one's dying and explains why euthanasia appears to offer death with dignity. Rather than active euthanasia these ancient religions advocate calm, control and compassion as a means of achieving dignity. Those who favour good palliative care in British hospices espouse very similar convictions.

The Hospice Movement

The network of hospices was established by Dame Cicely Saunders in 1967 after an inspiring encounter with a terminally ill cancer patient. The patient shared Cicely Saunders' vision of a caring environment for the dying and left £500 in his will so that she could begin fund-raising to transform the vision into a reality. There are now in excess of 200 hospices around the country, approximately 20 of which are dedicated to the care of children.

The hospice philosophy aims to provide a holistic approach to terminal care in response to the depersonalisation of traditional medical techniques. They treat total pain with total care in order to overcome the physical and psychological trauma of terminal and incurable disease. Dying patients, and their families are treated as individuals whose particular needs are related to their terminal condition rather than simply as the recipients of symptomatic therapy. A positive attitude to the dying process is encouraged. Cicely Saunders explains it thus:

> "To talk of accepting death when its approach has become inevitable is not mere resignation or feeble submission on the part of the patient, nor is it defeatism or neglect on the part of the doctor. For both of them it is the very opposite of doing nothing. Our work . . . is to alter the character of this inevitable process so that it is not seen as a defeat of living but as a positive achievement in dying; an intensely individual achievement for the patient".[45]

The development of the specialism of palliative medicine is directly attributable to the hospice movement[46] and hospices continue to carry out extensive research in the field of palliative care and the relief of pain. Advocates of the hospice ideal are vociferous in their defence of good palliative care for relief of the pain and distress associated with terminal illness. Such therapy is invaluable in assuaging distressing symptoms and is strongly defended as a means of achieving a *good death*, and as an alternative to euthanasia. The comments of Dr Thomas Nicholson-Lailey, following his participation in a survey of general practitioners on the subject of terminal care and euthanasia, demonstrate the success of the hospice model, "the priority should always be to provide palliative care of the highest

---

[45] Ciceley Saunders in S du Boulay, *Ciceley Saunders* (London, Hodder & Stoughton, 1994) at 174.

[46] N James, "From Vision to System: the Maturing of the Hospice Movement", in R Lee, D Morgan (eds.), *Death Rites: Law and Ethics at the End of Life* (London, Routledge, 1994) 102–130 at 125.

quality rather than legalise euthanasia".[47] Nevertheless the availability of good palliative care does not necessarily eliminate the appeal of euthanasia for the terminally ill.

Until recently in Britain hospices have been run on a voluntary basis with minimal Governmental financial support. Even now, when they receive around 40,000 new patients a year and support approximately 56,000 in patient admissions, approximately 95 per cent of their funding is received from charitable donations and voluntary organisations. They offer terminal and respite care to those suffering from cancer, motor neurone disease and recently AIDS but hospice care is not universally available to terminally ill and incurable patients. People dying from a range of commonplace diseases like, multiple sclerosis and chronic heart or lung disease have until very recently not been eligible. Moreover, the availability of hospice places is constrained geographically because not all eligible patients reside in the immediate vicinity of a hospice. The provision of hospice care may offer death with dignity to its recipients, but its limited availability means that it is unable to negate the need for euthanasia felt by many people suffering from terminal and incurable illness. And, even if a perfect service existed there would still be those who would prefer to opt for a quick, or immediate death, rather than palliation of symptoms.[48]

Furthermore, the nature of the hospice movement is changing as it is incorporated into mainstream medical services. The need for accountability and standardisation of care and services that has accompanied the growth of consumerism within health care and society in general has inevitably brought changes. Initially, not only were hospices funded entirely by the voluntary sector through charities and donations, but their staff were employed independently of the National Health Service. Now, in order to provide the increasingly formalised network of terminal care, "the initial hand-to-mouth financing of hospices has had to become more systematic".[49] Nicky James considers the implications of these changes at length,

> "With growing professionalism comes careerism and professional development. Inevitable though these may be, they bring about a change in emphasis. The early hospice pioneers who believed in the importance of their mission took it up without any assurances for their futures. These pioneers are being, and will be replaced by those who, albeit committed to their specialist discipline, work in a now established specialism and look for peer credibility and recognition in pay, status research and career prospects. Traditionally the biomedical system emphasises the physical. Hospice services which initially strived for a balance of 'total care' may observe the primacy of physical interventions re-emerge".[50]

---

[47] J Coulson, "G. P.s Oppose Mercy Killing for the Dying" *BMA News Review* March 8 1994, at 24.

[48] B Farsides, "Palliative Care—a Euthanasia Free Zone?" (1998) 24 *Journal of Medical Ethics* 149–50 at 150.

[49] N James, "From Vision to System: the Maturing of the Hospice Movement", in R Lee, D Morgan, *Death Rites: Law and Ethics at the End of Life* (London, Routledge, 1994) 102–130 , at 117.

[50] *Ibid*, at 123.

Research therefore indicates that the *good death* ideals of the hospice movement are beginning to be subverted by its institutionalisation and the consequent encroachment of mainstream medicine.[51] Similar concerns have long been expressed about the hospice movement in North America.[52] The infiltration of hospice care by medical technology emphasising treatment and cure may result in failure to achieve the *good death* that those who advocate palliative care as an alternative to euthanasia seek. The methods employed by conventional medicine to give symptomatic control of pain usually involve sedation, and require a level of compliance which necessarily negates the patient's control and choice. The intrusion of medical technology into terminal care is precisely what those pursuing death with dignity wish to escape and explains why some consider euthanasia to be an appropriate alternative. Bobbie Farsides has expressed concerns about the potential impact of portraying hospice palliative care as an alternative that is vehemently opposed to euthanasia.[53] For her, even though euthanasia is not yet a legal alternative, there is danger associated with marginalising present or potential patients who might favour euthanasia. Were euthanasia to become a legitimate option, it should ideally be available in an environment where palliative care options could be exhausted first, not as an alternative to good palliative treatment. The current hospice philosophy, which denies that there might be a place for euthanasia, appears to preclude such an option. Against this, and despite the close association between euthanasia and death with dignity, the hospice movement is presently applauded for providing dignity in dying without deliberately ending life, that is, as an alternative to euthanasia. So can euthanasia really deliver death with dignity?

DIGNIFYING DEATH

That dignity can be applied with equal effect on either side of the euthanasia debate demonstrates the fluidity of the concept and how nebulous it can be in application. Indeed, in another context, human dignity has been described as "comprehensively vague",[54] which may signal the fragility of dignity, and the limitations of relying on this concept to approve or refute arguments favouring euthanasia. However, in spite of its susceptibility to misinterpretation and sophistry, dignity clearly does play a valuable role in contextualising people's perceptions of death and dying, especially as it appears to embody a spirit of self-determination that advocates of voluntary euthanasia crave. But, whether or not euthanasia can provide a dignified death requires a multifaceted analysis

---

[51] N James, D Field, "The Routinisation of Hospice: Chrisma and Bureaucratisation", (1992) 34 *Social Science and Medicine* 1363–1371.

[52] E K Able, "The Hospice Movement: Institutionalising Innovation" (1986) 16 *International Journal of Health Services* 71.

[53] B Farsides, "Palliative Care—a Euthanasia Free Zone?" (1998) 24 *Journal of Medical Ethics* 149–50.

[54] J Harris, *Clones, Genes, and Immortality* (Oxford, Oxford University Press, 1998) at 31.

that depends largely on how euthanasia is performed in practice, both within present legal constraints and under any potential legal reforms.

Debates about the efficacy of euthanasia tend to regard the dignity of those who might die by euthanasia as of primary importance. Consequently, discourse that supports euthanasia as a means of achieving death with dignity is located within the dialogue of respect for individual autonomy, the need to provide alternatives to conventional modes of therapy and the desire to enable people to exercise choice in deciding when, where and how to die. Yet the debate is incomplete and inconclusive if this is the exclusive focus because the dignity of those who are, or might be, instrumental in performing euthanasia, and the wider implications for the dignity of society as a whole are of no less significance.

Evidently some communities, notably Buddhists, Hindus and Jains, and many within contemporary society, favour different methods of attaining dignity in dying and consider euthanasia an insult to human dignity. But, as the discussion of the hospice ideal demonstrates, these too may provide an inadequate response to the perceived need for dignity in dying. The societal failure to endorse euthanasia as a legitimate option may be regarded as destructive of human dignity for those who want it, but if it were permitted, preserving the dignity of some may be achieved only by compromising the dignity of others, most notably carers who perform euthanasia. To paraphrase Jinnet-Sack, emphasising euthanasia, which must be performed in the company of others, may fail to recognise the potential sacrifice of the dignity of the practitioner.[55] According to Sampaio, "to die with dignity should be a very private decision"[56] but, to die with dignity by euthanasia in the present legal environment, often involves not only privacy, but also complicity and subterfuge in order to avoid criminal liability.

The Voluntary Euthanasia Society graphically describes the effects of clandestine euthanasia, such that:

> "even when patients beg them for it—doctors tend to kill only when the dying are too far gone to consent. Thus, because voluntary euthanasia is taboo, a doctor makes the decision himself—and the patient is killed involuntarily in the night with a syringe. That is one price of keeping euthanasia secret".[57]

Others acknowledge that a conspiratorial duplicity often exists between doctor and patient because,

> "surveys suggest the practice of active euthanasia occurs covertly, most likely involving assertive patients who are able to convince the doctor to perform euthanasia in a private setting".[58]

---

[55] S Jinnet-Sack, "Autonomy in the Company of Others", in A Grubb (ed.) *Choices and Decisions in Health Care* (Chichester, Wiley, 1993) at 97.

[56] L Sampaio, "To Die with Dignity" (1992) 35 (4) *Social Science and Medicine* 433–441 at 434.

[57] The Voluntary Euthanasia Society, *Your Ultimate Choice: The Right to Die With Dignity* (London, Souvenir Press, 1992) at 106.

[58] R Hunt, "Approach of the GP to End-of-Life Decisions" (1997) *The RCGP Members' Reference Book 1997/8* 266, at 267.

For a person who seeks relief from the anguish of terminal or incurable disease active voluntary euthanasia may appear to be the most apposite means of achieving death with dignity. A decision to this effect may be rational, reasoned and appear entirely appropriate in the circumstances. Thus those caring for this patient are faced with a dilemma: how to respect the patients rational autonomous decision to die with dignity, without violating the law? Emotionally euthanasia might appear the best mechanism for achieving dignity in dying, and not only to the patient. Reason and emotion are both significant in treatment decisions, especially at the end of life where compassion is a natural response to appeals made on the basis of stifled self-determination. Where health care professionals are concerned Calman and Downie consider compassion to represent a collision of "imaginative insight" and empathy. Compassion is here distinguished from pity, which is regarded as "inappropriate to the dignity of the autonomous person, especially its overtones of paternalism",[59] because compassion is believed to provoke an active, and by implication positive, response.[60]

The case of Dr Nigel Cox[61] illustrates how this can occur in practice. Dr Cox cared for Lillian Boyes for thirteen years, he knew her and her family well. When she became desperately ill and repeatedly appealed to him to end her suffering, he empathised so completely with her that his compassionate reaction to her pleas took the form of direct action. He injected Mrs Boyes with strong potassium chloride, knowing that it had no therapeutic value, and intending to cause her death. Shortly afterwards she died. Her family believed that Dr Cox had provided her with a merciful release from the terrible pain and distress she was enduring and allowed her to die with dignity. However, Cox then suffered the indignity of a criminal prosecution which resulted in his professional integrity being questioned in court and by the General Medical Council.

A series of recent cases further illustrate the impact of the criminal justice system on the dignity of those who kill with compassion. They also raise the debate about the appropriateness of criminalising euthanasia.

Rachel Heath was a care worker who had witnessed the anguish of an elderly woman in her care. Kathleen Corfield, the seventy-one year old patient, had always been independent and lived alone until she became infirm and housebound because of lung cancer. Finding this existence too undignified Mrs Corfield tried unsuccessfully to starve herself to death and succeeded only in being hospitalised. Rachel Heath visited her in hospital and hastened her death by administering an overdose of diamorphine through her drip infusion. Heath was charged with attempted murder and was scheduled to appear for trial at Winchester Crown Court in March 1996. However, on the first day of the trial Ognall J requested that the Crown Prosecution Service reconsider the decision to

---

[59] R S Downie, K S Calman, *Healthy Respect: Ethics in Health Care* (Oxford, Oxford University Press, 1994) at 51–53.
[60] *Ibid.*
[61] *R v. Cox* (1992) 12 BMLR 38.

prosecute, after which no evidence was offered. The case was abandoned amidst comments from the judge that prosecution would not be in the public interest.[62]

In Scotland in October 1996 Paul Brady appeared before Glasgow High Court charged with the murder of his brother James. Brady had given his brother five times his usual dose of temazepam with alcohol and later smothered him with a pillow. James, who was dying from Huntingdon's disease, had pleaded for help to die on this and several previous occasions. The charge was later reduced to culpable homicide and Brady received a non-custodial sentence. Referring to the details of the case, Lord McFadyen is reported to have decided that "a custodial sentence would be neither appropriate nor necessary and would have the effect of adding to the considerable suffering already experienced by the family".[63] The family was later said to have found the criminal proceedings and media reporting of them, which exposed the details of the family's private life to the world, destructive of their dignity and the dignity of the memory of their brother.[64]

In 1999 Dr David Moore gained notoriety as a general practitioner who publicly claimed to have "helped a lot of people to die". He was tried for the murder of a Mr George Liddell, after it became known that the patient had died following a pain relieving injection of diamorphine. During the three week trial Dr Moore gave evidence that he had intended only "to relieve pain and suffering" and the jury took sixty-nine minutes to acquit him. Dr Moore, who claimed not to regret speaking out, took early retirement prior to the trial. One year later he died suddenly of a heart attack at the age of fifty-three, having suffered the breakdown of his marriage, alcohol problems and treatment for depression. Those who knew him professed that he seemed not to have fully recovered from the ordeal and indignity of the trial.[65]

While those who do find the courage to act suffer indignities associated with criminal and perhaps professional sanction, other carers may suffer the indignity of guilt, self-reproach, and remorse because they are unwilling or unable to perform the ultimate act of compassion. When a loved one or a respected patient professes to prefer the solace of euthanasia to enduring dependence, those who are unable to assist may suffer emotional turmoil which is destructive of their own dignity. Zoe Wanamaker has described being incapable of helping someone you care for to die as "being on an undignified, emotional and moral rack".[66] Jim Brady's sister reported similar feelings; "it was awful. He was crying and I was crying but I just could not do it. I used to try to fob him off and say, 'What if they find a cure?' "[67]

[62] See A Mollard, "Nurse Cleared of Mercy Killing", *The Daily Mail* 28 March 1996, 1, and "Euthanasia Charge Dropped", *The Guardian* 28 March 1996, 3.

[63] Cited in B Christie, "Man Walks Free in Scottish Euthanasia Case" (1996) 313 *BMJ* 961.

[64] See, H Mills, "The Courage to Kill", *The Guardian* 15 October 1996, 6–7, also, B Christie, "Man Walks Free in Scottish Euthanasia Case" (1996) 313 *BMJ* 961.

[65] N Smith, "GPs Face Ultimate Dilemma", (October 27 2000) *GP* 24.

[66] Z Wanamaker, *Woman's Hour* BBC Radio Four, 16 May 1995, and *The Long Goodbbye* BBC 2 TV, screened 17 May 1995.

[67] M Currie, in H Mills, "The Courage to Kill", *The Guardian* 15 October 1996, 6–7, at 6.

Euthanasia is seen by many as an immoral act which is an affront to the sanctity of life and humanity. The fact that it is also an illegal act prevents many professional and emotional carers from performing it even if they perceive it as a compassionate and otherwise appropriate response. Perhaps these turmoils and indignities might be avoided if voluntary medical euthanasia were permissible and regulated?

Passive euthanasia, whereby a patient dies as a result of selective non-treatment is, as we have seen, permitted in some circumstances, but that does not mean that death with dignity is necessarily forthcoming. Chapters three, four, and five, described the legal mechanisms designed to enable patients to endorse their autonomy by withholding consent to some or all forms of medical treatment, either contemporaneously or in advance through a living will. Hence, where a patient is competent and physically able to express a wish not to be treated she is, ". . . completely at liberty to decline to undergo treatment, even if the result of his doing so will be that he will die".[68] The Canadian cases of *McKay v. Bergstedt*,[69] and later, *B (Nancy) v. Hotel-Dieu de Quebec*[70] demonstrate this principle in practice.

Kenneth McKay was thirty one and had been a quadriplegic since he was injured in a swimming accident at the age of ten. He had been cared for by his devoted parents since the accident but his mother had died and at the time of the case his father was terminally ill. Kenneth requested that his artificial life support be withdrawn because he feared that his already poor quality of life would further deteriorate after his father died. He requested also that a sedative be administered when the ventilator was removed and that a court declare that his death was not from suicide but the result of his medical condition. Kenneth's right to die in this way was upheld.

Nancy B, was twenty-five years old and permanently paralysed from the neck down due to Guillain-Barre Syndrome. She was unable to even breath without mechanical life-support, and had been maintained by artificial respiration for two years when she petitioned the court to order her doctors to disconnect the ventilator. Like Kenneth McKay, Nancy B was not dying and could have survived for many more years. Endorsing the decision in *McKay*, Mr Justice Dufour granted her request, and affirmed that people have the right to decline treatment, or demand that it be withdrawn, if they perceive the conditions under which they survive to be intolerable The right exists even if the person concerned will die as a result of withdrawing the treatment but would not otherwise be considered terminally ill. A series of cases have defined the conditions under which courts will allow the selective non-treatment of people who are not competent to decide for themselves

The American case of *Re Quinlan*[71] concerned a young woman who was in a permanent vegetative state (PVS). The court decided that "there comes a point

[68] *Airedale NHS Trust v. Bland* [1993] 1 All ER 821, per Lord Keith, at 860.

[69] *McKay v. Bergstedt* (1990) 801 P 2d 617 (Nev Sup Ct).

[70] *B (Nancy) v. Hotel-Dieu de Quebec* (1992) 86 DLR (4th) 385, (Quebec Supreme Court).

[71] (1976) NJ 355 A 2d 647.

at which the individual's rights overcome the state's interest" and life support was discontinued on the basis that Quinlan herself would have sought this had she been able. Despite switching off the respirator however, Karen Quinlan survived for a further ten years. *Cruzan v. Missouri Department of Health*[72] addressed similar issues and allowed life support to be terminated, also on the principle of self-determination. In Britain, *Airedale NHS Trust v. Bland*[73] also concerned a decision to discontinue treatment for a patient who was not competent to decide for himself, but here the problem was solved through the application of the principle of best interests to determine the extent of a doctor's duty to this particular patient. The treatment was invasive by its nature, and futile because Tony Bland had no prospect of recovery. Allowing the patient to die by withdrawing treatment would amount to an omission which would only be unlawful if a duty of care existed between doctor and patient. The nature of the treatment involved allowed the House of Lords to determine that it would not be in Bland's best interests for it to continue. Once this was established no duty of care existed and the withdrawal of treatment was not unlawful.[74] But is it dignified to die in this way?

Decisions like these have been applauded as examples of preserving individual dignity by saving the respective patients from indefinite futile and degrading medical treatment. Comparatively it does seem certain that further indignity through worthless treatment has been avoided, but whether the nature of the dying that resulted was dignified is open to question. A patient who needs a ventilator to survive will suffocate if it is removed, and those who are deprived of food and fluid will die from the effects of dehydration, albeit sustained by adequate palliation of their symptoms. Kenneth McKay was aware of the fate that awaited him and requested medication to sedate him and ease his path; that was his choice. Karen Quinlan, Nancy Cruzan and Tony Bland were incapable of appreciating either the details about the manner of their demise, or the plight of the condition they existed in. This being the case it is difficult to ascribe human dignity to either their living or the method of their dying. Both appear inherently undignified for the patient.

Unlike active euthanasia, which exposes its practitioners to the potential indignity of criminal prosecution and sanction, passive euthanasia through selective non-treatment, can appear to preserve the dignity of the practitioner but perhaps at the expense of the patient's dignity. To avoid a Hobson's choice between the two some would argue that a death that results from double effect may be more dignified for all concerned. Hunt discusses the practice in the following terms:

> "The administration of sedatives for refractory symptoms and distress is common practice in terminal care. . . . It should be made clear that the treatment is likely to hasten

[72] (1990) 110 US Supreme Court 2841.
[73] *Airedale NHS Trust v. Bland* [1993] 1 All ER 821.
[74] More than twenty subsequent cases concerning other patients in PVS in the UK have been similarly decided.

death, the patient is less able to eat, drink, interact, mobilise, cough to clear secretions, and is prone to infections. . . . Terminal sedation which hastens death can be justified using the principle of double effect, or it can be regarded as slow euthanasia".[75]

He recognises here that double effect may be a less dignified option because "in some situations it is kinder to end the patient's life quickly", but considers it to be good medical practice in the present legal climate. He may however, be mistaken in his assumption that a doctor can be justified in *using* the doctrine of double effect to hasten a patient's death by terminal sedation. It has long been established that a doctor "is entitled to do all that is proper and necessary to relieve pain and suffering, even if the measures he takes may incidentally shorten human life".[76] But to *use* double effect to legitimate a treatment regime whose predicted outcome is death, is to imply that the effects are not purely incidental or anticipated, they are desired, purposeful and therefore intended. Should a criminal prosecution be brought against a doctor in these circumstances she may confront not only the indignity of a criminal prosecution and trial but also a conviction for murder or manslaughter.

Some of these indignities might be avoided if the law were reformed to permit voluntary euthanasia. Yet legal reform would also need to guard against other indignities and potential abuses in order to protect those who may fall victim to non-voluntary euthanasia in the guise of mercy killing. Relaxing the law too far in favour of euthanasia in order to protect practitioners might result in inadequate protection for vulnerable people and death with dignity would be equally illusive. Nevertheless the current legal approach to euthanasia serves nobody well, leaving many patients suffering against their expressed wishes and criminalising those who provide assistance in disregard of the law.

Furthermore, inconsistencies and uncertainties are readily discernible within the present legal framework. Would every jury have reached the same outcome in the cases of Dr Moore and Dr Arthur? Would every judge have insisted that the Crown Prosecution Service reassess its decision to prosecute Rachel Heath? Would the Brady's case have received similar attention had it been heard south of the border? And, how many clinicians expect that the terminal care they are providing will result in death and wonder whether their genuine motives might one day be called to account in a court of law? Answering these questions would not be necessary if the law were reformed to permit voluntary euthanasia in circumstances where there was no doubt about the patients desire, the practitioners motive and the compassionate nature of the action taken. The final section of this book will focus on how and why the law should be revised to facilitate death with dignity.

---

[75] R Hunt, "Approach of the GP to End-of-Life Decisions" (1997) *The RCGP Members' Reference Book 1997/8* 266, at 267.

[76] H Palmer, "Doctor Adams' Trial for Murder" (1957) *Crim LR* 365, per Lord Devlin at 375.

Conclusions

Dignified Life, Dignified Death and Dignified Law

Recent years have witnessed the further advancement of biotechnology and it seems clear that modern medicine's technical success at maintaining life increasingly results in no more than prolonging death. Concerns about medicine's ability to keep people alive inappropriately have been voiced as a result. The level of interest in advance directives demonstrates that most people would prefer not to be kept alive if they know they have no prospect of regaining their cognitive humanity. When faced with the reality of situations like this, most carers generally espouse similar sentiments, regarding the indefinite continuation of futile physical life as undignified. Doctors too appear apprehensive about merely postponing death in the face of terminal or incurable illnesses.

Consequently, the law is frequently being called upon to reinterpret the boundaries between life and death. The facts of the *Bland*[1] case were regarded as remarkable in 1993 when the House of Lords ultimately had to decide whether that young man should live or die. Since then however, the courts have been involved in well over twenty subsequent cases concerning patients with a diagnosis of permanent vegetative state. Human dignity is challenging medical science in the courts, and the courts have consistently endorsed the primacy of dignity over rigid legalistic interpretation and allowed life to be terminated.

Yet achieving the desired outcome has often required all the sophistry and sleight of hand the courts could muster. Creative manipulation of concepts like double effect and best interests has been required in order to tailor accepted legal arguments to unacceptable medical situations. In turn this has lead to the incongruous position where those who can no longer experience pain or any kind of suffering, and cannot speak for themselves, now or in the future, are legitimately allowed to die, while those who actively court death to relieve their continuing torment are not permitted the relief they desire. Aside from the well known objections from those who advance arguments promoting the right to life in all circumstances, or others who fear a slippery slope to eugenics, public sympathy appears to support the outcomes of the PVS cases. Scant attention is paid to the implications of how death will occur following the withdrawal of treatment, or why those who can articulate a wish for a similar outcome for themselves are not legally allowed it.

---

[1] *Airedale NHS Trust v. Bland* [1993] 1 All ER 821.

The chapters of this book have outlined the ways in which various clinical practices at the end of life relate to euthanasia, and the law's approach to them. Through an analysis of the law of consent and the legal response to advance directives, some of the mechanisms by which people can maintain control over their own dying within the present legal framework have been identified. The ability to exercise choice, has been established as central to the concept of death with dignity, but the limitations on available choice in the current legal climate reveals a need for legal reform in favour of euthanasia. The shape and extent of any reform is largely dependent upon how euthanasia is defined and, what kind of conduct is accepted as proper medical care rather than clinical killing.

Under the present law, any kind of conduct that aims to cause death amounts to homicide. As active voluntary euthanasia can certainly be described as an intentional action that causes death it will clearly fall within this definition. Whether the conduct amounts to mercy killing or assisted suicide is immaterial. Both are proscribed and attract hefty custodial sentences. Mercy killing is regarded as murder and carries a mandatory life sentence, while a maximum sentence of fourteen years imprisonment attaches to assisted suicide. The consent or request of the "victim" offers no defence in either crime, neither does the fact that the action was performed for compassionate motives. According to the law, no person may deliberately end the life of another, even at the repeated request of that person or in the face of a considered and enduring decision. Yet as dying becomes more medicalised than ever, people continue to conflate euthanasia and death with dignity, resulting in a perceived need for permissive reform.

Chapter five described how the preservation of dignity through autonomous choice has in recent years been the stimulus for much interest in living wills, or advance directives. As a result, some jurisdictions have introduced legislation supporting the use of advance directives or living wills, confirming their legitimacy. In Britain, living wills have been discussed in a number of cases,[2] prompting the Law Commission to give careful consideration to their use in specific medical circumstances. Comprehensive recommendations have subsequently been made with regard to their potential operation and legal status.[3] Additionally, a Code of Practice has been formulated by the British Medical Association and the Royal College of Nursing, advising medical practitioners how to respond to patients with advance directives.

The possibility of legislative intervention supporting the use of living wills has also been mooted however, with an opinion poll conducted in 1998 demonstrating a high level of public support for the potential enactment of legislation to give living wills the binding force of law.[4] Specifically, 1,960 adults were

---

[2] *Airedale NHS Trust* v. *Bland* [1993] 1 All ER 821, *Re T (Adult: Refusal of Treatment)* [1993] Fam 95, *Re C (Adult Refusal of Treatment)* [1994] 1 WLR 290.

[3] Law Commission Report 231, *Mental Incapacity: Item 9 of the Fourth Programme of Law Reform: Mentally Incapacitated Adults* (London, HMSO, 1995) at paras 5.1–5.39.

[4] See C Dyer, "UK Public Calls for Legislation over Living Wills" (1998) 316 *BMJ* 9551.

asked their views on whether Parliament should pass an act to ensure that doctors comply with advanced treatment decisions made in writing by people who could no longer speak for themselves. Sixty-five per cent of those surveyed favoured the introduction of a law making the provisions in advance directives binding on doctors, while 21 per cent disapproved. In practice the effect of such a law would of course be minimal, since common law already requires medical professionals to observe valid and applicable living wills.[5] Accordingly, if the results of this poll represent a true reflection of public understanding of the issues, a widespread public awareness campaign explaining the relevance and applicability of living wills would be more apposite than a statute reiterating principles that are already enshrined in common law.

Increased use of advance directives would certainly facilitate easier and more reliable terminal decision-making, especially where selective non-treatment or passive euthanasia was being considered, but they would be of little benefit to those who retain competence. The actions of clinicians accused of homicide following treatment withdrawal or double effect might be legitimated if the presentation of a valid living will were able to provide evidence of a patient's intentions prior to becoming incapacitated, but no advance directive can sanction deliberate acts that lead to death. Perhaps more pressing then, is the need to safeguard the interests of those who still have capacity and seek voluntary euthanasia, while simultaneously protecting the medical professionals who assist them from criminal sanction. A variety of methods of achieving this end have been suggested in recent years.

For example, the creation of an entirely new criminal offence of mercy killing would avoid labelling those who perform euthanasia as murderers. In 1980 the Criminal Law Revision Committee[6] discussed this possibility within the terms of a proposal made two years previously in the Twelfth Report of the Committee. That proposal suggested that a person who unlawfully killed another out of compassion, believing them to be either "subject to great pain or suffering", or "permanently helpless from bodily or mental incapacity", or "subject to rapid and incurable bodily or mental degeneration", should be liable only for a maximum of two years imprisonment. A significant level of public dissent resulted from the proposal however, leading the committee to conclude in the Fourteenth Report that:

"when we came to examine our suggestion again for the purposes of this report, we decided unanimously that we should withdraw it, if only on the ground that it is too controversial for the exercise in law reform on which we are engaged. We do not recommend that there should be an offence of mercy killing".[7]

---

[5] Ch. 5 offers a detailed discussion of the legal status of advance directives.
[6] Criminal Law Revision Committee, 14th Report, *Offences Against the Person* (1980) Cmnd 7844, section F, at 53.
[7] *Ibid.*

The 1994 House of Lords Select Committee on Medical Ethics, considered a similar proposal for the creation of a new offence of mercy killing, and also failed to recommend it.[8] Their position was endorsed in the Government Response to the Report of the Select Committee on Medical Ethics.[9] But the opinions and practices prevalent then may be less entrenched in the early years of the twenty-first century.

The series of high profile cases where the courts have sanctioned clinical decisions to allow patients to die, coupled with greater awareness of end of life issues, suggest that the political and social climate within which the Criminal Law Revision Committee and the Select Committee on Medical Ethics decided against introducing a new offence of mercy killing is no longer wholly applicable. However, if the creation of an entirely new offence of this type is still too radical then a more acceptable alternative might be to introduce euthanasia or mercy killing as a special defence in cases of homicide, as Tim Helme and Nicola Padfield have postulated.

According to their model, culpability could be defined without the need to analyse issues of causation or to distinguish between acts and omissions.[10] Clearly, if such a defence were available, there would be less of a need for the court to agonise over whether the cause of death had been a positive act which was outside of the scope of proper medical care, or an omission that constituted a breach of the duty of care. But it would remain essential to establish the factual cause of death before liability could be attached. If the death could be attributed to natural causes there would be no need for a sophisticated defence to apply. In practice this defence could operate in one of two ways; it might reduce a charge of murder to manslaughter, allowing for flexibility in sentencing, or it might provide a complete defence. Either way it would still leave clinicians vulnerable to the vagaries of the criminal justice system.

The same problem arises with one further possibility for legal reform, that is the abolition of the mandatory life sentence for murder. Here judges would be empowered to exercise discretion in sanctioning those convicted for practising euthanasia.[11] Such a reform could operate for all cases of murder so that the mandatory life sentence was abolished absolutely, or it might operate selectively whereby judges were given the option to dispense with the mandatory life sentence only in murder cases where a mercy killing had obviously occurred.[12] Leniency could be extended due to the particular circumstances of the case but

[8] House of Lords Select Committee on Medical Ethics, (1994) HL 21-II Para 260.

[9] Government Response to the Report of the Select Committee on Medical Ethics Cmnd 2553 (1994).

[10] T Helme, N Padfield, "Setting Euthanasia on the Level" (1993) XV (1) *Liverpool Law Review* 75.

[11] The 1994 House of Lords Select Committee on Medical Ethics strongly endorsed the recommendations of an earlier select committee that the mandatory life sentence for murder be abolished, at *Para 294*, but the Government Response to the Select Committee Report was equally vociferous in its opposition to this suggestion.

[12] M Otlowski, "Active Voluntary Euthanasia" (1994) 2 *Med LR* 161.

a criminal conviction would attach, and with it the inevitable stigma and professional consequences would follow.

Each of these proposed reforms could help to provide greater dignity for some of the participants in the dying process, but perhaps not all. The dying would benefit if reform allowed for greater openness so that they felt more able to voice their concerns about dying or to request assistance, and the carers could benefit from increased protection against criminal conviction. However, it is clear that without effective safeguards people who might already be vulnerable to abuse could be placed in greater jeopardy if the law were relaxed too far in favour of euthanasia. Opponents of euthanasia argue that no legislative framework could provide sufficient protection to save the vulnerable from abuse, or society from a decline into moral decay. George Fletcher's concerns about the ability of individuals to resist the corrupting influences of performing actions that society has regarded as taboo are relevant here:

> "the self-destructive individual who induces another to kill or mutilate him implicates the latter in the violation of a significant social taboo. The person carrying out the killing or mutilation crosses the threshold into a realm of conduct that, the second time, might be more easily carried out. And the second time it might not be particularly significant whether the victim consents or not".[13]

For Cicely Saunders, concerns focus more on the dangers that particular groups within society might be exposed to if voluntary euthanasia were permitted and she argues that

> "to make voluntary euthanasia lawful would be an irresponsible act, hindering help, pressuring the vulnerable, abrogating our true respect and responsibility to the frail and old, the disabled and the dying".[14]

Regardless of the apparent dangers however, the need for dignity in dying continues to be expressed through the demands of patients for greater autonomy to select the time and method of dying. Conventional medical treatment is constrained by the law and failing to adequately address these concerns. While the arguments for and against the legalisation of euthanasia are polarised on the basis of religion, ethics and politics, dignity in dying remains inexplicably linked with euthanasia in the public consciousness. Physical pain constitutes just one factor in the equation, with emotional pain assuming greater significance for those who wish to avoid dependence and therefore pursue death with dignity through euthanasia. But calls for reforms permitting euthanasia are also set against the backdrop of dissent about unauthorised "do not resuscitate orders", and concerns about under-valuing some lives in favour of others. Within the context of caring for the dying, neither example is necessarily dignified, but the criminal law may not be the most appropriate mechanism for achieving justice either for those who want euthanasia for themselves, or for those who assist its recipients.

---

[13] G P Fletcher, *Rethinking Criminal Law* (Boston, Little Brown, 1978) at 770–71.
[14] Cited in, Lord Goff, "A Matter of Life and Death" (1995) *Med LR* 1–21, at 17.

Alan Norrie has considered the limitations on the ability of the criminal just-ice system to deliver justice generally.[15] He argues that the theoretical basis of the criminal justice system and the practicalities of modern life have diverged in such a way that the accepted rationale that crime deserves punishment may not always be legitimate. It may not always be appropriate simply to apportion blame and allocate punishment to the individuals involved in criminal conduct. Norrie argues that society as a whole may be required to shoulder some of the responsibility through what he describes as "relational justice", where the social, moral and political context of the conduct in question is considered alongside its criminal definition. This conception of justice involves:

> "a sense of the particularity of human life, a sense of social engagement, and a sense of responsibility that is contextualised both in terms of looking at the wrongdoer's past acts and their provenance, and to his relationship with a community that includes his victim".[16]

Euthanasia presents a perfect example of conduct that is decontextualised by the law in this way, and demonstrates the hesitance with which the law reflects and responds to the moral and political contexts within which changes in social atti-tudes occur.

Recent technological advances have provided a context within which many ordinary people are calling for legal reform because they fear that they may be robbed of their autonomy and dignity as their lives draw to an end. In an age when people value their independence and strive to live independent and ful-filled lives it is important "that life ends *appropriately*, that death keeps faith with the way we want to have lived".[17] Here Ronald Dworkin observes that death is "not only the start of nothing but the end of everything"[18] and therefore it should be accomplished in a manner compatible with the ideals sought during life. In many respects his interpretation reflects the *good death* ideal of the reli-gious philosophies discussed earlier and those of the founders of the hospice movement. Both are contrary to the kind of death often achieved through the practice of modern medicine and within the law, yet Dworkin's proposals for immediate resolutions are more in accord with those of Derek Humphry and The Voluntary Euthanasia Society than with Buddhism and the Christian tradi-tion of the hospice movement. A quick and certain death may be more dignified than a slow lingering one.

The tensions inherent in Dworkin's approach are also visible in society more generally, causing James to marvel at the fact that these quite distinct approaches have developed simultaneously. In his view,

---

[15] A Norrie, "The Limits of Justice: Finding Fault in the Criminal Law" (1996) 59 *Modern Law Review* 540–556.

[16] *Ibid*, at 555.

[17] R Dworkin, *Life's Dominion* (London, HarperCollins, 1993) at 179.

[18] *Ibid*.

"it will be interesting to see how history interprets the morality of a society in which two contrasting groups, each with deeply committed views on human dignity, develop in parallel".[19]

Perhaps this diversity of opinions and approaches is due to the complex relationship between dignity and dying, which cannot be explained simply in terms of medical care or symptomatic relief. The dignity debate revolves around questions of how, where and when to die as much as to die or not to die. People fear a slow lingering death because such a death tends to be associated with a gradual loss of control and dignity. So some will respond by wishing for an immediate release in an effort to retain their dignity, while others consider the process of dying over an extended period of time as providing, "a chance to be able to come to terms with dying and with yourself, and other people, to sort things out in your life over a period of time; to round off your life".[20] Both may be dignity enhancing.

Of course, if euthanasia were available one could make dignified plans about the time and place of dying in advance, which in itself might facilitate the opportunity to make financial and emotional preparations for the inevitable death, as well as avoiding unwelcome suffering. Equally, one might find solace and dignity in resisting euthanasia, preferring to exercise choice by living every moment that life offers.

It is the fluidity of the concept of human dignity that enables the hospice movement and the pro-euthanasia lobby to share the common goal of avoiding pointless pain and suffering at the end of life. The solutions they offer remain poles apart however, and euthanasia remains an intractable problem which apparently defies social or legal resolution. The need for individual dignity in dying is strongly felt within society but can be achieved in vastly different ways, depending on the medical, religious and philosophical imperatives of those concerned. Individualistic solutions however focus on the needs of the dying, often to the detriment of others who share the experience. Sampaio articulates the nature of the problem of death with dignity very eloquently:

"Guidelines of how to die with dignity cannot be built on the individualism of John Locke or the humanitarianism ideals of Jean Jacques Rousseau but rather on a sense of civil responsibility to oneself and to others. Most of all, they must be based on never losing sight of the fact that their basic 'raison d'etre' is not to leave the helpless to their misery".[21]

One conclusion to draw from Sampaio's inference is that legal reform permitting euthanasia is necessary so that society as a whole can take responsibility for

---

[19] N James, "From Vision to a System: the Maturing of the Hospice Movement", in R Lee and D Morgan, *Death Rites: Law and Ethics at the End of Life* (London, Routledge, 1994) 102–130 at 125.

[20] N Kfir, M Slevin, *Challenging Cancer—From Chaos to Control* (London, Tavistock, 1991) at 53.

[21] L Sampaio, "To Die with Dignity" (1992) 35 (4) *Social Science and Medicine* 433–41, at 433.

easing people gently into that good night. However even to do so from his altruistic motivation may present dangers for some groups within society.

Located within the context of euthanasia, Fletcher's words above warn against crossing the Rubicon that separates mercy from killing, suggesting that once a practice that was stigmatised becomes accepted it presents dangers for society as a whole, not just for individuals. Cicely Saunders is more precise in her fears, believing that legalising euthanasia will undermine the position of particular groups. This is also a theme that recurs in Sampaio's analysis of euthanasia and death with dignity. He concludes that whether or not euthanasia will ultimately gain legitimacy is likely to be determined mainly by economic imperatives. For him:

> "in the industrialized part of the world there is the danger that as the economic problems worsen the powers that be might undergo an overnight 'conversion' and encourage the death of those who are not economically productive".[22]

Such a conversion is, he believes, likely to be informed by the kind of arguments made here and based upon notions of enhancing the dignity of the dying and protecting those who help others to die, but have a more sinister hidden agenda. With escalating costs placing market pressures on over extended health-care services this concern is only too valid. Euthanasia could become a method of resource-led population control, in much the same way as infanticide has been practised in various societies throughout the ages.[23] Furthermore, Cicely Saunders is right in her assessment that the impact may well be greater on some groups within society than others. Life expectancy in the United Kingdom has increased by twenty-five years during this century, and in recent years the number of people aged eighty and over has nearly trebled.[24] The numbers of people suffering disabling, chronic, and terminal disease is inevitably rising as the population ages. Simultaneously statistics demonstrate that women live longer than men so that in 1992 for example, 25 per cent of men who died did so in their own homes compared with only 19 per cent of women, with 13 per cent of men dying in communal establishments as opposed to 25 per cent of women.[25]

Cuts in welfare impact crucially upon the elderly who are now required to provide for more of their own care, either through contributions during their working lives or by the clawing back of their accumulated assets. The indignity of dependence coupled with the perceived financial burden to family and the state may be sufficient to encourage "the frail and old, the disabled and the

---

[22] L Sampaio, "To Die with Dignity" (1992) 35 (4) *Social Science and Medicine* 433–41, at 433.

[23] For an exposition of the prevalence of infanticide see M Harris, *Cannibals and Kings: The Origins of Culture* (London, Collins, 1978).

[24] *Social Trends*, Table 1.2, Age sex structure of the population (London, HMSO, 1990) at 24.

[25] Office of Population Census and Surveys, *Mortality Statistics, General: Review of the Registrar General on Death in England and Wales 1992* (London, HMSO, 1994) Table 7.

dying"[26] to consider euthanasia as an alternative.[27] If active euthanasia were to be permitted as a right, what is to prevent the endorsement of this *right* being translated into a social duty? How long will it be before those who seek euthanasia in order to avoid being a burden lose the right to continue living until the natural end of their lives?

Despite these valid concerns the pressure to relax the law and permit euthanasia for individuals remains, while the ability of medicine to maintain life beyond what many perceive to be dignified bounds raises questions that go to the root of defining what kinds of human behaviour ought to be criminalised.[28] Killing is rightly proscribed but voluntary euthanasia may be slipping beyond the scope of the criminal law if society's morality is no longer opposed to its practice. Yet the law needs to protect the vulnerable at the same time as enabling the dying to exercise their autonomy through euthanasia and protecting those who compassionately assist them.

Earlier in this chapter various types of reforms were discussed ranging from a new statutory offence of mercy killing, through the introduction of a special defence to homicide, to the abolition of the mandatory life sentence for murder. Either a new offence or a new defence would require a legislative resolution which would be entirely dependent upon political will. The emotive nature of the euthanasia debate and the voracity of its opponents dictate that Parliamentary intervention of this nature is unlikely to be forthcoming in the near future. Equally, the rigidity of statutory composition may not provide the most accessible format for sympathetic judicial interpretation of the issues arising from euthanasia. An incremental approach, like that adopted in the Netherlands in recent years, would give the opportunity to determine how much sustained support there is for euthanasia in practice, beyond the purely theoretical endorsement it currently attracts. In this way a gradual relaxation of the present legal restrictions could facilitate a highly regulated system of medically assisted dying for those who require it, while providing a high level of protection for everybody. It should be possible to adopt a model similar to the one that operates in Holland, where, in appropriate circumstances, and subject to strict guidelines, euthanasia could be made available to those who truly and consistently desire it. In the meantime, judicial discretion in sentencing would appear to offer the most immediately socially acceptable solution. This would enable the strengths of the common law to prevail, while offering maximum flexibility in order to safeguard the needs of the vulnerable. In combination with greater recognition and adherence to individual advance directives, personal autonomy would be enhanced without compromising compassion or caring. Ultimately a

---

[26] See Lord Goff, "A Matter of Life and Death" (1995) *Medical Law Review* 1–21, at 17.

[27] For further discussion see, H Biggs, "I Don't Want to be a Burden! A Feminist Reflects on Women's Experiences of Death and Dying" in S Sheldon & M Thomson (eds.) *Feminist Perspectives on Health Care Law* (London, Cavendish, 1998) at 277–293.

[28] For a discussion of some of the tensions present when one conduct is either criminal or legitimate depending on the context, see Jean Davies, "Raping and Making Love are Different Concepts; so are Killing and Euthanasia" (1988) 14 *Journal of Medical Ethics* 148–9.

more dignified alternative could be accessible to those who seek euthanasia for themselves and those who practice it. Nobody would need to feel as though they are dying in an age of eternal life.[29]

---

[29] B D Cohen, *Karen Ann Quinlan; Dying in an Age of Eternal Life* (New York, Nash, 1976).

Select Bibliography

E K Able, "The Hospice Movement: Institutionalising Innovation" (1986) 16 *International Journal of Health Services* 71.

Age Concern Institute of Gerontology and Centre of Medical Law and Ethics King's College London, *The Living Will: Consent to Treatment at the End of Life* (London, Edward Arnold, 1988 .

M Allen, "Consent and Assault" (1994) 58 (2) *Journal of Criminal Law* 183.

P Anderson, "Good Death: Mercy Deliverance and the Nature of Suffering" (1992) *Tricycle, The Buddhist Review* 36–42.

K Andrews, L Murphy, R Munday, C Littlewood, "Misdiagnosis of the Vegetative State: Retrospective Study in a Rehabilitation Unit" (1996) 313 *British Medical Journal* 13–16.

M Angell, "The Supreme Court and Physician-Assisted Suicide—the Ultimate Right" (1997) 336 *New England Journal Of Medicine* 50–3.

P S Applebaum, C W Lidz, A Meisel, *Informed Consent: Legal Theory and Clinical Practice* (New York, Oxford University Press, 1987).

W Arney, B Bergen, "The Anomaly, the Chronic Patient and the Play of Medical Power" (1983) 5 *Sociology of Health and Illness* 12.

A Ashworth, *Principles of Criminal Law* (Oxford, Oxford University Press, 1995).

M Barnes, "Euthanasia: Buddhist Principles" (1996) 52 (2) *British Medical Bulletin* 369–75.

B Barraclough, "The Bible Suicides" (1990) 86 *Acta Psychiatrica Scandinavia* 64–69.

H Beecher, "The New Definition of Death, Some Opposing Viewpoints" (1971) 5 *International Journal of Clinical Pharmacology* 120–1.

H K Beecher, "A Definition of Irreversible Coma" (1968) 205 *Journal of the American Medical Association* 337–340.

H Beynon, "Doctors as Murderers" [1982] *Crim LR* 17.

L Bibbings, P Alldridge, "Sexual Expression, Body Alteration, and the Defence of Consent" (1993) 20 (3) *Journal of Law and Society* 356.

H Biggs, "Decisions and Responsibilities at the End of Life: Euthanasia and Clinically Assisted Death" (1996) 2 *Medical Law International* 229–245.

—— "Euthanasia and Death with Dignity: Still Poised on the Fulcrum of Homicide" (1996) *Crim LR* 878–88.

H Biggs, K Diesfeld, "Assisted Suicide for People with Depression: an Advocate's Perspective" (1995) 2 (1) *Medical Law International* 23.

BMA, *Advance Statements about Medical Treatment*, BMA Publications April 1995.

—— *Assessment of Mental Capacity: Guidance for Doctors and Lawyers*, (London, BMA Publications, 1995).

—— "Diagnosis of Death" (1979) 1 *British Medical Journal* 332.

M Brazier, M Lobjoit, *Protecting the Vulnerable* (New York, Routledge, 1991).

—— *Medicine, Patients, and the Law* (London, Penguin, 1992).

J Bridgeman, "Medical Treatment: The Mother's Rights" [1993] *Family Law* 534.

—— "Because We Care? The Medical Treatment of Children" in S Sheldon and M Thomson (eds.), *Feminist Perspectives on Health Care Law* (London, Cavendish Publishing, 1998) at 97.

D W Brock, *Life and Death* (Cambridge, Cambridge University Press, 1993).

B Christie, "Man Walks Free in Scottish Euthanasia Case" (1996) 313 *British Medical Journal* 961.

C Clarkson & H Keating, *Criminal Law: Text and Materials* (London, Sweet & Maxwell, 1994).

B D Cohen, *Karen Ann Quinlan: Dying in an Age of Eternal Life* (New York, Nash Publications, 1976).

R Cooper, Comment "Withdrawal of Life Support—Lawful?" (1993) *Journal of Criminal Law* 283.

G M Craig, "On Withholding Nutrition and Hydration in the Terminally Ill: Has Palliative Medicine Gone too Far?" (1994) 20 *Journal of Medical Ethics* 139–143.

R Cranford, H Smith "Some Critical Distinctions Between Brain Death and Persistent Vegetative State" (1979) 6 *Ethics in Science and Medicine* 199.

R Cranford, "Misdiagnosing the Persistent Vegetative State" (1996) 313 *British Medical Journal* 5.

J Davies, "Raping and Making Love are Different Concepts; so are Killing and Euthanasia" (1988) 14 *Journal Medical Ethics* 148–9.

Dept. of Health and the Welsh Office *A Guide to Consent for Examination and Treatment*, and *The Patient's Charter*.

J A Devereux, D P H Jones, D I Dickenson, "Can Children Withhold Consent to Treatment?" (1993) 306 *British Medical Journal* 1459.

P Devlin, *Easing the Passing* (London, Bodley Head, 1985).

D Dickenson, M Johnson, J Samson Katz, *Death Dying and Bereavement* (London, Sage, 2000).

R S Downie, K S Calman, *Healthy Respect: Ethics in Health Care* (Oxford, Oxford University Press, 1994).

L Doyal, "Medical Ethics and Moral Indeterminacy" (1990) 17 (1) *Journal of Law and Society* 1.

A Duff, "Intentions Legal and Philosophical" (1989) 9 *Oxford Journal of Legal Studies* 76.

P Dundas, *The Jains* (London, Routledge, 1992).

R Dworkin, *Life's Dominion* (London, Harper-Collins, 1993).

B Farsides, "Palliative Care—a Euthanasia Free Zone?" (1998) 24 *Journal of Medical Ethics* 149–50.

J Feinberg, *Harm to Others* (Oxford, Oxford University Press, 1984).

—— *Harmless Wrongdoing* (Oxford, Oxford University Press, 1988).

R Fenigsen, "The Case Against Dutch Euthanasia" (1989) *Hastings Centre Report*, Special Supplement, 22–30.

P Fennell, *Treatment Without Consent* (London, Routledge, 1996).

Fleming, *Law of Torts* 8th edn. (London, Sweet and Maxwell, 1992).

G P Fletcher, *Rethinking Criminal Law* (Boston, Little Brown, 1978).

J Fletcher, "Medicine and the Nature of Man" (1973) 1 *Science, Medicine and Man* 93.

C Fried, *Right and Wrong* (Cambridge, MA, Harvard University Press, 1978).

R Gillon, *Philosophical Medical Ethics* (Chichester, Wiley, 1985).

—— "Autonomy and Consent" in M. Lockwood (ed.) *Moral Dilemmas in Modern Medicine* (Oxford, Oxford University Press, 1985).

J Glover, *Causing Death and Saving Lives* (London, Penguin, 1977).

B Goebel, "Who Decides if There is 'Triumph in the Ultimate Agony?' Constitutional Theory and the Emerging Right to Die with Dignity" (1995) 37 (2) *William and Mary Law Review* 827.

Lord Goff, "A Matter of Life and Death" (1995) *Med Law Review* 1–21.

R Gordon, C Barlow, "Competence and the Right to Die" (1993) 143 *New Law Journal* 1719–20,

J Griffiths, "The Regulation of Euthanasia and Related Medical Procedures that Shorten Life in the Netherlands" (1994) 1 *Medical Law International* 137–58.

A Grubb, "Commentary on *Re T (Adult: Refusal of Treatment)* (1993) 1 *Medical Law Review* 83.

E Grundy, "Future Patterns of Morbidity in Old Age" in F I Caird, J Grimley-Evans, (eds.), *Advanced Geriatric Medicine* (Bristol, John Wright, 1987).

S Gutmann, "Dr Kevorkian's Woman Problem: Death and the Maiden" 24 June 1996 *New Republic* 1.

A Halpin, "Intended Consequences and Unintentional Fallacies" (1987) 7 *Oxford Journal of Legal Studies* 104.

J Harris, *The Value of Life* (London, Routledge, 1985).

—— *Clones, Genes, and Immortality*, (Oxford, Oxford University Press, 1998).

M Harris, *Cannibals and Kings: The Origins of Culture* (London, Collins, 1978).

H L A Hart, "Intention and Punishment" (1967) *The Oxford Review*.

H L A Hart & A M Honeré, *Causation and the Law* 2nd edn. (Oxford, Clarendon Press, 1985).

I Haverkate, B D Onwuteaka-Philipsen, A Van Der Heide, P J Kostensa, G Van Der Wal, P J Van Der Mass, "Refused and Granted Requests for Euthanasia and Assisted Suicide in the Netherlands" (2000) 321 *British Medical Journal* 865–6.

T Helme, "Euthanasia Around the World" (1992) 304 *British Medical Journal* 717.

T Helme, N Padfield, "Setting Euthanasia on the Level" (1993) XV (1) *Liverpool Law Review* 75.

Higashi, Sakato, Hatano, "Epidemiological Studies on Patients with a Persistent Vegetative State" (1977) 40 *Journal Neurology, Neurosurgery, and Psychiatry* 876.

T Hope, D Springings and D Crisp, "Not Clinically Indicated: Patients Interests or Resource Allocation?" (1993) 306 *British Medical Journal* 379.

J Horder, "Mercy Killings—Some Reflections on Beecham's Case" (1988) 52 *Journal of Criminal Law* 309.

D Humphry, *Final Exit* (Oregon, Hemlock Society, 1991).

R Hunt, "Approach of the GP to End-of-Life Decisions" (1997) *The RCGP Members' Reference Book 1997/8* 266.

R Hunt, I Maddocks, D Roach, A McLeod, "The Incidence of Requests for a Quicker Terminal Course" (1995) 9 (2) *Palliative Medicine* 167–8.

I Illich, *Medical Nemesis: The Exploration of Health* (Delhi, Rupa, 1975).

F J Ingelfinger, "Arrogance" (1980) 303 *New England Journal of Medicine* 1507–11.

"Institute of Medical Ethics Working Party on the Ethics of Prolonging Life and Assisting Death. Withdrawal of Life Support from Patients in PVS" (1991) 337 *The Lancet* 96–98.

K V Irerson, "Forgoing Hospital Care: Should Ambulance Staff Always Resuscitate?" (1991) 17 *Journal of Medical Ethics* 19–24.

N James, "From Vision to System: the Maturing of the Hospice Movement" in R Lee, D Morgan (eds.), *Death Rites: Law and Ethics at the End of Life* (London, Routledge, 1994).

N James, D Field, "The Routinisation of Hospice: Chrisma and Bureaucratisation" (1992) 34 *Social Science and Medicine* 1363–1371.

B Jennet, F Plum, "Persistent Vegetative State After Brain Damage" (1972) 1 *The Lancet* 734–7.

S Jinnet-Sack, "Autonomy in the Company of Others" in A Grubb (ed.), *Choices and Decisions in Health Care* (Chichester, Wiley, 1993).

I Kant, *Groundwork of the Metaphysics of Morals,* in H J Paton, (ed.), *The Moral Law* (London, Hutchinson University Library, 1964).

M Kelner, 1 Bourgeault, "Patient Control Over Dying: Responses of Health Care Professionals" (1993) 36 *Social Science and Medicine 757–765.*

I Kennedy, "Alive or Dead" (1969) 22 *Current Legal Problems* 102.

—— *Treat me Right: Essays in Medical Law and Ethics* (Oxford, Clarendon, 1991).

—— *The Unmasking of Medicine* (London, Paladin, 1983).

I Kennedy, A Grubb, *Medical Law: Text with Materials* 2nd edn. (London, Butterworths, 1994).

D Keown, *Buddhism and Bioethics* (London, Macmillan, 1995).

J Keown, "Courting Euthanasia? Tony Bland and the Law Lords" (1993) 9 (3) *Ethics and Medicine.*

—— "The Law and Practice of Euthanasia in the Netherlands" (1992) 108 *Law Quarterly Review* 51–78.

E W Keyserlingk, "Sanctity of Life or Quality of Life" Law Reform Commission of Canada, Protection of Life Series Study Paper (1979) 62.

N Kfir, M Slevin, *Challenging Cancer—From Chaos to Control* (London, Tavistock, 1991).

R Klein, "Dimensions of Rationing: Who Should Do What?" (1993) 307 *British Medical Journal* 93.

A Kolnai, "Dignity", in R S Dillon (ed.) *Dignity, Character, and Self-Respect* (London, Routledge, 1995).

R Lam, "Who is Concerned about the Right to Die with Dignity? A Postal Survey of Exit Members" occasional paper, (London, Institute for Social Studies in Medical Care, 1981).

L Lamb, "Refusal of Life-prolonging Therapy" (1995) 1 (2) *Res Publica* 147.

Law Commission Consultation Paper No.128, *Mentally Incapacitated Adults and Decision-Making* (London, HMSO, 1993).

The Law Commission Consultation Paper No.129, *Mentally Incapacitated Adults and Decision Making: Medical Treatment and Research* (London, HMSO, 1993).

Law Commission Report No. 134, *Consent and Offences Against the Person* (London, HMSO, 1993).

—— No. 139, *Consent in the Criminal Law* (London, HMSO, 1995).

—— 231 Mental Incapacity. *Item 9 of the Fourth Programme of Law Reform: Mentally Incapacitated Adults* (London, HMSO, 1995).

P A Lecso, "Euthanasia: A Buddhist Perspective" (1986) 25 *Journal of Religion and Health* 51–7.

R Lee, D Morgan, *Death Rites: Law and Ethics at the End of Life* (London, Routledge, 1994).

R Leng, "Consent and Offences Against the Person: Law Commission Consultation Paper No. 134" (1994) *Criminal Law Review* 480.

P A Lewis, M Charney, "Which of Two Individuals Do You Treat When Only Their Ages are Different and You Can't Treat Them Both?" (1989) 15 *Journal of Medical Ethics* 28.

Louis van Loon, "A Buddhist Viewpoint", in G C Oosthuizen, H A Shapiro, S A Strauss (eds.) *Euthanasia* (1978) 65 Human Sciences Research Publication (OUP, Cape Town) 73–79.

J Lynn, "Why I Don't Have a Living Will" in A Capron (ed.) "Medical Decision Making and the 'Right to Die' After Cruzan" (1991) 19 *Law Medicine & Health Care* 101.

T N Madan, "Living and Dying", in *Non-Renunciation: Themes and Interpretations of the Hindu Culture* (1987) New Delhi: Oxford University Press.

—— "Dying with Dignity" (1992) 35 (4), *Social Science and Medicine* 425–32.

Manitoba Law Reform Commission Report No. 74 June 1991, *Self-determination in Health Care (Living Wills and Health Care Proxies)*.

J K Mason, R A McCall Smith, *Law and Medical Ethics* 4th edn. (London, Butterworths, 1994).

J McHale, M Fox, *Health Care Law: Text and Materials* (London, Sweet & Maxwell, 1997).

S A M McLean, *A Patient's Right to Know* (Aldershot, Dartmouth, 1989).

—— *Old Law, New Medicine: Medical Ethics and Human Rights* (London, Pandora Press, 1999).

B McNamara, C Waddell, M Colvin, "The Institutionalisation of the Good Death" (1994) 39 (11) *Social Science and Medicine* 1501–8.

The Medical Defence Union, *Problems in General Practice: Consent to Treatment* July 1996.

D W Meyers, *The Human Body and the Law* (Edinburgh, Edinburgh University Press, 1990).

J S Mill, *On Liberty* (London, Parker, 1859).

—— *On Liberty* in M Warnock (ed.) *Utilitarianism*, (Glasgow, Collins/Fontana, 1974).

S Millns, "Dwarf-throwing and Human Dignity: A French Perspective" (1996) 18 (3) *Journal of Social, Welfare, and Family Law* 375–80.

K R Mitchell, I H Kerridge, T J Lovat, "Medical Futility, Treatment Withdrawal and the Persistent Vegetative State" (1993) 19 *Journal of Medical Ethics* 71.

M Molloy, V Mepham, *Let Me Decide* (London, Penguin, 1993).

J Montgomery, "Power Over Death: The Final Sting" in R Lee, D Morgan (eds.) *Death Rites: Law and Ethics at the End of Life* (London, Routledge, 1996) 37–53.

D Morgan, "Odysseus and the Binding Directive: Only a Cautionary Tale?" (1994) 14 *Legal Studies* 411.

J Murphy, "W(h)ither Adolescent Autonomy?" (1992) *Journal of Social Welfare and Family Law* 529.

Lord Nathan, *Medical Negligence* (Oxford, Oxford University Press, 1957).

C Newdick, *Who Should We Treat? Law, Patients and Resources in the NHS* (Oxford, Oxford University Press, 1995) 297.

Geshe Ngawang Dhargyey, *Tibetan Tradition of Mental Development* (Dharamsala, Library of Tibetan Works and Archives, 1974).

A Nicolson, "Caught Between Life and Death", *Sunday Telegraph Review* May 26 1996 1–2.

E Nord, "An Alternative to QALYs: The Saved Young Life Equivalent (SAVE)" (1992) 305 *British Medical Journal* 875.

M Norden, "Whose Life is it Anyway? A Study in Respect for Autonomy" (1995) 21 *Journal of Medical Ethics* 179.

R Norman, *Ethics Killing and War* (Cambridge, Cambridge University Press, 1995).

A Norrie, "The Limits of Justice: Finding Fault in the Criminal Law" (1996) 59 *Modern Law Review* 540.

A D Ogilvie, S G Potts, "Assisted Suicide for Depression: the Slippery Slope in Action?" (1994) 309 *British Medical Journal* 492.

S D Olinger, "Medical Death" (1975) 27 Baylor Law Review 22.

O O'Niell, "Paternalism and Partial Autonomy" (1984) 10 *Journal of Medical Ethics* 177.

M Otlowski, "Active Voluntary Euthanasia" (1994) 2 *Medical Law Review* 161.

C Pallis "Return to Elsinore" (1990) 16 *Journal Medical Ethics* 10.

Palmer, "Dr Adams on Trial for Murder", *R* v. *Adams* [1957] Crim LR 365.

J Parry, *Death and the Regeneration of Life* (Cambridge, Cambridge University Press, 1982).

R Pearlman, K Cain, D Patrick, M Appelbaum-Maizel, H Starks, N Jecker, R Uhlmann, "Insights Pertaining to Patient Assessments of States Worse than Death", in L Emanuel (ed.) *Advance Directives: Expectations, Experience and Future Practice* (1993) 4(1) *Journal of Clinical Ethics* 33.

Poole, "Arthur's Case: A Comment" [1986] *Crim LR* 383.

D Price, "Euthanasia, Pain Relief and Double Effect" (1997) 17 (2) *Legal Studies* 323.

C Pritchard, *Suicide—The Ultimate Rejection* (Buckingham, Open University Press, 1995).

T E Quill, "Death and Dignity: A Case of Individualized Decision Making" (1991) 324 (10) *New England Journal of Medicine* 691–4.

E Roberts, "*Re C* and the Boundaries of Autonomy" (1994) 10 (3) *Professional Negligence* 98–101.

J Roberts, C Kjellstrand, "Jack Kevorkian: a Medical Hero" (1996) 312 *British Medical Journal* 1434.

S du Boulay, *Ciceley Saunders* (London, Hodder & Stoughton, 1994).

L Sampaio, "To Die with Dignity" (1992) 35 (4) *Social Science and Medicine* 433–441.

J Sanders, "Medical Futility: CPR", in, R Lee, D Morgan (eds.), *Death Rites: Law and Ethics at the End of Life* (1994) London: Routledge, 72–90.

R E Sartorius, (ed.) *Paternalism* (Minneapolis, University of Minnesota Press, 1983).

C Seale, J Addington-Hall, "Euthanasia: Why People Want to Die Earlier" (1994) 39 *Social Science and Medicine* 647–54.

S Sheldon, "Subject Only to the Attitude of the Surgeon Concerned: The Judicial Protection of Medical Discretion" (1996) 5 (1) *Social and Legal Studies* 95.

T Sheldon, "Judges make Historic Ruling on Euthanasia" (1994) 309 *British Medical Journal* 7.

M M Shultz, "From Informed Consent to Patient Choice: a New Protected Interest" (1985) 95 *Yale Law Journal* 219.

P Singer, *Practical Ethics* 2nd edn. (Cambridge, Cambridge University Press, 1993).

—— *Rethinking Life and Death* (Oxford, Oxford University Press, 1995).

P D G Skegg, "Justifications for Medical Procedure Performed without Consent" (1974) 90 *Law Quarterly Review* 512.

—— "The Case for a Statutory Definition of Death" (1976) *Journal of Medical Ethics* 190.

—— *Law, Ethics and Medicine* (Oxford, Clarendon, 1984).

C Smith, "Disabling Autonomy: The Role of Government, the Law, and the Family" (1997) 24 (3) *Journal of Law and Society* 421–39.

N Smith, "GPs Face Ultimate Dilemma", (October 27 2000) *GP* 24.

K Stern, "Advance Directives" (1994) *Medical Law Review* 57–76.

The Terrence Higgins Trust and King's College London, Living Will 2nd edn. in M Molloy, V Mepham(eds.), *Let Me Decide* (London, Penguin, 1993).

M Thomson, "After *Re S*" (1994) 2 *Medical Law Review* 127.

K Tickner, " *Rogers* v. *Whitaker*—Giving Patients a Meaningful Choice" (1995) 15 (1) *Oxford Journal of Legal Studies* 110

K Toolis, "A Death for Thomas", *The Guardian Weekend*, Feb 3 1996 18–23.

R G Twycross, "Assisted Death: a Reply" (1990) 336 *The Lancet* 796–798.

C Wells, "Patients, Consent and Criminal Law" (1994) 1 *Journal Social Welfare and Family Law* 65.

R Weir, "The Morality of Physician-Assisted Suicide" (1992) 20 *Law Medicine and Health Care* 116.

K Wheat, "The Law's Treatment of the Suicidal" [2000] 8 *Medical Law Review* 182–209, at 208.

E Wilkes, "On Withholding Nutrition and Hydration in the Terminally Ill: Has Palliative Medicine Gone Too Far? A Commentary" (1994) 20 *Journal of Medical Ethics* 144–5.

A Williams, "The Economic Role of 'Health Indicators'" in G Teeling-Smith (ed.) *Measuring the Social Benefits of Medicine* (London, Office of Health Economics, 1983).

G Williams, "Euthanasia" (1973) 41 *Medico-Legal Journal*.

—— *Textbook on Criminal Law* 2nd edn. (London, Stevens, 1983).

—— *The Sanctity of Life and the Criminal Law* (London, Faber & Faber, 1957).

Voluntary Euthanasia Society, *Your Ultimate Choice: The Right to Die with Dignity* (London, Souvenir Press, 1992).

C Zinn, S Potts, "Australians to log on for the Final Exit" *The Observer* 9 June 1996, 23.

Index

Printed in the United Kingdom
by Lightning Source UK Ltd.
107555UKS00001B/172-186